PREFABULOUS WORLD

PREFABULOUS WORLD

ENERGY-EFFICIENT AND SUSTAINABLE HOMES AROUND THE GLOBE

SHERI KOONES   FOREWORD BY ROBERT REDFORD

Abrams, New York

To all of those who work to make the world green,
and to my dear friends, who keep my world rosy.

ACKNOWLEDGMENTS

I wanted to write this book because the inefficient usage of energy and water, limited resources, and an abundance of waste are global problems that are not restricted to any particular country. Because the world's energy and resources are not being used optimally in so many locations, it continues to be an important issue for us all. I believe people from all countries can learn a great deal by sharing information on how efficiency in construction is being achieved in many different ways, in many different places.

This book was more challenging to write than all of the others I've written so far because of language barriers, the complexities of different local and national codes and requirements, and just plain distance. I want to thank all of the architects, builders, homeowners, and other professionals who were so helpful and patient working with me—many of them whose first language is not English.

Thank you to all the photographers who graciously shared their beautiful photographs with me.

Many thanks to my "building" friends who continue to inspire and help me with technical issues: Dave Wrocklage, John Connell, and Adam Prince with his colleagues at Zero Energy Design. And to Denise Marcil and Lucy Hedrick for your friendship and great support for all of my book projects. Thanks to Michelle and Alexander Kolbe, who have been my European "connection" and have been so helpful.

Thank you to Mary Doyle-Kimball and the members of NAREE for your continuous support for my books.

My thanks to Robert Redford—you have been such an inspiration to me and a huge gift to this country. Thank you to Joyce Deep—your work inspires me, and your support brings me joy.

My family—Rob, Alex, and Jesse—provide much of the incentive for wanting to improve the environment. I wish for a cleaner, healthier environment for them, and for all living things that reside on this planet.

My gratitude to my brother, Mark Warman, and my sister, Barbara Corpuel—you are both wonderful friends and great supporters of my life and work.

Special thanks to Chuck Lockhart for your efforts, beyond the call of duty, in creating meticulous graphics.

Thank you to Eric Himmel. I'm so appreciative of your continued support for my work. And thanks to Laura Dozer for your fine editing and Darilyn Carnes for your magnificent graphic design.

PAGES 2-3 The view from the many windows of the Lugano House in Switzerland (see page 230) is of the surrounding mountains—Monte Lema, Monte Tamaro, and Monte Rosa. On a clear day, you can see all the way to Italy, a distance of about 112 miles (180 km). (Photo courtesy of Grandpierre Design GmbH)

PAGE 4 The green[r]evolution Plus Energy House, located in Cologne, Germany (see page 140), has a powerful photovoltaic array, which produces clean solar energy.

BELOW Casa Locarno in Solduno, Switzerland (see page 236), was panelized with parts that could be flown in by helicoptor because of the limited accessibility of the site.

CONTENTS

An important part of my life's work has been to preserve this land we hold so dear, conserve our natural resources, keep the air we breathe healthy, and protect all living things from the disasters associated with obtaining fossil fuel. Although much of the work I have done has been focused in North America, environmental threats know no boundaries, and all countries must work to reverse the results of global warming and halt the decimation of our land in the name of energy.

One of the best ways to deal with these overwhelming goals is to reduce the amount of fossil fuel required to heat, cool, and ventilate our homes and other buildings. With about 40 percent of the energy used in this country and others around the world toward this end, reducing the need for fuel in our buildings and substituting renewable energy for fossil fuel can make a tremendous difference in our environment. The availability of technology to reduce energy consumption in homes is better than it has ever been in the past, and the mechanisms to capture renewable energy are also more readily available and at a lower cost.

Some countries around the world have taken the challenge to reduce the use of fossil fuel very seriously. One of the important goals of the European Union (EU), for example, has been to improve energy efficiency and to meet their commitments on climate change, made under the Kyoto Protocol originally adopted in 1997. In 2008, the EU agreed on an integrated approach to climate and energy policy called the Climate and Energy Package with the aim of transforming Europe into a highly energy-efficient, low-carbon economy. Its midterm targets, known commonly as the 20-20-20 targets, include a 20 percent reduction in greenhouse gas emissions from the 1990 levels, an increase to 20 percent renewable energies (in the total energy consumption in the EU), and a 20 percent improvement in energy efficiency across all EU countries by 2020.

Other countries around the world have also been working toward reducing the use of fossil fuel and, like the EU, are attempting to reduce the wasting of natural resources and increase the preservation of land. There are a multitude of certification programs for homes around the world, which were created to help reduce energy consumption. Several of the houses certified by these programs are profiled in this book.

In North America, we have established numerous guidelines and certification programs for home construction, as well as other types of construction. These have inspired homeowners, architects, and builders to meet the challenges established by these programs, such as LEED for Homes, ICC National Green Building Standard certification, and Passive House.

Sheri Koones's books have inspired professionals and homeowners to consider using prefabrication methods that reduce waste, inherently conserve energy, and limit the need for fossil fuel. This latest book, *Prefabulous World*, demonstrates the valiant efforts by builders around the world to use prefab methods to build houses that not only are beautiful but also substantially reduce energy usage and drastically reduce construction waste. I hope these examples will inspire you as they have inspired me.

—Robert Redford
Environmentalist, Actor, Director

OPPOSITE Villa Langenkamp (see page 80), seen here nestled among tall pine trees, was the first certified Passivhaus in Denmark. (Photo by Thomas Søndergaard)

As a society we are becoming increasingly concerned about this planet we inhabit. We need the water we drink to be clean, the air we breathe to be unpolluted, and the homes we reside in to be healthy. We all want to leave this earth intact so future generations will have resources and be able to enjoy the natural beauty of our planet.

A crucial step in protecting our environment is to build houses that reduce the need for heating and cooling using fossil fuel. Building more energy-efficient homes in the United States and around the world can have a significant effect on the high consumption of fuel used for heating and cooling, on the environment, and in perserving our natural resources.

Fossil fuels are a fraught subject. There are political ramifications to acquiring the fuels, as well as environmental issues in extracting them from the earth. Making use of the fuels emits greenhouse gases and pollution. There is also the growing financial expense for their use to fuel both our cars and our homes.

We have learned over the years that there are better ways to build a house to drastically reduce the amount of fossil fuels necessary to heat and cool it. These methods can also create healthier environments for us to live in.

A GLOBAL EFFORT

This book includes some of the most energy-efficient and environmentally friendly houses in nineteen countries around the globe. My previous books demonstrate the ingenuity and creativity of architects and builders in the United States. By expanding this book to include houses all around the world, we can see a wider range of styles, climates, and techniques. A worldwide survey introduces practices that might not be familiar or common to us but are ones we can all learn from. It's exciting to see how the global efforts being made to reduce energy consumption are improving the environment.

The variety of styles and methods used around the world is truly inspiring. As many countries work to reduce energy usage in the home, architects and builders have developed a huge range of methods and materials to make energy efficiency a reality. We can all benefit from sharing this information and technology.

WHY PREFABRICATION?

Prefabrication offers huge benefits in terms of construction duration, quality, and cost.

Most people would prefer to have their home built quickly, limiting the need for an alternative residence while waiting for the house to be completed and reducing the time required for the construction loan. With prefab construction, the foundation and house structure can be built simultaneously, reducing the overall building time. Depending on the prefab method, components for the construction in the factory can be completed in a few days to several months—far less time than is generally required on-site.

Often there are cost advantages for factories, which purchase materials in bulk, decreasing the product and shipping costs. Factories are also often located in areas where construction costs are more advantageous.

Computer controlled machinery is often used in factories, reducing construction time and making wood cuts more precise. These machines are faster

OPPOSITE The welcoming entrance area of the Eliasch House in Austria (see page 38) is accessible via a light-colored natural stone staircase. The wine-red front door has a large glass frame, which lets natural light flood into the interior. All materials used to build the home were tested by organic biologists for pollutants. (Photo courtesy of Anton Stefars)

The Facit House in Hertfordshire, England (see page 110) was constructed with digitally prefabricated components.

and more accurate than those used by site-based workers using conventional hammers and saws.

During prefabrication, professionals supervise the construction of these houses inside factories, which limits the opportunities for error and prevents the homes from being compromised by weather or excessive moisture. Materials left out in the rain and snow—as they often are during typical on-site construction—can easily rot and decay after they are used to build the house. This leads to the threat of air infiltration and mold, which can cause health problems. Prefabricated houses avoid this threat because they are built in controlled environments, with ideal conditions for the construction materials, as well as for the workers. And in terms of limiting the construction duration, weather conditions also do not limit work in factories, which can operate regardless of the weather or extremes in temperature.

Many factories have also incorporated methods of building more efficient homes with advanced framing techniques and additional insulation. Some factories own their own equipment for spray foam installation, reducing the cost for this very efficient means of insulating a house.

Prefabrication has been my mantra for a long time because it is such a superior way to build. In addition to saving time and money and reducing site disturbance, prefabrication saves materials. The materials that often end up in Dumpsters on-site are, instead, reused for other houses or returned to the manufacturer and recycled.

I believe saving energy and saving materials go hand in hand. So, when I searched for the most energy-efficient houses for this book and my previous ones, I selected only prefabricated homes because I cannot consider a structure fully efficient when it is built with excessive material waste.

The benefits of prefabrication are numerous and always evolving. An ingenious variation, which maintains the advantages listed above without the

BELOW   In this rear view of the Portland HOMB (see page 260), the back deck is visible. It is an example of a home built by modular construction. (Photo courtesy of Michael Cogliantry)

BOTTOM   The Montana Farmhouse (see page 254) was built using structural insulated panels. (Photo courtesy of Holly Donoven Seion Studio)

existence of a permanent factory, is a new technology exhibited in England that brings the factory, with a computer-controlled machine, to the site in a shipping container. In England, Facit House (see page 110) was built using digitally prefabricated components. This process saved time, created components that were easily handled without a crane or hoist, and resulted in minimal waste and minimal damage to the site.

A WIDE VARIETY OF METHODS

Many different kinds of prefabrication methods are being used around the world. Modular construction is popular in the United States and beyond, with exciting new designs being seen in homes like the Portland HOMB (see page 260) and the Elsternwick in Australia (see page 22). In addition to being energy efficient, modular houses have been shown to be more resilient. After Hurricane Andrew, the Federal Emergency Management Agency (FEMA) determined that modular housing "provided an inherently rigid system that performed much better than conventional residential framing."[*] With the rise in dramatic hurricanes and tsunamis, building stronger and more durable houses is increasing in importance.

Building with structural insulated panels (SIPs) is another method, which is growing in popularity because the panels create such a tight and efficient envelope, also reducing construction time and energy costs. The SIP Panel House in Chile (see page 70), the Positive Energy ECOXIA House in France

[*]   "Building Performance: Hurricane Andrew in Florida," FEMA, December 1992

BELOW The kitchen and library of the Solar Tube house in Austria are on the ground floor. The flooring is stone, which functions as thermal mass (see Glossary, page 290), to help maintain comfortable temperatures inside the house. (Photo by Bruno Klomfar)

BOTTOM In the Camden Passivhaus in England (see page 98), the insulated timber front door has a triple-glazed panel to allow natural light and solar energy into the entrance area. The door was manufactured in Germany and has two layers of continuous seals to prevent drafts. (Photo by Tim Crocker)

(see page 134), and the Montana Farmhouse in the United States (see page 254) are examples of highly efficient houses built with SIPs.

The overabundance of maritime shipping containers is now being put to good use in houses such as the worldFLEXhome in Denmark (see page 86), which is both more attractive and more efficient than many of the earlier versions of this type of construction.

There are also wonderful hybrid systems that have developed around the world. Beautiful examples include Austria's Solar Tube (see page 42), which is designed to collect light and make use of renewable energy like a solar panel or tube, and Archway Studios in England, which is created out of steel components to adapt to a brownfield environment (see page 92). France's Fusion Bretagne (see page 130) is built with a new hybrid log system that uses airtight and strong cross-laminated logs.

Manufacturers and builders around the world have also found more efficient ways to build timber frames and panelized systems, which create homes that are not only attractive but also function at a high level of energy efficiency and comfort. The Camden Passivhaus in England (see page 98) and the green[r]evolution Plus Energy House in Germany (see page 140) are examples of this type of home, which are both incredibly energy efficient.

Additionally prefabricated methods aid in the building of homes in difficult places. The lack of skilled workers, shortage of materials, and limited access on roads create roadblocks in construction. But houses such as the Dangar Island House (see page 28) on an island in Australia and Casa Iseami (see page 74), built in a remote area of Costa Rica, are made possible with the use of prefabrication

Two modular homes are shown here in the late stages of construction in South Boston, Virginia. One of them is built to the highly energy-efficient Passive House standard, and for comparison, the neighboring house looks the same but was built to the normal building code. The homes were designed by the ecoMOD Project— a research and educational initiative at the University of Virginia. After occupation in the fall of 2013, the units will be monitored and evaluated to assess the return on investment for the use of the Passive House standard in affordable housing. (Photo courtesy of Michael Britt)

methods that take into account the limitations of the environment where the house will be set.

It is exciting to see the ongoing developments in prefabricated construction, which have continued to occur so rapidly, even since my previous book was published in 2012. The homes in this book illustrate the positive impact and efficiency of these construction methods and how this vibrant industry continues to evolve and adapt to an endlessly varied list of homeowner needs.

CERTIFYING GREEN

Architects and builders in countries worldwide have taken steps to reduce the use of fossil fuels and greenhouse gas (GHG) emissions, and a variety of systems are being used to help accomplish this reduction. Some countries offer tax incentives to offset the cost of renewable energy systems. This is true in the United States, the United Kingdom, Germany, and Italy, among others.

Labeling programs, in the United States and Europe as well as other countries, help reduce energy demand: "Labeling acts as an incentive for manufacturers to differentiate themselves from their competitors and stimulates the introduction of new, more efficient models. Standards remove from the market the less efficient appliances."* A few examples of labeling systems include the ENERGY STAR label in the United States, the EnerGuide in Canada, and the European Union energy label.

Establishing certification programs has also encouraged the construction of more energy-efficient structures by creating guidelines for better building methods. In North America, we've adapted several guidelines to define environmentally friendly construction. Each year more houses are certified by the LEED for Homes program established by the United States Green Building Council. Examples of these homes include the Morris Island House (see page 64), the Beachaus (see page 54), and the Nexterra LivingHome (see page 48), all in Canada. ICC 700 National Green Building Standard certification is also growing in the United States.

Passive House (or Passivhaus) standards, which originated in Germany, are now being used to build houses in the United States and in many European countries, New Zealand, and other locations around the world. These standards focus on the efficiency of the building envelope and interior heath of the structure, as opposed to other environmental factors included in other certification programs. Austria's Plus Energy Passivhaus (see page 34); the Passivhaus in Bessancourt (see page 126), the Evolu-

---

* *Energy Efficiency Policies around the World: Review and Evaluation, Executive Summary World Energy Council 2008*

BELOW At the Team Israel house, the living wall, where a variety of vegetation can be grown, creates a private outdoor area. (Photo courtesy of TEAM ISRAEL ALL [E] LAND)

BOTTOM Construction of the Team Israel house was completed with a prefabricated and recyclable light steel frame and insulated panels constructed of two galvanized and prefinished steel sheets bonded to a noncombustible mineral wool core. The house was inspired by traditional Mediterranean homes, which make use of outdoor areas; however, unlike many houses in Israel, this house was built to be highly insulated and requires minimal energy for heating and cooling. (Photo courtesy of TEAM ISRAEL ALL [E] LAND)

tive Home in France (see page 120); and England's Camden Passivhaus (see page 98) are examples of houses meeting this standard. The Passive House concept is also growing in the United States with such examples as the Island Passive House in Washington (see page 248).

There are a multitude of national and regional programs around the world, which are covered in the pages to follow, that limit the use of fossil fuels by recognizing energy-efficient structures and identifying healthy and more efficient products. For instance, the Minimum Energy Performance Standards (MEPS) of Australia, the BBC Effinergie in France, and Italy's CasaClima demonstrate the growing dedication to the construction of energy-efficient homes.

THE GLOBAL SOLAR DECATHLON

Since its inception in 2002, the Solar Decathlon, a collegiate competition that recognizes environmentally friendly home design, has always included international prefabricated houses, but the event has substantially expanded. In addition to the several Solar Decathlons that have occurred in Washington, DC, the event has gone truly global and now takes place in Madrid, Spain, as well as in Datong, China. The United States Department of Energy challenges students from all over the world to explore energy efficiency and prefab construction firsthand by developing their own innovative houses for these events. Participants from the Madrid event in 2012, Romania's PRISPA (see page 212), and the DC event in 2011, New Zealand's First Light (see page 202), are profiled in this book.

The houses built for the China event in 2013 were also very technologically sophisticated and environmentally friendly, and a few examples are

BELOW The Green Sun House is reminiscent of the classic yurtlike habitats indigenous to inner Mongolia and other parts of Central Asia. The design takes advantage of the traditional benefits of these structures, such as good ventilation and convenience of assembly, while also employing modern architecture and technology. (Photo courtesy of Inner Mongolia University of Technology, Team Green Sun)

BOTTOM The structure of the Green Sun House is made of a prefabricated steel frame. (Photo courtesy of Inner Mongolia University of Technology, Team Green Sun)

BELOW The shape of the E-Concave House, designed by Team SCUT for the Solar Decathlon is based on the traditional Chinese courtyard houses. In order to resist the cold wind in winter, the house's exterior wall has few openings. The kitchen, living room, and bedroom all open up to a central courtyard. (Photo courtesy of Team SCUT)

BOTTOM The atrium of the E-Concave House changes with the seasons. In the summer, it is a water pool, which will help cool the house with the windows and doors open. In the winter, the water is drained and the atrium will serve as a sunroom, which absorbs the heat from the sunlight with the windows and doors closed. (Photo courtesy of Team SCUT)

shown here. For instance, an Israeli team participated for the first time in a Solar Decathlon. The house was built by students from four universities: Shenkar College of Engineering and Design, Tel Aviv University—The Porter School of Environmental Studies, The College of Management—Academic Studies, and The Neri Bloomfield School of Design and Education.

Team SCUT, from the South China University of Technology, finished second in the overall Solar Decathlon contest. Team SCUT used module design and construction methods for their E-Concave House, which made industrial prefabrication possible. The structure was convenient to transport, assemble, and disassemble. The main body of the house is divided into three modules. All the modules were prefabricated in a factory and then assembled on-site in ten days. The team choose environmentally friendly materials and energy-saving products to create a healthy and comfortable interior environment.

The many houses that have been designed and built by students around the world for the Solar Decathlon demonstrate the ingenuity and creativity that we can expect from the next generation of architects, engineers, and builders.

NEW, MORE EFFICIENT MATERIALS AND SYSTEMS

The growing interest in energy efficiency has encouraged the development of creative new solutions and more efficient products, which help limit air infiltration and reduce the need for heating and cooling. This book features some of the most effective and innovative uses of these products.

In particular, windows and doors have become more efficient. Triple-glazed windows and more efficient double-glazed windows are becoming increasingly popular around the world. Mechanical systems that operate with less fuel and renewable energy sources are also more readily available and varied. Combined heating, cooling, ventilation, and water heating products are coming of age and have been used in the Plus Energy Passivhaus in Austria (see page 34) and the Edge in England (see page 116), among others.

Advanced framing techniques, which vastly reduce air infiltration, are being used by companies like Method Homes to build structures, such as the Portland HOMB in Oregon (see page 260). The Energy Neutral Residence in the Netherlands (see page 194), and Spain's Villa EntreEncinas (see page 226), both have incorporated cross-laminated wood, a new product that reduces construction time and is structurally very stable. Metal structural insulated panels, once used only for commercial construction, are now being used for building homes such as the Casa Iseami in Costa Rica (see page 74).

Various materials are being used to enhance insulation. Blown-in spray foam and cellulose insulation are popular in the United States. But there are many other materials being used around the world, such as glass wool insulation in Denmark's Villa Langenkamp (see page 80) and PRISPA in Romania (see page 212) and wool insulation in First Light in New Zealand (see page 202). Laurel Hollow, in the United States (see page 242), was built with a polyisocyanurate rigid insulation with very high performance.

Other new and exciting materials are slowly being introduced into home construction, such as Aerogen, which was developed for NASA, and was used for insulation in the Energy Neutral Residence (see page 194).

Manufacturers are increasingly focused on the life cycle of products and making use of recycled materials. The world's resources are finite, and the well-known solution for this is "Reduce, Reuse, Recycle." Adhering to this motto can be accomplished in a multitude of ways, an important one of which is by using products that contain recycled materials and purchasing items from companies that use less water in their production and less packaging in their shipping.

Luckily the choices for these kinds of products have never been greater. As you'll see in many of the houses in the pages to follow, there are many products available today that are made from recycled materials and are also recyclable at the end of their use, adhering to the concept of Cradle to Cradle®.*

BUILDING MORE EFFICIENT HOMES

Profiling fifty energy-efficient prefabricated houses around the world, this book demonstrates a variety of prefab methods, architectural styles, and techniques used to meet high-energy standards. Despite the diversity of homes showcased in this book, they all have one thing in common: They were built with careful construction of the building "envelope." Many types of insulation, windows, roofing, and foundations were used to build these houses, but all of them were planned as systems to create the most efficient structures. Popular strategies featured in these pages that limit the use of fossil fuels and guarantee an efficient envelope include: optimal solar orientation; more abundant windows on the side of the house getting the most solar gain;

---

* A concept developed and popularized by William McDonough and Michael Braungart with their 2002 book *Cradle to Cradle: Remaking the Way We Make Things.*

BELOW This is the side view of the Dream House in Germany (see page 162) with a patio on the second level used for outdoor dining. The external smoke pipe adds a design feature to the house. (Photo courtesy of Peter Kiefer)

The six modules of the Nexterra LivingHome (see page 48) are delivered to the site on flatbed trucks. The site where the house was set includes a big ravine with many large-growth trees. Only a few of the trees were removed to make room for this house and the three other houses that will follow on this same site. (Photo courtesy of Nexterra Green Homes Ltd.)

fewer windows on the side where heat may be lost; large overhangs to block the sun in the summer and encouraging sunlight in the winter; excellent, efficient insulation throughout the entire structure; and energy-efficient windows.

The book stresses the above themes throughout, as I believe these are particularly crucial to improving home construction. As I have tried to do with prior books, with these examples of new, exciting home design I hope to increase consumer understanding of energy efficiency, show some healthy options for the home, and increase awareness of designs that can be achieved within these parameters.

According to a research study done in the United Kingdom by the NHBC Foundation, "Today's Attitudes to Low and Zero Carbon Homes," there are several methods that could be implemented to encourage people to buy and realize the benefits of low- and zero-carbon homes. The report suggests that we need to improve understanding of zero carbon homes, develop consumer-friendly terminology, and provide better information to consumers regarding the materials and systems available, and I see this book as a part of that process.

Beautiful and efficient designs have been created by architects and builders around the world to build the houses in this book, and I believe we can all benefit from sharing their expertise and creativity. Building more efficient and healthy homes is a win-win situation for everyone. We create a better environment for the world as a whole by limiting greenhouse gas emissions and protecting our natural resources, while we are creating a healthier, more comfortable, and cost-effective home for ourselves.

As the documentary *A Fierce Green Fire* elo-

quently suggests, "Over the course of fifty years, environmentalism has shifted from saving wild places to saving human society. How we find a path to a sustainable future will involve reinventing not just the way we make and do everything, but reinventing the way we think about our place in the natural world."*

Changing how we build our homes is one of the most crucial improvements we can make in how our societies function, in order to shape a more sustainable future and redefine our place in the natural world. Deciding where we live, and what kind of house we call home, is a personal choice that we all have to make—and it's a choice that can have a significant impact on our environment.

I hope this book will inspire you to consider the many home construction options that can improve our world.

* www.afiercegreenfire.com

Elsternwick

Modular/SIPs/Steel Frame

PHOTOGRAPHER:

Ben Johnson (unless otherwise
noted)

**ARCHITECT/MANUFACTURER/
BUILDER:**

Modscape

LOCATION:

Elsternwick, Melbourne, Australia

SIZE:

2,626 square feet (244 sq m)

CERTIFICATION:

FirstRate5—7 Stars
(see sidebar, page 25)

▶ **GREEN ASPECTS:**

Dual-flush toilets

Engineered limed oak flooring

Low-VOC paints

Small footprint

Structural plywood cladding

WELS-rated 4.5 star water fixtures
and appliances

▶ **ENERGY ASPECTS:**

Ceiling fans

High-efficiency windows

Hydronic heating system

LED lighting

No cooling system

Optimal solar orientation

Solar hot water panels

Structural insulated panels (SIPs)

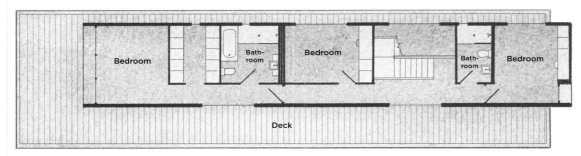

SECOND FLOOR

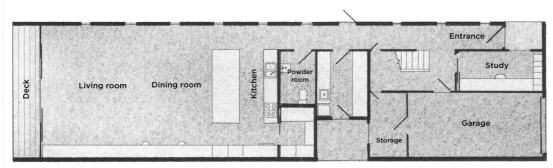

FIRST FLOOR

OPPOSITE The hundred-year-old Victorian house that previously sat on the property had unsteady floors, leaked, and was too small for Jan, Blair, and their two sons. (Photo courtesy of the owners)

BELOW By constructing a modular house, Jan and Blair were able to preserve the trees that were on-site since the lot was only minimally disturbed with the demolition and construction. The siding is an EcoPly, a structural plywood that is manufactured from sustainably grown New Zealand plantation pine.

With their two sons and their cat, Jan and Blair began to feel their one-hundred-year-old Victorian house was too small. In addition, the house was leaky and the floors unsteady. Because the house was central to multiple types of public transport, near great schools, and a short walk to retail stores and parks, they wanted to remain at that location.

BUILDING MODULAR AND LIMITING CONSTRUCTION TIME

With modern houses on either side of their house, Jan and Blair decided to have their new house built modular and with a modern aesthetic to fit in with the neighborhood. They watched their neighbors' houses being built on-site, in nine and twelve months respectively, and were excited to learn their own house would be completed in just three weeks, from demolition to move-in.

CONSTRUCTION CHALLENGES

It was a challenge to install this house on a lot just 24 feet and 7 inches (7.5 m) wide. An additional challenge was to demolish the old house without disturbing the two houses so close on either side. A third challenge was to lift the modular units over the many power lines above the street.

A SEAMLESS EXPERIENCE

Jan and Blair chose Modscape to build their home because the company was able to offer a seamless experience—designing, building, installing, and finishing the construction of the house. All the modules were constructed to completion in the factory before being transported to the build site. This includes plastering, painting, tiling, and installing the cabinetry, a hydronic heating system, lighting, water systems, blinds, flooring, decking, pergolas, and all internal electrical wiring and plumbing fixtures. They also installed appliances, such as refrigerators, washing machines, televisions, and more. Only fixtures and fittings that required the modules to be connected before being finished were installed on-site—such as floorboards that sit directly above the join lines between the modules, cladding that covers module joins, exterior baseboards that run around the bottom edge of the modules to prevent rodents from getting in, etc.

Other than a minor water-main problem on installation day that delayed the set by two hours, the house came together seamlessly in two days. Blair was very concerned that the modules would not line up, since the placement of the staircase left no room for being off by even a millimeter. But when the installation was completed everything lined up perfectly. The house was built very strong, with a steel frame, and very energy efficient, with structural insulated panels to form the roof, walls, and floors. There are six modules that comprise the first floor and two for the second. Jan and Blair chose the bold safety-jacket orange for the top floor and a more subtle gray for the first floor.

Jan says, "Building from scratch meant I could do all the things I wanted in the house—Modscape doesn't have any limits on that. I was able to design everything to suit my family's needs. We would not have done it any other way."

BELOW The flooring throughout the first floor is engineered limed oak. All the cabinetry in the house was built in the factory.

BOTTOM LEFT The floor in the shower is tilted toward the drain in the bathroom so the floor is seamless and flush with all other surfaces.

BOTTOM RIGHT The sliding closet doors allow some storage areas to be hidden from view.

FirstRate5

FirstRate5 is Victoria's leading residential thermal performance assessment software. It is used by the majority of the industry to rate the energy-efficiency compliance of residential dwellings under the National Construction Code (NCC) of Australia. The standard applies to all new homes and major renovations and extensions. It is used to generate the home rating and can be used to rate an existing structure or as an interactive tool to optimize a new design for or beyond compliance. FirstRate5 is one of three software packages in Australia to be accredited with the NatHERS protocol for national regulatory compliance, which is administered by the Commonwealth Department of Climate Change and Energy Efficiency. The software tool generates ratings based on the NatHERS 0–10 star scale for homes, with 6 stars being the current regulatory requirement for new homes, major renovations, and extensions. For further information about this software, see www.sustainability.vic.gov.au.

Water Efficiency Labeling and Standards (WELS)

WELS is the mandatory labeling system used in Australia for providing water efficiency information to purchasers of certain household products. The products covered by the scheme are plumbing products (showers, certain tap equipment, stand-alone flow controllers, toilets, and urinals) and whitegoods (washing machines, the dryer function of combination washer/dryers, and dishwashers). Further to this minimum, water efficiency requirements are applied to toilets and washing machines. WELS was established to reduce water consumption in Australia, provide water efficiency information to purchasers of water-using products, and encourage efficient and effective water-using technologies. For additional information see www.waterrating.gov.au

BELOW The large sliding doors at the rear of the house allow natural ventilation and let in natural light.

OPPOSITE Beautiful primary colors can be seen throughout the house, including in the children's room, on the factory-built cabinets and desk. Floor-to-ceiling windows allow in a great deal of light.

Dangar Island House

Kit House/Steel Frame

PHOTOGRAPHER:
Patrick Bingham-Hall

ARCHITECT:
Sue Harper

STRUCTURAL ENGINEER:
Max Irvine

ENVIRONMENTAL ENGINEER:
Andy Irvine

MANUFACTURER:
Mecando

BUILDER:
Liam Flood

LOCATION:
Dangar Island, Australia

SIZE:
1,722 square feet (160 sq m)

▶ **GREEN ASPECTS:**

6,600-gallon (25,000-liter) rainwater tank
Dual-flush toilets
Low-flow faucets
Minimal waste with prefabrication
Wastewater treatment
Water recycling

▶ **ENERGY ASPECTS:**

CFL lighting
Cross-ventilation
Energy-efficient ceiling fans
Gas cooking (with propane)
Heat pump
High-efficiency appliances
Large overhangs
Low-combustion stove
Wool-polyester blend insulation

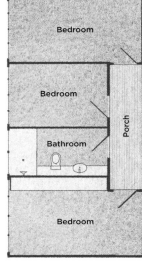

LOWER FLOOR

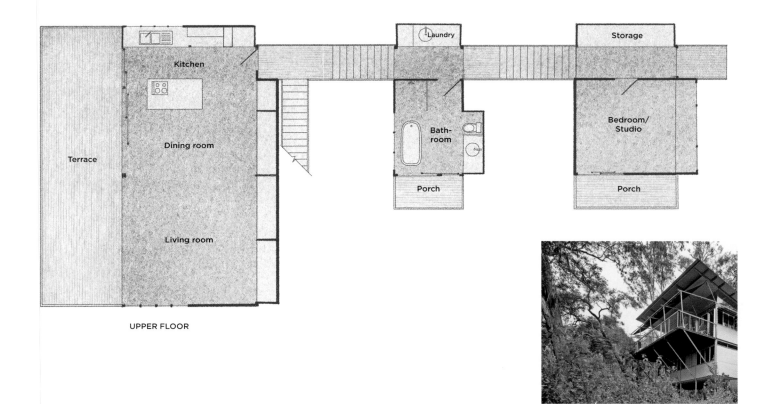

UPPER FLOOR

OPPOSITE The roofs are slanted to collect rainwater, which is channeled to and then stored in a large tank next to the bathhouse pavilion. The roofs can also be opened to the north to allow sunlight to penetrate the main living space in the winter and closed to keep the sunlight out in summer.

BELOW East elevation showing two of the three pavilions on the hillside among the tall gum trees.

After watching local builders struggling with on-site construction in the rural communities of the outback, architect Sue Harper and her husband, engineer Andy Irvine, decided there had to be a better way to build. They developed a prefab method of building that would be ideal for remote construction sites, which also allowed them to create homes that are flexible, durable, affordable, and environmentally friendly.

They design houses that require minimal maintenance and that can be expandable for a homeowner's changing needs, with parts that can be disassembled and moved to another location as needed. The Dangar Island House is one example of their work.

RESTRICTIONS ON DANGAR ISLAND

Building on Dangar Island presented many challenges. There are limited craftsmen and materials on the island. Thus, materials, produced in Sydney, had to be brought to the island by boat and connected on-site. With only one truck and a small crane on the island to move materials, the components had to be light. It took approximately six trips to bring most of the components to the island. The large portions were moved by truck and crane, while wheelbarrows were used to move the smaller parts. Andy said, "I worked with Liam, the builder, to put the Dangar House together, and we always laugh about how many wheelbarrows of gear we took across in the ferry and pushed up that hill!"

With limited services available on the island, the house had to be equipped with full on-site wastewater treatment equipment, a rainwater tank, and water recycling. There is also a high-energy, efficient hot water system.

The tight budget required that tradespeople such as electricians and plumbers could only be employed for a limited time. Systems were kept simple and adaptable so there was a limited need for highly skilled professionals on the project.

A PREFABRICATED SYSTEM

The house is built on steel pilings that minimally disturb the natural flora below. Connected to these components is a system consisting of braced steel "picture frames" that enables all walls and windows to be easily interchanged without any structural changes. Building with a steel frame eliminates the necessity of load-bearing walls that restrict the interior configuration and size of rooms, as well as offering the ability to easily expand the design.

The walls were prefabricated on the mainland with a timber frame, wool-polyester insulation, and a hoop-pine ply interior wall. The precut exterior cladding was attached on-site.

The design called for the Australian standard sheet size for materials for the floors, walls, and ceiling, which meant that a minimal amount of cutting was required on-site, limiting waste. In the future, the house can be easily expanded or additional pop-outs can be added because the materials are standard and easily available. Pop-outs, also known as bump-outs, are cantilevered microadditions to a room, which protrude out (like a bay window), expanding the footprint of the room, without requiring a foundation to be built to support it. The double doors and windows were easily connected with these prefabricated wall panels by a simple internal fixing system.

Materials were carefully chosen to balance environmentally responsible design and ease of

Large awnings protect the house from summer sun. Sliding doors with screens allow the full length of the living space to be opened for natural ventilation. Decking is made of blackbutt (*Eucalyptus pilularis*), a tree native to Australia. Public water is used for bathing; rainwater is used for the toilets and the laundry.

maintenance, while also meeting the new, stringent bush fire regulations.

A tightly scheduled program of work was implemented, which enabled site impact, waste, and construction time to be minimized, so as to disturb the other island residents as little as possible. The project was completed within three and a half months.

A TRIO OF BUILDINGS

Sue Harper's design for the Dangar Island House consists of three separate elevated buildings, linked by open, suspended walkways. The main living area and kitchen extend out to a full-length, covered hardwood deck set high in the treetops overlooking the Hawkesbury River.

The studio and bathhouse have complete privacy from the main section of the house and can be opened up to the surrounding bush land. Pop-outs from the main structures provide abundant storage and additional floor space.

All pavilions have decks allowing for outdoor living and beautiful views.

PASSIVE HEATING AND COOLING

Passive heating and cooling principles were adopted to minimize the need for any mechanical systems. Wide roof overhangs open up to the north, allowing maximum winter sun exposure and minimizing heat gain in the summer. Cross-ventilation is achieved throughout with an abundance of well-placed windows and doors throughout the structures. Fans help to keep residents cool in warm weather (see Glossary, page 288). As a result, the house is kept very comfortable without sophisticated mechanicals.

Since the Dangar Island House was built, Sue and Andy have developed a series of beach and country houses, studios, eco resort accommodations, home offices, school buildings, music rooms, kids' rooms, and so on, called *mihaus*. These are based on the principles developed during the construction of the Dangar Island House.

In this view of the kitchen from the main deck, the pop-out, which houses the sink, dishwasher, and cabinets and was added to expand the size of the kitchen, is visible.

BELOW The rear of the pavilion with the bedrooms, studio, and home office opens to the south and the bush beyond. This is a very private, secluded, and peaceful place to be.

BOTTOM This open shower has a timber slatted shower base with a stainless steel shower tray below to collect the shower water. The pop-out in the bathroom contains the toilet and vanity. At the opposite side of the walkway is another pop-out for a washer, dryer, and laundry storage space.

Plus Energy Passivhaus

Panelized

ARCHITECT/MANUFACTURER/BUILDER:

Elk Fertighaus AG

LOCATION:

Vienna, Austria

SIZE:

1,700 square feet (158 sq m)

CERTIFICATION:

Passivhaus

BLOWER DOOR TEST:

0.06 ACH @ 50 Pascals

▶ GREEN ASPECTS:

Low-flow faucets and showerheads

Low-VOC paints

Native plantings

Small footprint

▶ ENERGY ASPECTS:

All-in-one system (see sidebar, page 37)

Energy-efficient appliances

Energy recovery ventilator (ERV)

Glass wool insulation (see sidebar, page 85)

LED and CFL lighting

Optimal solar orientation

Photovoltaic panels

Triple-glazed windows

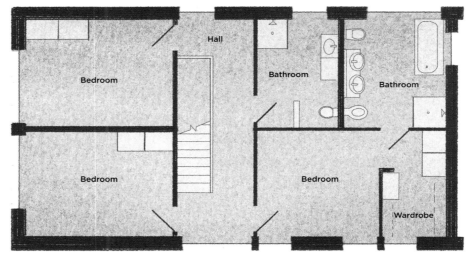

SECOND FLOOR

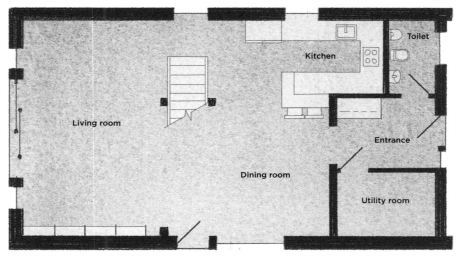

FIRST FLOOR

The Plus Energy Passivhaus, in the foreground of this image, is located at Blue Laguna, a park of show homes. The facade of the house is a high-pressure laminate, which is composed of acrylic/polyurethane/resin-impregnated paper and then pressed under extreme pressure and high temperature. It is scratch resistant and also resistant to graffiti. The photovoltaic panels on the house produce 7,000 kilowatt-hours of electricity per year. An average household in that latitude uses 3,000 to 4,000 kilowatt-hours per year.

The Plus Energy Passivhaus took just one day to build and approximately three and a half weeks to complete on-site. It was built in a factory that claims an 80 percent reduction in material waste because of its careful recycling of materials.

The turnkey cost for this house is €209,423 (which is approximately $280,000). This includes the structure and interior finishes like flooring, tiles, sanitary equipment, interior doors, plumbing, and wallpaper hanging.

PREFABRICATION

The quick construction time is due to the prefabrication. The wall panels, which are 9 feet by 44 feet (2.7 m by 13.4 m), were produced in one piece in the factory. The panel size was restricted by the dimensions of the trailers that delivered the panels. The external walls are timber frames that are 8 inches (203 mm) thick with glass wool insulation between the timber studs. The interior walls are plasterboard that is about ¾ inches (19 mm) thick, and on the exterior of the wall is gypsum fiberboard that is about 12 inch (15 mm). Onto this gypsum fiberboard a polystyrene layer is mounted and then the siding is installed. Electric conduits and pipes are also installed in the walls in the factory.

As much of the material as possible is prefabricated in the factory to avoid exposing the materials to weather conditions. The walls are loaded onto trailers vertically so that the siding will not get damaged and then they are lifted into place with a crane on-site. Ceilings and floor panels that are about 8 feet by 44 feet (2.4 m by 13.4 m) are also prefabricated at the factory, so the house can be waterproofed on-site as quickly as possible.

A GROWING PHENOMENON IN EUROPE

The house was set at Blue Laguna, a park that includes more than eighty other show houses—nine of them built by Elk Fertighaus. Several versions of the house have been sold as a result of this model house.

Elk Fertighaus maintains its show houses at the Blue Laguna Park for about five to ten years. About two hundred people visit the show houses every week. The houses are then dismounted and reassembled at another location. Passivhaus construction is very popular in Austria, Germany, and Switzerland (see Glossary, page 289). Elk Fertighaus has erected about 450 Passivhaus in these countries.

BELOW The floor plan is very open, which is a popular trend in Austria.

BOTTOM The floors are laminate, and the appliances are energy efficient.

OPPOSITE The bathroom's design is characterized by clean lines. The shower is on-grade so there is no step getting into it. LED lights are built into the shower enclosure.

All-in-one Systems for Heating/Cooling/Heat Recovery/Ventilation, or "Magic Boxes"

All-in-one systems are often called Magic Boxes; they combine all the functions of an HVAC system in one unit. The Compact P Heat Pump used in this house functions as a ventilation system with heat recovery, but also includes space heating and cooling, as well as domestic hot water. This type of system is compact, provides healthy indoor air, and reduces energy costs. While heat recovery can recapture a portion of space heating energy before it is exhausted and replaced with fresh air, the additional heat pump in this system can also increase the fresh air temperature on the coldest days directly within the supply air ducts. Separately, the same heat pump also provides 47.5 gallons (180 liters) of hot water for domestic use. This unit has additional options to incorporate a geothermal heat pump or outdoor air-to-water heat pump, which can supplement air heating with radiant floor heating. The Compact P system is certified by the Passivhaus Institut in Germany. For further information on this system, see www.nilan.dk, or for a similar system by Drexel & Weiss in Austria, see www .drexel-weiss.at.

Eliasch House

Timber Frame/Panelized

PHOTOGRAPHER:

Anton Stefan

ARCHITECT:

Georg Schauer

MANUFACTURER/BUILDER:

Baufritz

LOCATION:

Salzburg, Austria

SIZE:

3,310 square feet (308 sq m)

CERTIFICATION:

Min effezienzhaus 70

BLOWER DOOR TEST:

1.5 ACH @ 50 Pascals

▶ **GREEN ASPECTS:**

Dual-flush toilets

Low-flow faucets and showerheads

Low-maintenance landscaping

Low-VOC paints and stains

Xeriscape (low-maintenance
  landscaping)

▶ **ENERGY ASPECTS:**

Electrically operated window blinds

Large overhangs

LED lighting

Pellet boiler

Triple-glazed windows

Wood shaving insulation
  (see sidebar, page 151)

OPPOSITE The floor-to-ceiling glazing on the first floor catches the sun's warming rays in the winter, cutting expensive heating costs. In summer, the room can be shaded by using the electrically operated window blinds.

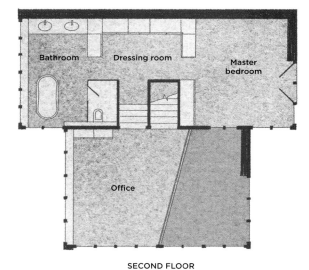

SECOND FLOOR

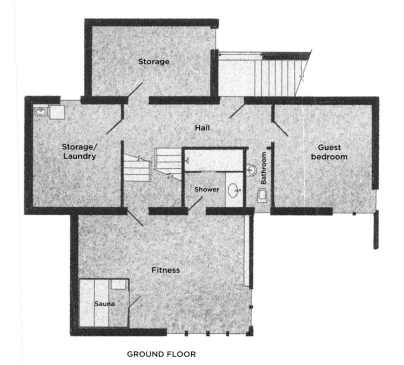

GROUND FLOOR

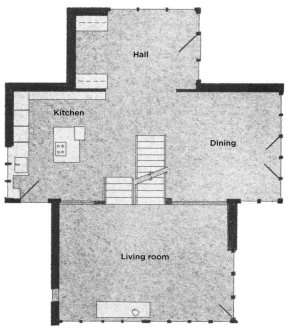

FIRST FLOOR

Everyone is familiar with the anticipation of the weekend after a long, demanding week at work. For a long time Mr. and Mrs. Eliasch dreamed of making the best of their time away from the office in a weekend home of their own design. A splendid plot of land on a slope near Salzburg provided an ideal location for achieving this wish.

The Eliasches chose this location because they could be surrounded by nature. The house was designed to best reflect the features of the land and the Eliasches' personal requirements.

Faithful to their motto for this home, "Relax, recuperate, and refresh," a wellness and sport area with its own sauna and quiet surroundings was incorporated into the basement level. This area was designed to be very comfortable, with soothing lighting, a charming arrangement of colors, high-quality materials, and meticulous attention to details.

Linked to the bathroom with a comfortable dressing room, the bedroom nestles under the slopes of the pitched roof. The room is flooded with light due to a glazed gable, which also provides a panoramic view. On the second floor is an office with a terrace with an inspiring view.

ECOLOGICAL CONSIDERATIONS

The owners wanted their vacation house to be not only architecturally interesting but also ecologically friendly. This was always foremost in their minds when making purchasing decisions. All the materials were tested by trained organic biologists for pollutants. "It is only by testing that we are able to ensure that we could hand over a pollutant-free healthy home to our customers. Thanks to the integrated electro-smog protection sheets, we are also able to hand over a home which is largely radiation-free," says builder Dagmar Fritz-Kramer.

BELOW The Eliasches wanted an open floor plan, so that the dining, kitchen, and living rooms were all conveniently linked to one another.

BOTTOM One of the most striking features of the house is the staggered single pitch roof. The steep plot necessitates multilevel living.

OPPOSITE The floor of the living room and all other rooms, other than the bath and anteroom, are furnished with maple vulcano, a special wood that is put into a stove and roasted on low temperature until it becomes a warm honey color.

Pellet Heating

Wood pellets are carbon neutral, renewable fuel, and usually made from 100 percent wood: cut-offs, sawdust, bark, and shavings, without any adhesive additives. Some are also made from agricultural crop waste, nutshells, and other organic materials. Most are made by compressing dry natural wood waste into cylindrical pellets with a diameter of ¼ inch and 1 to 1¼ inches in length (6 mm in diameter and 25 to 30 mm in length). Wood pellets take up very little space compared with logs, and because of their high heat value, they burn more efficiently and produce very little air pollution or creosote (a type of tar-like residue).

Pellet fuel appliances are available as freestanding appliances or as fireplace inserts. Pellet wood and regular, solid wood are more eco-friendly alternatives to nonrenewable fossil fuels, such as oil, coal, and natural gas.

Pellets are used for the heating system in the Eliasch House. The electronically controlled wood pellet boiler with its automated pellet feed system and modulating burner, is easy to use. A dosed delivery system gently transports the pellets to the burner. Dosed delivery means that only the correct amount of fuel goes to the burner when it is required. It does not continuously feed pellets. The boiler has a temperature set-point that it is attempting to maintain.

The burner features a fully automated cleaning mechanism to ensure long intervals between emptying of the system. The 211-gallon (800-liter) tank provides primary heated water to be circulated around the heating system and also instantaneous hot water via a plate heat exchanger.

In the Eliasch House, the wood pellets are stored in a canvas hopper with a capacity of 80.7 square feet (7.5 sq m). The hopper is made of tightly woven canvas on a metal frame and has a supply pipe. For additional information about pellet heating see www.windhager.com.

Solar Tube

Hybrid

PHOTOGRAPHER:
Bruno Klomfar

DESIGN ARCHITECT:
driendl*architects

LOCATION:
Dobling, Austria

SIZE:
3,315 square feet (308 sq m)

▶ **GREEN ASPECTS:**
Central manifold plumbing system
Clerestory windows
Composite materials for countertop and siding
Engineered wood
Fireplace with renewable energy source
Flexible interiors (to reduce need for future
    renovations)
Locally sourced materials
Low-flow faucets and showerheads
Native plantings
Natural ventilation
No-VOC paints and stains

Rain garden
Separate garage (no fumes or gas can
    permeate into house)
Walkable community

▶ **ENERGY ASPECTS:**
Concrete flooring
Daylighting
Large overhangs
Optimal solar orientation
Shaded property in summer
Sliding roof opens, creating chimney effect
Trombe wall

OPPOSITE Most of the frontal facade is
glazed. The front door is made of Oregon
pine and walnut.

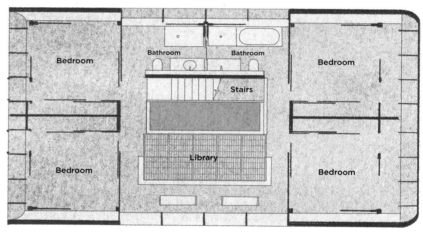

SECOND FLOOR

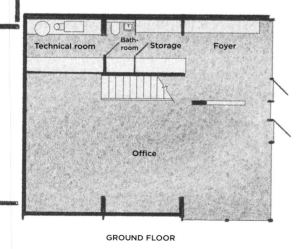

GROUND FLOOR

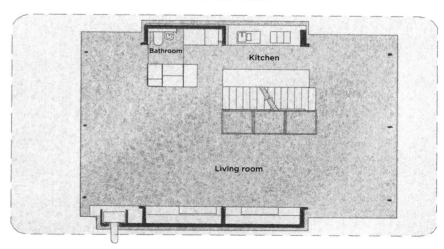

FIRST FLOOR

The design concept of the Solar Tube was to create a structure that functions similarly to a solar tube, a device that is usually installed on the roof, capturing heat and light on all sides. The goal according to the architect was "to lead solar energy in a passive way into the masses, capable of heat storage and releasing heat indoors." Therefore, the energy required for generating heat is minimized.

This mostly glazed design also offers "intimacy with the surrounding nature, therefore giving the feeling of living in a tree house. It's a symbiosis between nature and architecture," according to driendl*architects.

With a roof that slides open, warm air can escape with a chimney effect and cool air can be brought into the house. Trees that surround the house create shading in the summer, and when the leaves are off the trees in winter, warm sun can heat the compact house.

PASSIVE ORIENTATION

Before design and construction could begin on this house, careful information was collected on the location, the landscape, the sun's position at various times of the day and year, the number of hours of sunlight, and the typical weather conditions. The design of the house allows the structure to serve as a collector, open to light and heat on all sides. Since the roof and floors are also partly transparent, the core of the house works like an integrated atrium. A Trombe wall (see sidebar, page 46) helps to passively even out the heat in the house. Utilizing passive solar energy instead of fossil fuel substantially reduces the cost of heating the home.

PREFAB CONSTRUCTION

The house was built in just five months, which was made possible because of the use of mostly prefabricated or in-stock materials. The components of the house, which were built off-site in a controlled environment, are made of steel, timber, and glass. Choosing this alternative construction solution saved money, energy, and time. The architects point out that building this way, with parts that can easily be separated, also makes it more feasible to recycle the parts of the house in the future.

LIVING IN A GLASS HOUSE

The look of the "solar tube" is quite a unique design when seen from the street. The remarkable shape of the house and the glass facade attract the attention of passersby. So to provide privacy for the residents, the part of the house that faces the street is not as transparent as the sides facing the garden.

The integrated atrium that forms the core of the house is open to all sides. Even from the ground level one can see through to the sliding roof above, giving the feeling of "open living." This is possible due to the partially transparent floors and the bedrooms in the uppermost level, which are reached by crossing a see-through gallery. All of the interior furniture, in the kitchen, library, bathrooms, and so on, was designed by the architects; therefore, they fit in perfectly with the design of the house itself.

LEFT Because of the transparency of the construction, the different
levels of the house are visible from each floor.

RIGHT The second floor contains four bedrooms and a library.

BELOW A Trombe wall, the dark-colored siding on the first floor, can be seen on the side of the house and will help to warm the house passively.

BOTTOM The metal tube coming out of the side of the house, which can be seen from this rear view of the house and garden, is a stainless steel exhaust for the open fireplace in the living room.

OPPOSITE The view through the library on the second floor reveals the transparency of the structure.

Trombe Wall

A Trombe wall is a wall facing the sun (on the south side in the northern hemisphere and the north side in the southern hemisphere). It is separated from the outdoors by glass, with approximately ¾ to 2 inches (20 to 50 mm) of air space. The glazing reduces heat loss and allows more of the solar energy to transfer to the inside of the home. The wall, which is typically 4 to 16 inches (100 to 410 mm) thick and a dark, heat-absorbing material (such as masonry or concrete), absorbs solar energy and releases it toward the interior at night when the sun goes down. Some Trombe walls have vents at the top and bottom to allow heat to transfer earlier in the day, before the wall is able to release heat. Air enters the interior of the home from the warmed air space in the top vent and is replaced by air from the outside, entering through the lower vents, creating a convection loop. These vents should be closed at night to avoid the reverse of this convection loop.

These walls work particularly well in areas that have large temperature swings between the day and night. There is generally an overhang extending over the Trombe wall, which blocks the sun in the hot summer and allows the rays to enter in the winter when the sun is lower in the sky. Trombe walls decrease the need for conventional heating and provide a very even heat.

Nexterra LivingHome

Modular

PHOTOGRAPHER:
Finn O'Hara
(unless otherwise noted)

ARCHITECTURAL AND TECHNICAL CONSULTANT:
LivingHomes

ARCHITECT:
Ray Kappe

BUILDER/DEVELOPER:
Nexterra Green Homes Ltd.

MANUFACTURER:
Hi-Tech Housing Inc.

LOCATION:
Toronto, Ontario, Canada

SIZE:
2,130 square feet (198 sq m)

CERTIFICATION:
LEED Platinum (pending)

BLOWER DOOR TEST:
0.79 ACH @ 50 Pascals

ENERGUIDE RATED (ERS):
88 (see sidebar, page 58)

▶ **GREEN ASPECTS:**
Bio-organic, soy-based composite tubs and sinks
Cement fiber panel exterior rain screen system
Dual-flush toilets
FSC-certified flooring and lumber
Green roof ready (for the owner to install)
Landscaping that requires no irrigation
Low-flow water fixtures
Porcelain tile in all bathrooms
Quartz countertops with up to 35 percent
recycled content
Recycling of all possible demolition and
construction waste
Zero- and low-VOC paints and stains

▶ **ENERGY ASPECTS:**
ENERGY STAR–rated appliances
ENERGY STAR–rated fiberglass windows
ENERGY STAR–rated lighting, including LED
downlights and ENERGY STAR LED/CFL
light fixtures
Geothermal heating and cooling
Heat recovery ventilator (HRV)
Insulated concrete form basement
Solar-ready (for the owner to install)
Spray foam insulation (soy-based, for R38
walls and R50 in the roof)

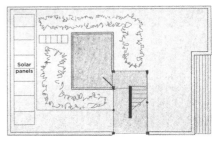

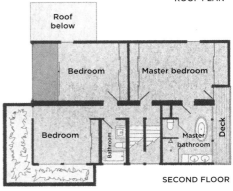

ROOF PLAN

SECOND FLOOR

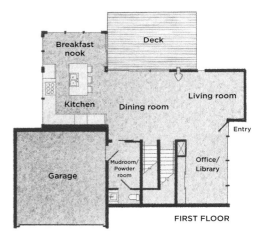

FIRST FLOOR

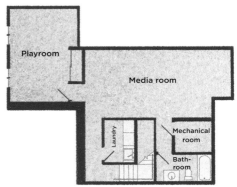

BASEMENT FLOOR

OPPOSITE A crane carefully lifted the modules into place on the foundation, limiting any disturbance to the site. (Photo courtesy of Nexterra Green Homes Ltd.)

BELOW The exterior of the home is a combination of Eternit fiber cement panels and custom-colored HardiePanel. They make up the rain screen system (see sidebar, page 48). A rain screen system is a double wall construction that uses an outer layer to keep the rain and snow away from the inner layer of thermal insulation. The outer layer breathes, while the inner thermal layer reduces energy loss. The shell of the building is kept dry as water never reaches it or the thermal insulation. This system is very durable and long lasting.

Gary Lands, the developer of the Nexterra LivingHomes, knew that it would be a challenge to sell a contemporary home in this traditional, residential community. However, he thought this contemporary design would allow more open spaces and more spacious livable areas. The house was built relatively small to meet the demands of the site and also to create cozier spaces that people will actually use on a regular basis and feel comfortable in.

TEAMING UP WITH LIVINGHOMES

Gary's company, Nexterra Green Homes Ltd., teamed up with LivingHomes, the builder of the first prefabricated LEED Platinum house in the United States. Gary was intrigued by the modular building method being used by LivingHomes, which he says creates tighter houses, less waste, and supports the use of better materials. He decided that modular was the way he wanted to build this first spec house and the three additional ones he plans to build at this location.

The modules were fabricated by Hi-Tech Housing about 450 miles (724 km) away in Bristol, Indiana, in just ten days, set in two days in January 2012, and completed about three and a half months later on-site.

BUILDING GREEN

Building the house as green as possible was a primary goal. With green consultant Laura Felstiner, the company was able to find the greenest materials available. As an example, instead of using Caesarstone's typical quartz material for the countertops, they opted for material made out of the company's offcuts, recycled mirrors, and glass from cars. The

kitchen appliances are not only ENERGY STAR–rated but also RoHS compliant (see sidebar, opposite).

Gary decided to incorporate a geothermal heating and cooling system, although it was more expensive than some other systems, because it is so efficient and creates minimal cost to operate.

GETTING CERTIFIED

Because the house was being built to such high green standards, Gary decided to have it certified by the Canada Green Building Council's LEED Canada for Homes program. He expects the house to meet the Platinum level, which is the highest standard possible in this program. LEED is still relatively new to Canada, but Gary believes it will be more widely recognized in time and that the future owners will appreciate having the certification.

OPPOSITE The light-filled home office/library is conveniently located off of the front entrance. A reclaimed wood desk and Second Life rug provide a colorful and clean space, with ample room in the cupboards for electronics and storage.

BELOW In this bedroom, there is a clerestory window and a west-facing, wide, floor-to-ceiling window (not seen in the photo) that looks over the future green roof.

BOTTOM The kitchen cabinets were produced by a very green company that powers their factory with a solar array, uses nontoxic materials, and follows life-cycle practices (produced by taking into consideration not only the raw materials and processes they require, but also how the products are shipped and disposed of by the customer). The downlights and under-cabinet lights are LED, and the faucet is low flow. The wood of the stools is FSC certified.

RoHS Directive

RoHS aims to restrict certain hazardous substances commonly used in electrical and electronic equipment. Any RoHS compliant component is tested for the presence of lead (Pb), cadmium (Cd), mercury (Hg), hexavalent chromium (Hex-Cr or Cr_6), polybrominated biphenyls (PBB), and polybrominated diphenyl ethers (PBDE) flame-retardants. For additional information about this directive, see www.rohscompliancedefinition.com.

FSC Certification

The Forest Stewardship Council (FSC) is one of fifty worldwide organizations that have developed standards for good forest management with third-party auditors, assuring end users that the wood comes from responsibly managed forests. All programs promote chain of custody certification, which follows the wood during every step of its production. The FSC is one of the largest and most commonly used certification programs in the world and assures that areas of special conservation value are protected, that workers' rights are respected, and that no illegal logging is occurring. For additional information, see www.fsc.org.

WETSTYLE'S WETMAR BiO™

This is a proprietary, patent-pending, and environmentally responsible material made from soy-based resin and a natural mineral stone granulate. It offers an alternative to the solid surface and composite sanitary ware materials made with petrochemical-based ingredients. WETMAR BiO offers strength, durability, slip resistance, heat retention, resistance to stains, ease of cleaning, and a superior finish. WETMAR BiO is renewable and easily repaired, and the surface is brought back to its original luster with just a light sanding and buffing. The material keeps replacement and energy expenditures to a minimum. WETMAR BiO is available in a high gloss or matte white finish. For more information see http://wetstyle.ca/wetmar-bio.

The gas fireplace meets LEED standards and is a great space saver in comparison to traditional gas fireplaces, which can take up a lot of valuable wall space. This one has glass on three sides so you can see the fire from most rooms on the first floor, and also has a Scandinavian look that appealed to the owners.

LEFT The bathtub and sinks are made from WETMAR BiO™ (see sidebar, page 51). All the wood is sustainably sourced.

RIGHT The open stairs not only let in southern light, but also allow for air to easily flow to the penthouse for passive cooling in the summer.

Beachaus

Modular

PHOTOGRAPHER:
Courtesy of InHaus Development

ARCHITECT:
PB Elemental Design

MANUFACTURER:
Method Homes

BUILDER:
InHaus Development

LOCATION:
White Rock, British Columbia,
   Canada

SIZE:
2,085 square feet (193.70 sq m)

CERTIFICATION:
LEED Platinum

BLOWER DOOR TEST:
1.75 ACH @ 50 Pascals

ENERGUIDE RATED (ERS):
86 (see sidebar, page 58)

▶ GREEN ASPECTS:
Dual-flush WaterSense-rated toilets
FSC-certified bamboo flooring
FSC-certified wood cabinetry and built-ins
Green roof
Integrated rainwater harvesting system
Large office with private entrance (promotes
   work-from-home)
Low-flow faucets and showerheads
Native plantings
No hallways or wasted space
Optimal solar orientation
Permeable paving
Soft-close drawers with FSC-certified solid
   wood drawer boxes
Xeriscape (low-maintenance landscaping)
Zero- or low-VOC paints and stains

▶ ENERGY ASPECTS:
Automatic skylight (with rain sensors) for
   passive ventilation
Automation system (wireless smartphone
   remote operation)
Cross-ventilation
DWHR system (drain water heat recovery)
Electric vehicle charging (prewired)
Energy monitoring
ENERGY STAR–rated appliances
Heat recovery ventilator (HRV) air-exchange
   system (HEPA filtered)
High-efficiency fiberglass windows and doors
Indirect hot water tank (uses heat from in-floor
   heating system to keep domestic hot water warm)
In-floor radiant hydronic heating throughout
Integrated Apple iPad® touch controller
On-demand pilot gas fireplace
Photovoltaic panel ready
Prewired for automatic blind system
Smart Wiring/Cat-5/HDMI throughout
Spray foam insulation (soy-based)
Ultraefficient ENERGY STAR–rated laundry
   with steam-dry
White TPO membrane roof (reflects heat)

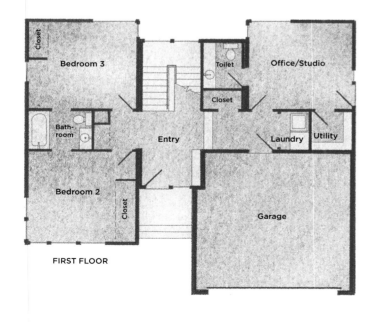

FIRST FLOOR

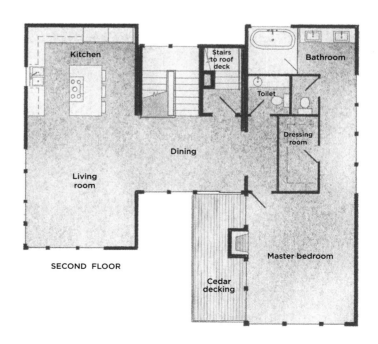

SECOND FLOOR

The house was sited to take the best advantage of the sun. The siding is a sandwich panel with aluminum on both sides and a plastic core for added strength. It is very durable and has a high recycled content. The home is surrounded with a permeable blue limestone to help promote drainage. A similar product was used on the walkways in conjunction with spaced-out pavers, rather than traditional impermeable concrete. Plants are all 100 percent native, drought-tolerant plants, and a thick layer of bark mulch was used to retain moisture in summer months and minimize erosion in the wetter winter.

The Beachaus was inspired by the modern homes that are seen along the California coastline. The developers wanted this house to be durable, extremely efficient, and very comfortable for the residents. They kept the footprint relatively small, selected sustainable materials, and designed the house to be as energy and water efficient as possible.

A DECISION TO BUILD "GREEN"

Developer-builder Dave deBruyn and his wife spent ten years refurbishing, renovating, and redeveloping single-family homes and condominiums. Years ago they grew conscious of the waste that the renovation process was generating and challenged themselves to recycle more than 90 percent of the materials they were removing from the properties. Dave says, "We became quite good at this process, eventually managing whole-home gut remodels with very little waste ever hitting a landfill. We decided at that point we wanted to look at certification programs (one of which was LEED) in order to start backing up our claims and providing verification of our processes for the eventual homebuyer. In 2010 we launched InHaus Development, a company solely focused on the development of sustainable homes, and Beachaus was the first project."

Dave commissioned designer Chris Pardo of PB Elemental Design to create Beachaus. Since Chris had an existing relationship with Method Homes, that company was an obvious choice to build the house when Dave decided he wanted to build modular. Method Homes is a CSA A-277 Canada-certified modular manufacturer (a Canadian code for factory certification of buildings). Beachaus was the first Method Home built in British Columbia.

AN EVOLVING INDUSTRY

Heating and cooling are kept to a minimum with optimal solar orientation, excellent insulation, high-energy windows and doors, and a smart home system, which allows the eventual owners to maximize energy efficiency based on the seasons by programming the shades and thermostat to automatically adjust for the time of day or outside temperature. These systems can also be controlled by a smartphone. The efficiency of the Beachaus makes it an excellent model for the homes that InHaus Development designs in the future.

Dave says, "There is no question that the industry has to evolve in response to the realities of our world in terms of environmentally friendly construction. Change is always a slow process, but we are still proud to be a part of it."

Floor-to-ceiling windows offer beautiful views, natural ventilation, and light. The natural lighting is supplemented by a combination of LED and halogen bulbs.

EnerGuide Rating System

The EnerGuide Rating System is administered by Natural Resources Canada's Office of Energy Efficiency (OEE) and shows a standard measure of a new or existing home's energy performance. This rating (from 0 to 100) provides current and future homeowners with information on the energy efficiency of the home (at the time when the energy evaluation was performed): 0 represents a house with significant air leakage, no insulation, and high fuel consumption, whereas 100 represents an airtight, well-insulated, and well-ventilated house that produces as much energy as it consumes over a year. The Beachaus achieved an EnerGuide rating of 86. Canada considers an EnerGuide score of 90 to be completely net zero, while 86/87 is considered the highest you can get without the use of renewable energy. To obtain a rating for new homes, a certified energy advisor conducts detailed modeling of the home (based on building plans, construction specifications, and equipment to be installed), then provides advice on potential upgrades to increase its efficiency, and finally conducts an assessment of work done and a blower door test (see Glossary, page 288) once the home is built. A label with the EnerGuide rating is then affixed to the home's electrical panel. For additional information see http://oee.nrcan.gc.ca/energuide/15896.

In addition to home ratings, the EnerGuide label can also be used to make informed buying decisions about different products.

A mandatory EnerGuide rating is provided in Canada for: clothes dryers, integrated clothes washer-dryers, clothes washers, dehumidifiers, dishwashers, electric ranges and ovens, refrigerators and freezers, and room air conditioners.

A voluntary EnerGuide rating is provided in Canada for air-source heat pumps, central air conditioners, gas and oil furnaces, gas fireplaces, and gas unit heaters. Coming soon, you may also be able to find an EnerGuide rating for water heaters and boilers.

Water Heat Recovery

Water heating accounts for approximately 20 to 30 percent of household energy demand. Much of the energy is expended warming the water coming into the shower. By transferring some of the heat from the drain water to the incoming water, reduced energy is required. Beachaus has Power-Pipe, a patent-pending system, incorporated into the plumbing. This system uses copper tubing, which wraps around the drainpipe and recovers approximately 17°F (45°C) to heat the incoming water using residual heat from wastewater leaving the home. The company claims the pipe can save up to 40 percent of water heating costs in the typical home. For further information see www.renewability.com.

BELOW To save space, the corridor from the master bedroom to the living room was enlarged to create a gracious dining room, which can easily accommodate a table to seat ten people. Floor-to-ceiling windows in this area allows "sneak peeks" of the kitchen area from the master bedroom, giving the illusion of a much larger space. The deck is set up for barbecuing, with gas and power hookups.

BOTTOM The master bedroom is showered with natural light from the floor-to-ceiling windows. The on-demand pilot gas fireplace helps to heat the room on cold nights. Typical gas fireplaces have a standing pilot light, which burns natural gas twenty-four hours a day, seven days per week—one of the reasons that many homeowners manually turn their fireplace pilot lights off in the summer. An on-demand pilot system lights the pilot light only when the fireplace is turned on. This one change can save up to $25 per month in natural gas costs, depending on the location.

Beachaus, Canada

Kitsilano

Modular/Steel Frame

PHOTOGRAPHER:

Jacob McNeil

Platinum HD Canada

ARCHITECT:

Balance Associates

MANUFACTURER/BUILDER:

Karoleena Inc.

LOCATION:

Naramata, British Columbia, Canada

SIZE:

1,520 square feet (141 sq m)

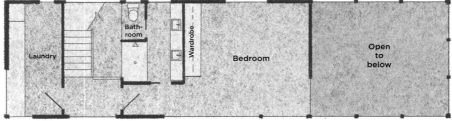

GREEN ASPECTS:

Low-flow water fixtures

Recycled content steel frame

Zero-VOC paints

ENERGY ASPECTS:

Automation system

ENERGY STAR–rated appliances

Energy-efficient heating and cooling

Geothermal heating and cooling

High-efficiency windows

Hi-Velocity air handler

Radiant floor heating (see Glossary, page 289)

LED and CFL lighting

Optimal solar orientation

Pressurized HVAC system

Spray foam insulation

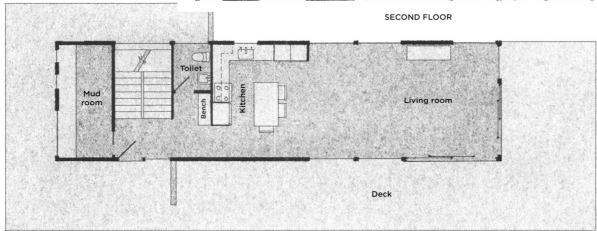

SECOND FLOOR

FIRST FLOOR

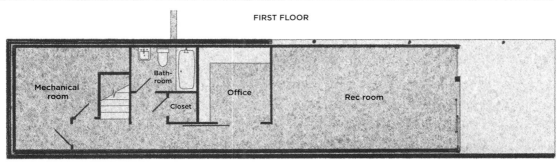

BASEMENT

The front of the house is south facing, so it has large overhangs to protect it from solar gain in the warmer months. The siding is a combination of cedar, fir, and steel.

The Kitsilano house was first displayed in the Vancouver Home and Garden Show in February 2012. It was then transported and assembled on-site in Naramata, British Columbia, where it will be sold.

According to Kris Goodjohn, a founder of Karoleena homes, "The house was designed for middle-aged people who enjoy beautiful architecture and have a passion for energy-efficient and smart spaces."

CONSTRUCTION OF THE HOUSE

Construction of the house was completed in five weeks from start to finish in the Karoleena warehouse. It was assembled in BC Place (a domed stadium) for the Home Show in four days and completed on-site for occupancy in just three weeks. The foundation was finished at the same time that the factory was building the modules.

BUILDING GREEN

Karoleena Homes is committed to building their houses very green. In so doing they claim that their average house creates less than 400 pounds (181 kg) of waste, which is far less than the typical 8,000 pounds (3,629 kg), as reported by the NAHB. They also create less wood scrap because they use steel for their frames and recycle cutoffs from the wood they use. They believe the energy cost savings for their homes will be excellent because of the insulation used in their walls, ceilings, floors and their advanced framing techniques.

HEATING AND COOLING

The house has a geothermal heating and cooling system. Heat is provided to all three floors through the in-floor hydronic system, which is run off the geothermal pump. Cooling is achieved using an air handler (with a small duct system), which also runs completely off the geothermal system. The home is both heated and cooled for a fraction of the cost of the other homes in the area. The geothermal HVAC system, combined with the fact that all the walls, floors, and roof are completely insulated with 2-pound spray-foam insulation in staggered stud walls that are 8 inches (200 mm) wide, provides an efficient building envelope

A LUXURY CONSTRUCTION

The house was built as a luxury home with several special features, which brought the cost of the house to over $300 a square foot. However, Kris says that by removing some of these add-ons, such as the geothermal system, home-automation, and sliding glass walls, the cost of the house could be reduced closer to the $200-a-square-foot range.

The house is a product of several different engineered systems using a steel and spray foam construction to achieve an extremely strong and efficient basic building structure. Kris says, "The construction methods (such as full steel frame and spray foam insulation), as well as careful attention to on-site assembly techniques and systems, allowed this very high-end home to easily be transported through the rocky mountains and subsequently assembled and disassembled two different times with literally zero damage to any of the structure or even the fully finished tile, hardwood, and drywalled interiors."

BELOW All of the appliances in the house are high efficiency.
The countertops of the island are made of quartz.

BOTTOM Beautiful views of the Okanagan Lake waterways and the
Okanagan Valley wineries can be seen from the house.

The Morris Island House

Timber Frame/Panelized

PHOTOGRAPHER:

Mathieu Girard

Studio Versa

ARCHITECT:

Jeff Armstrong

DAC International

MANUFACTURER:

DAC International

BUILDER:

Wade & Drerup

LOCATION:

Morris Island, Ontario, Canada

SIZE:

2,200 square feet (204 sq m)

CERTIFICATION:

LEED Platinum

BLOWER DOOR TEST:

1.5 ACH @ 50 Pascals

▶ GREEN ASPECTS:

Dual-flush toilets

Exterior wood siding from beetle-kill pine

Low-flow faucets and showerheads

Low-VOC paints and finishes

Permeable paving

Porcelain tile with recycled content

Recyclable steel roofing

Vented rain screen (see sidebar, page 69)

▶ ENERGY ASPECTS:

Blown-in cellulose roof insulation

Concrete slab for thermal mass

ENERGY STAR–rated appliances

Heat recovery ventilator (HRV) with an Electronically Commutated Motor (ECM)

Large overhangs

LED and CFL lighting

Low-power air handler

Passive solar glazing orientation

Photovoltaic panels

Polyisocyanurate wall sheathing

Radiant floor heating

Solar water heater

Spray foam insulation

Triple-glazed windows

Wood–cement ICF foundation

Wood-fired masonry heater

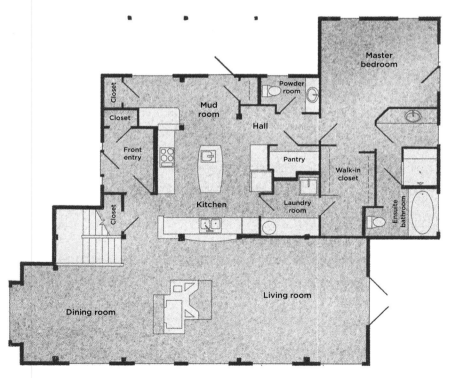

FIRST FLOOR

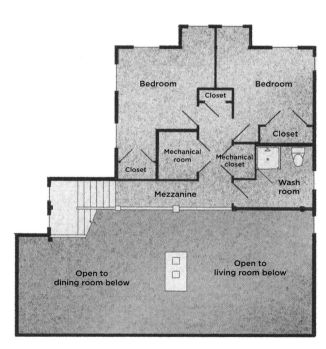

SECOND FLOOR

By converting sunlight to electricity and burning site-sourced firewood to heat it, this house meets most of its energy demands from renewable sources.

Owner and architect Jeff Armstrong designed and helped build his new house on Morris Island, which juts into the Ottawa River in eastern Ontario.

The prefabricated panels were produced in DAC International's plant in Ottawa and were erected in about two weeks. It took about eighteen months to complete the balance of the house.

Jeff decided to have the house certified LEED, a program that had just recently been introduced in Canada. Since he had been promoting energy and environmental standards to his clients for many years, he wanted to have firsthand experience with this new standard.

Factory-built as a panelized "kit," the house was designed with open high-efficiency walls, ceilings, and foundation.

LIFE WITHOUT AIR-CONDITIONING

Jeff's focus in the construction was to build an excellent insulated envelope that limits the need for heating and cooling, rather than installing technology to produce energy. Jeff says, "In the world today, conserving energy turns out to be cheaper in the long run, more reliable, and less harmful to the environment than buying it or even using technologies like wind power or photovoltaics to harness energy. While such renewables are clearly useful in reducing dependence on fossil fuels, they make little sense in drafty, poorly insulated buildings. By building a very good thermal enclosure, it is possible to reduce the amount spent on the mechanical system. In this case, the space-heating load is so low, and the masonry heater so effective that an electric boiler—a relatively inefficient but low-cost device—easily does the job."

The combination of strategic window placement, thermal mass, the presence of large deciduous trees, and ground-tempered ventilation air ensures that the house is comfortable without mechanical air-conditioning even in the hottest weather.

A CREATIVE NEW WAY TO USE AN HRV

With vast experience in the design and building industry, Jeff took the opportunity to employ many of the creative methods he had learned over the years for his own house. For instance, below the ground floor slab, insulated by 4 inches (10 cm) of polystyrene (XP5), is roughly 48 inches (122 cm) of compacted crushed stone. The foundation walls, which also contain that crushed stone, are insulated with ICF (see sidebar, page 69), so the temperature of the crushed stone stays close to a constant 50°F (10°C) year round. Two smooth-wall ducts embedded in that stone bring fresh outdoor air to the HRV. About 40 feet (12 m) of the journey from outdoors to the HRV is through these ducts. As the air travels through them it is "tempered," which means it is either preheated or precooled (depending on the season) by the constant temperature of the stone. In the winter, this has the effect of improving HRV efficiency by raising the temperature of fresh outdoor air before it reaches the HRV. In the summer, the cool stone dehumidifies the incoming warm, moist air, and lowers its temperature. Humidity that condenses out of the air runs down the sloping ducts and drains harmlessly to the outdoors. The cooling effect achieved is typically in the range of 18–20°F (10–12°C).

A multizone ground-floor radiant slab powered by an electric boiler also provides baseline winter

The wood-burning fireplace insert is faced with slate. The lighting is created with low-voltage halogen bulbs.

heating, and an air handler with a low-power motor distributes warm air from the vicinity of the masonry heater to the upstairs rooms during the winter.

Jeff estimates that the energy consumed for space and water heating for his house is about half of that of similar-sized houses.

BELOW The kitchen cabinet doors are solid birch and finished in the factory with low-VOC paint. The flooring is cork, which is a renewable resource. The countertops are durable quartz, which is hygienic because of its natural bacteriostatic protection.

BOTTOM The beautiful timber frame is made of Douglas fir; the staircase and handrails are solid cherry; and the flooring is engineered cherry. The masonry heater with a bake oven is faced with slate. The dining table is a slab of fossil-filled stone, and the built-in bookcases and buffet are solid bird's-eye maple.

OPPOSITE Large covered decks provide all-weather outdoor living spaces where firewood for the masonry heater can also be stored.

Vented Rain Screens

Vented rain screens are an approach to building exterior walls that deters rainwater intrusion, reducing the potential for mold and fungus growth. Building a vented rain screen involves creating a gap between the exterior siding and the layers that sit behind it—such as house-wrap or insulated sheathing. Installing vertical furring strips or rolled rain screen materials (such as Home Slicker) on the wall before installing the exterior siding are typical ways to create this gap.

There are several advantages to this strategy. The cavity provides a path for wind-driven rain that gets through cracks or holes in the exterior siding to drain away before it travels farther into the wall. The air space also promotes faster drying of the exterior cladding, adding to its longevity.

The effectiveness of a rain screen depends in part on the cavity being open, or "vented," to the outdoors at the top and bottom. When the cavity behind the siding is vented and the rest of the wall is airtight, the pressure in the cavity will equalize with the wind pressure on the siding, preventing water from moving through the cracks and holes. Insect screening is required at the top and bottom to prevent bugs and other critters from getting into this space and to ensure that air can flow freely through this area.

The vented rain screen approach involves more labor and material than traditional methods of wall construction, but it is an excellent way to avoid durability problems and extend the life of the house. For additional information, see www.toolbase.org.

Wood Fiber ICF

Typical Insulated Concrete Forms (ICFs) are made with expanded polystyrene (EPS) or extruded polystyrene (XPS), set in place, connected with ties, reinforced with rebar (steel), and filled with concrete. The foam functions as the insulation, and the steel and concrete, the structure. Using ICFs is an excellent method of constructing a foundation and in some cases an entire house. ICFs are very energy efficient, sound deadening, termite resistant, high wind and fire resistant, and fast to erect. The ICFs used for the foundation of this house are not made with polystyrene or foam. Instead they are composed of a cement-bonded wood fiber with a semi-rigid mineral wool core. The blocks have lower embodied energy than conventional ICFs; they sequester carbon (with the wood fiber) and they can be cut with a circular saw, nailed, screwed into, drilled, etc. The exterior surface can be left unfinished or coated with a cement mixture. For further information about this product, see http://durisolbuild.com.

This is the wood fiber ICF foundation of the house.

SIP Panel House

Structural Insulated Panels

PHOTOGRAPHER:

Felipe Fontecilla (unless otherwise noted)

ARCHITECT/BUILDER:

Alejandro Soffia

Gabriel Rudolphy

PANEL MANUFACTURER:

Tecnopanel

STRUCTURAL ENGINEER:

Jose Manuel Morales

LOCATION:

Santo Domingo, Chile

SIZE:

1,496 square feet (139 sq m)

▶ **GREEN ASPECTS:**

Dual-flush toilets

FSC-certified wood

Low-flow faucets and showerheads

▶ **ENERGY ASPECTS:**

Double-glazed windows

Large overhangs

Movement control lighting

Natural cross-ventilation

SIPs

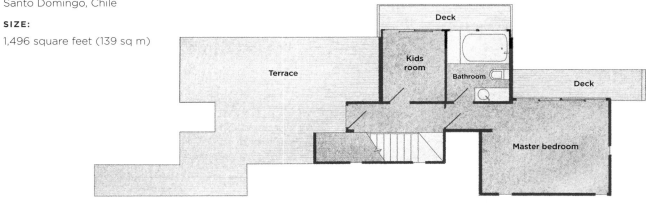

SECOND FLOOR

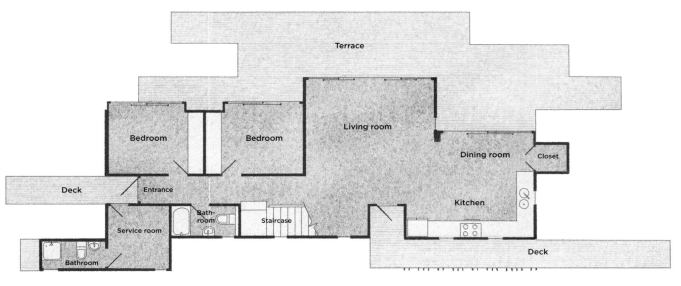

FIRST FLOOR

OPPOSITE The dark gray siding is made of an elastomeric membrane. Generally used for roofing, this material was used here as "wet" proofing and for its ease and speed of construction and low price.

BELOW The northern side of the house is mostly glazed to offer beautiful views of the Pacific Ocean.

This holiday house, designed for a family with two small sons, is located on the central coast of Chile, an hour and a half from Santiago. In order to complete the house for the summer and to lower construction costs, the architect suggested the use of prefabricated panels.

Built with structural insulated panels (SIPs), the house was designed to achieve maximum energy efficiency and strong dimensional stability. It was assembled in just ten days with panels that were erected quickly and with minimal waste. Seventy-one wall panels and forty flooring panels were used.

The house was designed to take the best possible advantage of the ocean views. Most of the rooms face the northern side of the house with decks on the lower and upper levels. The principal rooms are clustered toward the north, in the quest for an ocean view.

Both the first and second floors have terraces with beautiful views. From the terrace on the second floor the waves and the sand of the Pacific can be seen. The eastern facade of the house, close to a neighbor, is more closed-off, while the western facade also opens up to the light and the view. The northern and southern sides of the house, as well as the terraces, are enveloped in a wooden skin.

OPPOSITE The flooring of the first floor is concrete, which reduced the cost of construction and also serves as thermal mass to reduce the need for electrical heating. The concrete was polished to give it a more finished look.

LEFT The entrance to the home is located on the western facade.

BELOW The staircase was constructed with one steel beam in the center and solid native Rauli wood steps. The handrails run from the floor to the ceiling of the second floor. (Photo courtesy of Josefina Lopez Ovalle)

BOTTOM The house has an open floor plan with the kitchen, dining room, and living room flowing into one another.

Casa Iseami

Prefabricated Steel Frame/SIPs

PHOTOGRAPHER:
Sergio Puccí

ARCHITECT:
Robles Arquitectos

MANUFACTURER:
Cemtria

BUILDER:
CPS Construccion

LOCATION:
Península de Osa, Costa Rica

SIZE:
2,368 square feet (220 sq m)

GREEN ASPECTS:
Dual-flush toilets
Low-flow faucets and showerheads
Recycled materials

ENERGY ASPECTS:
Cross-ventilation
High-efficiency appliances
Horizontal sunshades
Hydroelectric generator
Large overhangs
LED lighting
Optimal solar orientation
Photovoltaic panels
Polycarbonate skylights
SIPs
Solar hot water tank and panels

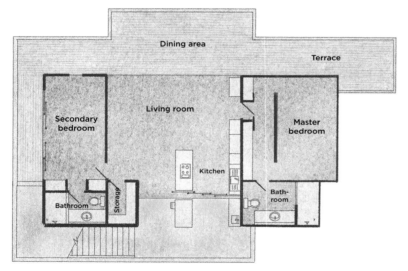

UPPER LEVEL

OPPOSITE ABOVE The upper level of the house is a residence, while the lower level is used for hosting meetings, yoga, and training. The house is elevated more than 3 feet (1 m) off the ground to allow water to permeate into the ground.

OPPOSITE BELOW This is the frontal view of the house and its large overhangs. The large recycled plastic louvers that circle the house reduce the amount of direct sunlight hitting the windows and deflect the rain.

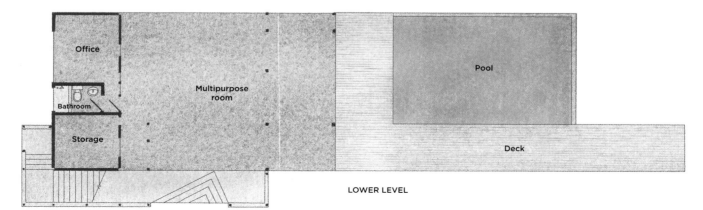

LOWER LEVEL

It was a major challenge to build a self-sufficient, low-impact house in the middle of one of the most biodiverse places on earth without disturbing the land. One major obstacle was the location, about 19 miles (30 km) from the nearest town, Puerto Jiménez. Bringing building materials to the site and accessing the site were challenging because the road to the site is overgrown with wild forest foliage and there are rivers to cross without bridges and twelve small creeks that are sometimes not crossable on very rainy days.

There were a variety of other practical and environmental issues to deal with in order to build this house. The project had ambitious goals in terms of achieving environmentally friendly construction, including minimally impacting the land, selecting materials with a low carbon footprint, and using materials that could someday be recycled.

Architect Juan Robles concluded that the house could only be built with prefabricated components because of its location and environmental requirements.

PREFABRICATION

The house is located a seven-hour drive from San José, the Costa Rican capital city. It is situated in a very dense and deep tropical jungle, just outside the borderline of Corcovado's National Park, where there is no public infrastructure or grid energy available. Robles decided the best option for building the house would be structural insulated metal sandwich panels (see sidebar, page 78), because of their low maintenance, high acoustic capacity, light weight, and thermal insulation.

The steel structure for the house was preassembled in San José, transported to the site, and quickly installed in about three months. The frame went up first, and then the roof and the walls were mounted to the frame. The panels came 100 percent ready for installation, including all wiring and installation accessories.

THE CHALLENGES

A major challenge in this location was the lack of water and energy utilities to the house. A strategy had to be devised that would use renewable energy to meet all the needs of the residents. To run appliances, lighting, and other small energy users, the house was equipped with photovoltaic panels on the roof and a hydroelectric power system.

Water for the hydropower system comes from a spring that runs down a nearby mountain. The owner was required to get authorization to use the water. A piping system collects the water, which is taken from the top to the bottom of the mountain, passing through the Pelton water wheel, a turbine that creates hydroelectric power.

Passive methods of ventilation, heating, and cooling were created with an abundance of windows and doors. Large overhangs prevent overheating from the hot summer sun. A horizontal grid was built around the house that limits the sun's rays and also diverts water from the house. The louvers offer protection against sun and rain and create a more visible boundary for birds in contrast to the glass beyond it.

WATER FOR ALL USES

The same water from the spring that is used to generate energy, after having gone through the Pelton water wheel, loses pressure and is then used for domestic water use. A solar hot water tank provides the warm water for the house.

Five-thousand-liter containers that hold 1,320 gallons of water are stored about 50 feet (15 m) from the house. They collect water that is used for irrigation of the gardens around the house.

IN TUNE WITH THE ENVIRONMENT

With so much humidity in the middle of the forest, Robles needed to select materials that were resistant to moisture. The thermal panels were a perfect solution since they are moisture resistant. All the rest of the materials used, such as the paints and coatings of the steel structure, are also moisture resistant.

To minimally disturb this rich ecosystem, the house was built on stilts, about 3 feet (1 m) off the ground, so water could flow beneath and the flora and fauna would not be disturbed.

Casa Iseami is used by the administrator of the Iseami Institute (see page 98) and is also available for rental if people want to experience the beautiful natural ecosystem in the area. The institute has since provided economic and technical help to a community effort for the building of a sea turtle hatchery.

Structural Insulated Metal Sandwich Panels

These panels are more often used for commercial construction but are beginning to be incorporated into residential construction as well. They are sandwich panels that include two metal sheets fused with a polyurethane center. The depth of the polyurethane depends on the needs of the project. This was an excellent product for the roofing of this house because it reflects the sun's rays and it could be walked on, if there was a need to service the photovoltaic panels situated on them. There were also numerous advantages to using these for the walls. The panels are light, and thus could be transported to this remote location, and are quick to install and weather resistant, which is particularly important in this highly humid climate. The panels form a thermal break, providing excellent insulation, are impact resistant, can span large expanses, and don't require special skill to erect.

For further information about the Versapanel and Versawall used in Casa Iseami see www.centriaperformance.com. Other companies that make similar products are Kingspan (www.kingspanpanels.us), Huntsman (www.huntsman.com), and ASI (www.asi-sd.com).

Iseami Institute

Seeking to promote sustainable development throughout communities in Costa Rica and set environmental standards worldwide, Iseami is an organization still in the process of forming and plans to eventually provide environmental education programs to local schools in order to raise conscientiousness about the environment. The word *Iseami* comes from the indigenous Costa Rican language Bribri, meaning "Our Mother," as in, mother earth. Each letter in Iseami stands for the following: I: Institute, S: Sustainability, E: Ecology, A: Art, M: Mind, I: Investigation. In this area rich with animals, birds, and foliage, there is a continuous threat of deforestation, pollution, and illegal poaching of wild birds and animals. The institute hopes to eliminate these practices through education. For further information, see http://iseami.com.

BELOW The house is nestled in a lush forest about 19 miles (30 km) from the nearest town, Puerto Jiménez.

BOTTOM The deck on the second floor, with its wide overhang, is a perfect place for outdoor dining. Polycarbonate sheets, which are lightweight and durable, are built into the overhang. The overhang allows natural light to pass through to the seating area below but blocks ultraviolet rays. This also allows more natural light into the interior of the house.

Villa Langenkamp

Panelized

ARCHITECT:

Langenkamp.dk architects

MANUFACTURER:

Ökologischer Holzbau Sellstedt

FOUNDATION:

Ole Vognstrup A/S

BUILDER:

UNS4

LOCATION:

Ebeltoft, Denmark

SIZE:

2,475 square feet (230 sq m)

CERTIFICATION:

Passivhaus (first certified
  Passivhaus in Denmark)

BLOWER DOOR TEST:

0.6 ACH @ 50 Pascals

▶ **GREEN ASPECTS:**

Dual-flush toilets

FSC-certified oak flooring

Low-flow faucets

Recycled insulation

▶ **ENERGY ASPECTS:**

ENERGY STAR–rated appliances

Geothermal heating

Heat pump

Heat recovery ventilator (HRV)

LED and low-energy bulbs

Optimal solar orientation

Radiant heating

Retractable blinds

Solar hot water panels

Triple-glazed windows

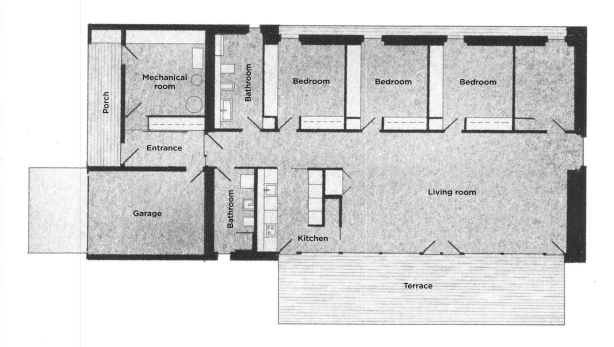

Douglas fir wood cladding covers most of the house. (Photo by Thomas Søndergaard)

Villa Langenkamp is the first certified Passivhaus in Denmark. Architect Olav Langenkamp designed the house and lives there with his wife, Lotte Dahl, and their family. The house is located in the grassy hills of Ebeltoft near the Mols Mountains.

The simple and modern wooden house is an example of minimal architecture with clean lines and a simple box shape. The linear design is in sharp contrast to the tall, majestic pines that surround it. The large glass windows in the living room offer panoramic views of the grasslands, bright yellow shrubs, and a small blue lake beyond.

PANEL CONSTRUCTION

A carpenter in Germany, with many years of experience building energy-efficient elements, constructed the prefabricated panels for the facade and roof. Since this was the first Passivhaus to be built in Denmark, there was no one with the expertise to build it locally. The panels were constructed using formaldehyde-free glue for the oriented strand board (OSB) wood panels. The panels were then shipped about 340 miles (547 km) from the factory in northern Germany to the construction site. It took just five days to assemble the prefabricated components of the house. Once the house was mounted and the roof was finished, the large glass facade was assembled. It took just four months to complete the balance of the construction.

DIVIDED HEATING STRATEGIES

Different areas of the house have different heating strategies. The parts of the house on the northern side—the porch, garage, entrance, and mechanical room—are all unheated, although well insulated.

Because these rooms face north, they do not contribute any heat gain, only heat loss. They would be too expensive to heat, but instead they serve as a thermal buffer for the insulated north-facing walls of the two bathrooms. Although these rooms are fully integrated into the overall design, the actual Passivhaus begins with the insulated walls between the bathrooms and the garage, entrance, and technical room. From there on, the house opens up into one large space containing the living room and kitchen, with the individual bedroom units on the opposite side distributed along the main axis.

KEEPING THE HOUSE WARM IN WINTER

The walls, roof, and flooring are super insulated, beyond the requirement of the Danish building regulations. Glass wool insulation (see sidebar, page 85) was used for the roof and walls, and expanded polystyrene (see sidebar, page 85) was installed under the floors.

A heat pump produces hot water, assisted by solar collectors on the roof. The solar collectors provide 60 percent of the warm water required in the house each year. When the sun is shining, the solar collectors produce hot water instead of the heat pump. The pump is connected to a 106-gallon (400-liter) storage tank to ensure there is always hot water available.

The house is equipped with a highly efficient Passivhaus-certified heat recovery ventilator. The ventilation system maintains a constant exchange of air to ensure high indoor air quality. Because the house is well insulated, the only necessary heat source is preheated inlet air from the geothermal system. This is achieved by means of tubes, buried at a depth of about 6 feet (2 m) around the house,

The red panels on the south elevation function as a passive solar wall. This solar comb facade is a thin honeycomb-like pattern of cardboard. In the winter the sunlight passes through the cardboard pattern and indirectly heats the interior, but is shaded from the high summer sun. (Photo by Martin Brandt)

through which all the inlet air passes before entering the building. The solar energy stored in the ground is thereby utilized to preheat the inlet air during wintertime, while during the summer the tubes can be used for cooling the inlet air. Radiant floor heating keeps the bathroom comfortable. The heating system in the house is cost efficient and simple to use.

Due to the effective insulation, if solar shading had not been taken into consideration, there would have been a risk of the house overheating during the warm summer months. This risk was overcome by the exterior blinds, which can block the sun (and also can be fully retracted and concealed in the roof construction during cooler months). In addition, the tubing used for the geothermal system can also be used to cool the inlet air in the summertime.

MULTIFUNCTIONAL DESIGN

The house was built to be compact and multifunctional. The extra wide wall that divides the living room from the bedrooms contains both closets and ventilation pipes, while also supporting the roof structure. The central walls function as the spine of the house. Workspaces can be hidden within the multiple storage closets and a workspace is also set within one of the kitchen walls, which can be opened as required. The kitchen area can be left open or closed off with sliding doors.

At the International Passivhaus Conference in Dresden, Germany, the innovative and efficient design of the house was formally recognized: Villa Langenkamp was awarded a prize by the Passivhaus Institut.

BELOW FSC-certified oak flooring is used throughout the house.
(Photo by Martin Brandt)

BOTTOM The dining room looks out onto the beautiful grass fields
and shrubs beyond. The lighting in the dining room is produced by
two fixtures; each includes six white transparent, low-energy glass
bulbs. (Photo by Thomas Søndergaard)

Glass Wool Insulation

Glass wool insulation is made from the fusion of natural sand with recycled glass. The materials are melted to about 2,642°F (1,450°C) in a furnace, and then forced through precision drilled holes in high-speed spinners, to form fibers that are similar in texture to wool. Binding products are then added as fibers fall onto moving collection belts. The glass wool mat is polymerized in a curing oven with compression rollers to provide a product of the required thickness and density. The finished products are packaged under high compression to reduce the volume and cost of storage and transportation. This product is light and offers good acoustic and thermal insulation. For additional information about the insulation used in this house in the solar comb facade, see www.isover.com.

Expanded Polystyrene (EPS) and Extruded Polystyrene (XPS)

EPS is closed-cell foam that is made of pre-expanded polystyrene beads that inflate with heat and then are placed in a mold or form where they bond and expand to fit the shape. Molded sheets of EPS are used for insulation (the small "peanuts" used for protecting fragile items inside packaging are also made of EPS). The R-value (see Glossary, page 289) of the insulation will depend on the density and thickness of the foam. EPS will not support mold or mildew growth, can be placed below grade, and has a high R-value (typically about R-4 per inch). Extruded polystyrene (XPS) foam is a similar closed-cell material but is denser (typically R-5 per inch) than EPS and is produced in a different way. Polystrene pellets are mixed with chemicals that liquefy them. A blowing agent is then injected into the mixture, forming billions of miniature air pockets. This frothing mixture is then pushed through a shaping die to give the required size and minimize waste. When the boards are cooled, they can be further shaped. Higher density means more cells and less space between the beads, which results in lower water absorption and higher compressive strength. Villa Langenkamp includes EPS in the outer walls and foundation.

Solar Comb Facade

This patented system consists of a red honeycomb facade of cellulose board protected behind one layer of glass; there is about ⅖ inches (1-cm) of space between the board and the glass. The board is about 1¼ inches (30 mm) thick. Behind the cellulose is a board about ¼ inches (6 mm) thick, and then 2 inches (50 mm) of glass wool insulation. The structure is delivered as a ready to install sandwich element. The low winter sun penetrates the cellulose and heats the wall behind the solar sandwich. During summertime, when the sun is high, the solar comb facade is shaded, which prevents overheating. Heat is ventilated away because of the space between the glass and board. This cost-effective system helps to create a uniform, comfortable temperature inside the house and also helps to dampen sound. For more details, see www.gap-solution.at/produkte/einzelansicht/article/isosolution.html.

The worldFLEXhome

Shipping Containers

PHOTOGRAPHER:

Jens Markus Lindhe

ARCHITECT:

Arcgency

MANUFACTURER:

worldFLEXhome and Nordisk Staal

BUILDER:

Nordisk Staal

TECHNICAL ENGINEER:

Esbensen, Henrik Sørensen

CONSTRUCTION ENGINEER:

Sloth Møller

LOCATION:

Horsens, Denmark

SIZE:

1,938 square feet (180 sq m)

▶ GREEN ASPECTS:

Bamboo facade

Dual-flush toilets

Green roof

Low-flow faucets and showerhead

Nontoxic oil stains on wood

Paint with Swan (Svanemærke) label
  (see sidebar, page 90)

Permeable paving

Rainwater harvesting

Recyclable plasterboards

Recycled shipping containers

▶ ENERGY ASPECTS:

Air-to-water heat pump

Class A+++ Appliances (see sidebar, page 109)

Cross ventilation

DWHR pipe (Drain water heat recovery system)

Energy monitoring system

Geothermal system

Glass mineral wool insulation

Heat recovery ventilator (HRV)

High performance fiberglass windows

LED lighting

Optimal solar orientation

Photovoltaic panels

Skylights

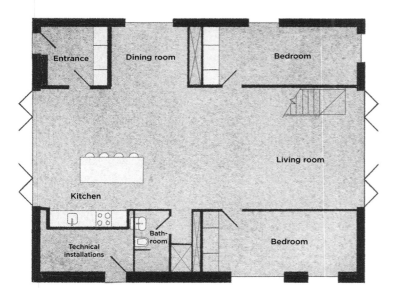

FIRST FLOOR

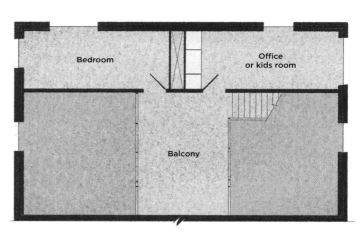

SECOND FLOOR

Built at the factory Nordisk Staal in Frederiksværk, Denmark, the house has been moved to the town of Horsens, Denmark, where it will undergo efficiency studies at the VIA University College. It is currently a living laboratory for sustainable housing solutions.

Arcgency, situated in Copenhagen, Denmark, designed this prototype container house as part of their goal to design Resource Conscious Architecture (RCA). Arcgency says, "In the making of architecture, a high percentage of the world's resources are used. As architects, it is our responsibility to create a better world, with better cities, without exploiting nature. At Arcgency we design and build sustainable architecture by using new building methods and always thinking of life cycle and reusability. We have a strong belief that better design lasts longer and creates less waste."

This current house is an attempt to develop sustainable housing in cooperation with FISH China, a program that aims to "provide a new and innovative business model that allows Danish companies and organizations to enter the Chinese market for sustainable buildings and urban development."

DEVELOPING THE CONCEPT FOR THE HOUSE

This prototype was developed for worldFLEXhome in collaboration with a wide range of producers, the Danish Technological Institute, and various technical advisors.

It was built in the factory Nordisk Staal in Frederiksværk, Denmark, and was later moved to Horsens, Denmark, where it is undergoing a variety of studies. WorldFLEXhome developed this house as a solution for individual housing using alternative building methods. The house uses less energy than it produces, is built of recycled 40-feet (122-m) long shipping containers, and can be transported by land or sea. It is a factory-built product, with endless opportunities for individual customization to suit different climates, cultures, and styles. The design can be configured online, and sixteen weeks later the homeowner can move in.

The company claims the structure, which includes the containers, steel frame, and steel decks, is strong enough to withstand earthquakes.

A FLEXIBLE, DURABLE DESIGN

The overall look of this sample house is to be minimalistic but playful. As suggested by its name, this prototype was designed to be flexible and to adapt to the needs of different individuals and various locations. The house was designed so that it can be taken apart and relocated or the parts can be recycled. Healthy materials, such as certified paint, were used as well as recyclable materials for items such as the plasterboards and insulation.

Care was taken to incorporate materials that will age well, such as the floors, which can be sanded many times and will not need to be replaced. The wood is also from only certified forests and cut in a sawmill that is certified to handle waste in a sustainable way (www.junckers.dk). The green roof was designed to maximize the life of the roof, slow water runoff, protect the roofing materials below, and add insulation.

Materials were also selected to minimize future maintenance. The bamboo facade, for example requires only oil treatment, and the aluminum window frames on the exterior are maintenance free.

HOMEOWNER ORIENTED

The house is designed to be a sustainable choice for middle-class Chinese families, with the initial cost and the future maintenance cost of the home as important considerations. The home is compact

OPPOSITE The open first floor is called the FLEX space, which includes the living room and kitchen; it can be used for multiple purposes. Parts of the room are double height, creating excellent lighting conditions. The rest of the space is one story in height, defined by the landing that allows access to the second floor. At each end of the FLEX space is access to the exterior and daylight from skylights, windows, and floor-to-ceiling doors. A connection to nature is a fundamental part of the design.

Shipping Containers

When there is an excess of import rather than export in a country, the shipping containers begin to stack up. Because the cost of the containers is so low, it is sometimes more cost effective for companies to buy new containers than to have the used ones returned. Old containers are then discarded. Shipping containers have several advantages for building homes. They are designed to carry heavy loads in harsh environments, are stackable, can be interlocked, and are standard in size. They can be easily transported by sea, truck, or rail and are readily available at a reasonable cost. Used containers may cost as low as $1,500; new ones cost up to $6,000, depending on the type and the location where they are being sold. Insulating containers, however, may be a challenge and costly. Because steel rusts, the containers need to be sealed well, and making attachments and alterations requires skill in metalworking. Building permits for houses made with shipping containers may also be a problem in some areas. For the worldFLEXhome, containers were used because of their strength and ability to be shipped. In the future, the company says they will create their own container that will be customized for the construction of homes.

Swan (Svanemærke) and Flower Labels

The Swan label is the official Nordic ecolabel that looks at the entire product life cycle and all of the environmental problems that may be related to different stages of the production chain. The Nordic Council of Ministers established the label in 1989. The Swan is used in all Nordic countries—Denmark, Norway, Sweden, Finland, and Iceland—and in other countries as well.

The Flower is the European ecolabel. The European Commission established this label in 1992. The flower is used throughout Europe. The European Flower and the Nordic Swan are the only two labels officially recognized in Denmark. The criteria, which a product or service must fulfill in order to use the label, are decided upon by the Nordic countries and the European countries respectively. These labels are part of the European Union's ecolabeling system, some of whose criteria is directly linked to preventing climate change. This system takes into account the amount of fossil fuel or energy consumption required to manufacture the product. Ecolabeled products must meet strict environmental requirements for health and good quality, and not contain harmful chemicals.

A wide range of products, such as kitchen towels, shampoo, furniture, and computers, can be labeled with the Flower or Swan. Services, such as hotels and car washes, can also have an ecolabel; however, food and medicine are not labeled with the Flower or Swan as of yet. Ecolabels make it easy for consumers to find environmentally friendly products. When a product is labeled with the Flower or Swan, the consumer is guaranteed to be purchasing products that were produced under strict environmental requirements, with concern for health and good quality. Certification for either of these labels is voluntary. The goal of this labeling system is to encourage environmentally friendly production and consumption. There are more than 6,500 products that are identified by either the Flower or the Swan. Ecolabeled products can be found at www.ecolabel.dk and http://ec.europa.eu/environment/ecolabel/index_en.htm.

BELOW To increase the flexibility of the house's layout, the wall separating this room from the main space can be partially or totally removed. Glass can be added, as shown here, to increase the light in the room and connect it visually with the rest of the house.

OPPOSITE The kitchen elements are built into the wall inside the technical module. This allows for more floor space and also makes connection to water and plumbing easy.

vided by solar cells. In Denmark, where the house is currently situated, the photovoltaic panels give electricity back to the grid when an excess is produced, and energy can also be taken from the grid when it is required. The geothermal system allows ground heat to be used for heating both water and air.

THE FUTURE OF THE PROTOTYPE

WorldFLEXhome is hoping to mass-produce these houses, providing many families with sustainable, energy-efficient housing options.

Although this prototype was built in Denmark, the first houses based on this design will be built in Wuxi, China. They are a low-carbon, resource-conscious solution for this fast-growing country.

"Early in the development phase we could see that we had something special with this house, so therefore we applied for a patent on the concept," says the CEO of worldFLEXhome, Anders Bach-Sørensen.

There has been a great deal of interest in this first prototype. Approximately 275 people have visited this home as of this writing. Bach-Sørensen says, "We believe there is a need for a product/house like this one, whereby the house performs economically over a period of years instead of just considering its initial cost. Energy is becoming more expensive, and this is something the homeowner should now care about."

The cost of the house is substantially less than a comparably sized house in Denmark. The company hopes the price will be competitive when they are sold in China in the future.

and designed to be placed on small lots. Additionally, adequate lighting was an essential part of the design. Large windows and skylights were strategically located to optimize natural lighting so the inhabitants can enjoy the nature around them.

LOW-ENERGY CONSUMPTION

The house is well insulated with glass wool insulation, and much of the energy required for the house is pro-

Archway Studios

Prefabricated Metal Components

PHOTOGRAPHER:
Candice Lake (unless otherwise noted)

ARCHITECT/BUILDER:
Undercurrent Architects

MANUFACTURER:
GZ Shipping

LOCATION:
London, England

SIZE:
1,722 square feet (160 sq m)

GREEN ASPECTS:

Built on a brownfield site (see sidebar, page 95)
Built with the goal of regenerating the community
Dual-flush toilets
Live/work home
Low-flow faucets and showerheads
Low-VOC paints and stains
Palmwood (see sidebar, page 95)
Recycled materials

ENERGY ASPECTS:

High-efficiency appliances
Highly efficient insulation
Highly insulated glass
LED and CFL lighting

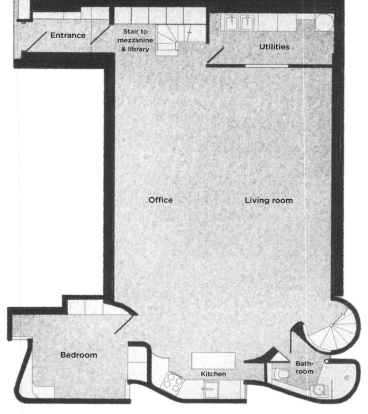

FIRST FLOOR

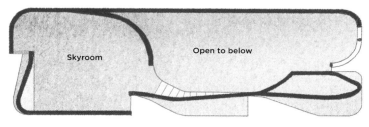

THIRD FLOOR

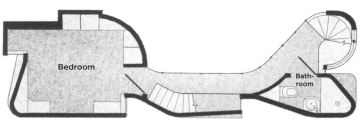

SECOND FLOOR

OPPOSITE The components of the house were built in a factory in China. The outer skin is COR-TEN steel plate that is ¼ inch (6 mm) thick, which acts as a sound barrier and a decorative screen. The concave shape of the wall helps to collect and bounce light into the deep recesses of the arch. This house was assembled with a "stressed skin" (an insulated building panel comprised of a core sandwiched between two outer "skins"), where the outer skin is hung almost independently from the inner skin. There is a continuous air gap between the inner and outer skins, with the only connection at the outer edges of the wall. This isolates the interior spaces from the exterior walls, preventing the transfer of noise and vibration. (Photo courtesy of Undercurrent Architects)

BELOW The building shell is made from weathered steel that fits in with the industrial nature of the area. With limited surrounding area views, a large skylight provides views of the sky and the distant treetops, while also flooding the interior with light.

Architect Didier Ryan had a vision to revitalize a brownfield (see sidebar, opposite) in Southwark, London, to create a live/work space. He chose a lot that by most standards would be considered too narrow to build on and too close to a train line to be viable. As a prototype for future construction in London and other inner cities, this type of structure could help revitalize underutilized spaces and connect them to other residential areas.

REVITALIZING BROWNFIELDS

Ryan points out that there is a large network of Victorian viaducts in London that divide neighborhoods, create corridors of conflict, and leave the inner city with a vast number of vacant brownfields. Ryan says this project "reuses redundant 'brownfield' land, turning wasteland into productive, aspirational use. We found opportunities in the constraints and developed a design that positively embraced the tough environmental surroundings." He continues, "Micro regeneration projects such as Archway Studios can pave the way for broad community change, matching macro scale initiatives where development clusters are being located over railway transport hubs."

AESTHETIC CONSIDERATIONS

The building shell is designed to complement the industrial heritage of the locality, with rust-oxide colored steel skin that matches the warm brown tones of the Palmwood cladding. This forms a striking relationship that helps the building stand out even when dwarfed by towering City neighbors, echoing the materials of the adjacent railway. Industrial assembly methods were consistent with this approach, using lots of metal and creating the components in the factory.

THE CHALLENGES OF THIS LOCATION

With very limited space (the site is about 10-feet [3-m] wide), Ryan needed the thinnest exterior shell possible to maximize the internal width of the house. A prefabricated steel shell allowed the wall thickness to be reduced to the minimum. To make use of every inch of space, Ryan says, "We studied ways to construct a thin but robust shell, applying stressed skin construction from ship and aircraft manufacturing and the prefab steel layers to dampen noise. Construction next to a live railway placed extreme limits on access, sequencing, methodology, and safety. Prefabricated methods minimized site unknowns."

THE CONSTRUCTION

The metal shell, which was fabricated in a factory in China, is about 28 feet (8.5 m) tall and 36 feet (11 m) long, with two bedrooms and two bathrooms and a central atrium that provides office space for Ryan and a photography studio for his partner. Sky views and tall trees can be seen through the glass ceiling. Sleeping alcoves are tucked into this area, making efficient use of space.

To protect the structure from the vibrations and noise of passing trains, the foundation has a rubber base under it, a stacked rubber and waffle pad above the foundation, and extensive insulation in the steel walls. The wall construction consists of two ¼-inch (6-mm) thick steel plates with a 6-inch (150-mm) thick steel grillage, a thermal insulation blanket, and an airspace in the wall's inner cavity. There are two types of insulation used in the construction: a bulk mineral wool, which resists the flow of heat by conduction, and an aluminum foil and foam blanket (made of nineteen layers), which resists the flow of heat by radiation.

The central atrium is brightly lit by the natural light coming in through the glass roof.

Brownfields

Brownfields are properties that have been abandoned or that are underused industrial sites, which may have the presence or potential of hazardous substances, pollutants, or contaminants. In order to reuse or develop this land, it must be cleaned up, removing any hazardous materials. By doing so, the environment is protected, and blighted areas are upgraded and made useable and productive. For additional information see www.epa.gov/brownfields.

Palmwood

Palmwood® is a registered product developed from "senile" mature coconut palm trees, which can no longer produce coconuts and in the past have been considered waste. After the trees are harvested, the stems are cut into planks, sticks, or columns, depending on their density. They are stacked to air dry for two to three months, then they are "cooked" in a self-powered kiln (the kiln is powered by burning the sawdust produced from cutting the palms), and then they are shaped and sanded. The coconut wood is impregnated with a nontoxic, oil-based preservative to add stability and longevity, while also making the wood resistant to termites and boring insects, as well as mold and rot. It is free from knots and other blemishes and has a golden textured appearance. The wood is then finished with natural plant oils. This wood can be used for interior and exterior applications. In the Archway Studios, Palmwood was used for the exterior cladding of the folds in the steel structure, window frames, doors, floors, and furniture. For additional information see www.palmwood.net.

LEFT The balcony connects the two ends of the narrow plot that is approximately 10 feet (3 m) wide, allowing light from the atrium to flood the ground floor and providing an overhang into which the kitchen was built.

RIGHT The skylight at the top of the structure is made from thick cavity glass consisting of two ¼-inch (6-mm) thick laminated panes of glass, a ⅝-inch (16-mm) thick argon-filled cavity, and two slightly less than ¼-inch (5-mm) thick laminated panes of glass, which help to block the train noise. Asymmetric glazing, using different thicknesses of glass rather than the conventional symmetrical systems, improves the acoustic attenuation properties of the insulated glass unit.

Didier Ryan works several days a week at the house, while his partner uses part of the structure for her photography studio.

A vibration-dampening membrane is adhered to the inner steel surface to prevent structural resonance and to provide additional sound absorption.

The house was fabricated in three months, erected in four days, but then took a year of site work to complete because the budget necessitated having a small team in order to control wages and cash flow.

A HOME TO LIVE AND WORK IN

A central atrium floods the interior with light. Sky views and tall trees can be viewed through the glass ceiling. Sleeping alcoves are tucked into the folds of the external wall, creating cozy spaces for rest.

The house not only serves as living space but also includes both an office for Ryan and a photography studio for his partner in the central atrium. As a live/work space, Ryan says this prototype shows the feasibility of limiting the use of crowded mass transit in London by spending at least some of the time working from a home office.

Live/work buildings relieve pressure on transit systems and save travel time and resources, making them a very sustainable land use. They offer work and jobs within residential areas, lowering overheads and logistics. In the case of Archway Studios, the dual uses of work and living have brought twenty-four-hour occupants and economic activity to a commuting neighborhood. Conversely to the adjacent industrial area, the residential aspect has brought supervision and activity around the clock, during non-business hours, improving safety.

Camden Passivhaus

Panelized/Timber Frame

PHOTOGRAPHER:

Tim Crocker

ARCHITECT:

bere:architects

SUPERSTRUCTURE ENGINEERING, FABRICATION, AND ERECTION:

Kaufmann Zimmerei

CONTRACTOR:

Visco

LOCATION:

London, England

SIZE:

1,270 square feet (118 sq m)

CERTIFICATION:

Passivhaus (the first in London)

BLOWER DOOR TEST:

0.4 ACH @ 50 Pascals

▶ **GREEN ASPECTS:**

Draft-free construction

Dual-flush toilets

Green roofs

Low-flow faucets and showerheads

Natural wood fiber and mineral wool insulation

Nontoxic materials

Rainwater harvesting

Water filtration

▶ **ENERGY ASPECTS:**

External venetian blinds

Heat recovery ventilator (HRV)

Optimal solar orientation

Solar hot water panels

Thermal bridge-free design

Triple-glazed windows

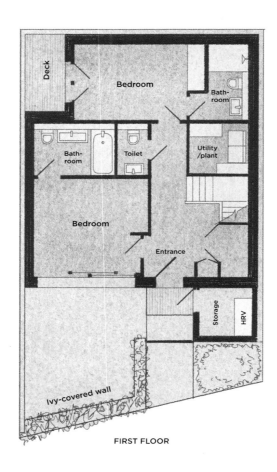

FIRST FLOOR

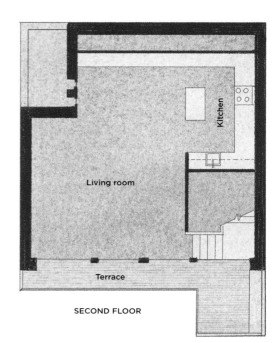

SECOND FLOOR

An ivy-planted wall provides privacy. The cladding is Austrian larch, which was attached to the panels in the factory.

The primary objective of this project was to construct a comfortable home that required minimal energy for a young family. The homeowners, along with bere:architects, worked to achieve this by building the house to Passivhaus standards. It became the first certified Passivhaus in London, combining energy-efficient design with comfort and high indoor air quality.

THE STRUCTURE

The structure of the house was built in Austria with the walls prefabricated as insulated timber framed panels that are 9½ to 11 inches (240 to 280 mm) thick. To reduce on-site construction time and minimize waste, these panels were clad with horizontal boards of Austrian larch and attached to untreated softwood battens in the factory. The precladding of the panels allowed precise details to be achieved around window and door reveals and minimized the disruption to the neighbors adjacent to the site, since the home extends right up to the site boundaries. The vapor barrier was also preattached to the wall panels, reducing time and waste on-site. After the panels were installed, 4-inch (102 mm) timber studs were fixed to the panels internally and the voids were filled with tightly packed natural wood fiber insulation, for a healthy indoor environment and to achieve U-values of 0.122–0.11W/(m²K) (see Glossary, page 289).

The first floor and flat roof were constructed out of structural glued solid wood timber panels that are 5½-inches (140-mm) deep and manufactured from European spruce. These provide additional thermal mass and the structural base for the roof insulation that is 15¾ inches (400 mm) thick.

BUILDING AN EFFICIENT ENVELOPE

The Passivhaus Planning Package (PHPP) was used in planning this house to determine the optimum position for the house on the site and the optimum size, quantity, and orientation of the glazing, taking into consideration the impact of building on the small site and the overshadowing of the adjacent buildings. The home was designed to have limited thermal bridging (see Glossary, page 289), excellent insulation, and be adequately shaded.

CONTROLLING SOLAR GAIN AND LOSS

Bright and airy rooms were achieved with large tilt-and-slide, triple-glazed windows on the south and west (there are no windows on the north and east facades, where heat would be lost). The design accounts for cross-ventilation with sliding doors that open to a south-facing terrace.

Summer shading is provided by means of retractable external venetian blinds (see sidebar, page 102) with automatic solar control on the south side of the house, limiting heat gain, while inward-tilting windows provide a secure way for warm air to be released.

The two wildflower gardens on the roof help increase local biodiversity, reduce water runoff, and protect the roof covering. Green roofs can reduce heat gain in the summer, but this house is so well insulated that this feature is unnecessary.

TIME-TESTED RESULTS

After a year of being occupied, continuous monitoring of the house found that it performed even better than anticipated in terms of energy consumption. The monitored space heating demand for the

The kitchen appliances were chosen for this house because of their high energy efficiency; the refrigerator/freezer is A+++ rated, which is the highest rating available in England. A clerestory south-facing window above the kitchen allows natural light to flood in creating a pleasant environment for preparing meals.

house was 12.1kWh/m^2 as compared to the typical new house in the United Kingdom, which consumes about 100 kWh/m^2 per year. The total gas and electricity consumption combined was only 54 kWh/m^2 for the year, compared to another monitored house in the United Kingdom widely considered a low-energy exemplar at 90 kWh/m^2. But the most significant factor was the comfort of the residents, whose average winter living room temperature was at 72.5°F (22.5°C). The house is also inexpensive to operate, saving 90 percent in heating, compared to other existing housing in the area.

A HEALTHY INTERIOR AND EFFICIENT WATER SYSTEMS

Nontoxic materials, such as low-VOC paints and stains, were used to avoid polluting the interior air and, together with a heat recovery ventilation system, keep the air quality high. A water filtration system ensures clean water for both drinking and bathing. An underground rainwater-harvesting tank provides water for the garden and limits the amount of municipal water required. A solar thermal panel supplies domestic hot water via a compact unit with a tiny backup gas boiler to supplement heating.

HOMEOWNER SATISFACTION

The homeowners say, "We absolutely love living in the house because it is warm and cozy. . . . The environment inside the house could not be better in terms of temperature, the air one breathes, and the low fuel costs. . . . The house works in a very efficient manner. It requires very little heating, even when it's subzero [outside], so it proves the Passivhaus concept works in reality."

BELOW All of the lighting in the house is from either LED or fluorescent bulbs. This low-energy lighting design includes a number of 7-watt LED downlights over the main living areas.

BOTTOM The open concept living and dining rooms form a bright and airy space.

External Venetian Blinds

Exterior venetian blinds can minimize heat gain, reducing or eliminating the need for air-conditioning, while controlling glare and pro-viding privacy. Some blinds are perforated to optimize exterior views, even when the blinds are closed. These exterior blinds are built to withstand the effects of wind, snow, ice, and other weather conditions. However, to protect blinds in extreme conditions, some systems will automatically retract when the wind reaches a certain velocity. Some will adjust blades automatically to maintain max-imum internal light and minimize heat trans-fer. These louvered blinds come in a variety of gauges, slat sizes, and colors. The slats can be adjusted from inside to any angle to ensure that the right amount of light enters the room at any time of day by a variety of methods, whether they are moved manually or by a motor that is activated by a remote control. The blinds can also be fully retracted to allow maximum light in and therefore max-imize solar gain during colder winter months. This feature also allows access to glazing for cleaning. For further information about the external venetian blinds used in this house, see www.hella.info.

LEFT A local joinery company fabricated the custom-made solid oak staircase.

RIGHT The modern bathroom with clean lines has low-flow water fixtures.

House Jackson

Timber Frame/Panelized

PHOTOGRAPHER:

Nicholas Yarsley

ARCHITECT:

Alexander Kolbe

MANUFACTURER/BUILDER:

Baufritz

LOCATION:

Marlow, England

SIZE:

3,109 square feet (289 sq m)

BLOWER DOOR TEST:

1.51 ACH @ 50 Pascals

▶ **GREEN ASPECTS:**

Dual-flush toilets

Low-flow faucets and showerheads

Low-VOC paints and stains

Permeable paving

Rainwater harvesting

▶ **ENERGY ASPECTS:**

A-rated appliances (see sidebar,
  page 109)

LED and CFL lighting

Photovoltaic panels

Solar hot water panels

Triple-glazed windows

Wood shaving insulation
  (see sidebar, page 151)

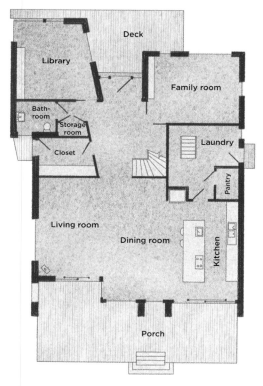

FIRST FLOOR

SECOND FLOOR

OPPOSITE The siding for the house is made from mineral-based render or external plaster. The plantings around the house are all indigenous to the area. The pool is heated with an air source heat pump, which in turn is connected to photovoltaic panels.

BELOW Three doors (one at the front and two at the back) provide access from the outdoors to the raised ground floor. The impressive entrance hall serves as a central focus of the house.

When regattas are staged on the Thames in summer, Stephanie and Neil Jackson and their two children shout encouragement to the rowers from the bank, since their new home is just a stone's throw from the river. They live in Marlow, a small town with about 14,000 residents, 30 miles (48 km) west of London. This location is highly sought after because of its setting on the banks of England's second longest river, and its outstanding transport links to London. The journey takes just forty minutes by car if the traffic is light.

SELECTING A MANUFACTURER

In contrast to their immediate neighbors, who live in a half-timbered Victorian house, the American and her British husband wanted to live in a new house. Both Stephanie and Neil are enthusiastic viewers of *Grand Designs*, a program broadcast on British television that presents unusual private-sector dwellings, and they are readers of the journal of the same name. In one of the issues, they came across the company Baufritz.

The Jacksons decided that Baufritz was the right company to build their home when they found out that they use only nontoxic building materials and are able to construct highly energy-efficient dwellings. "Because our children are still small it is important for us that they grow up, at home at least, without being exposed to dangerous substances," explains Stephanie. "In addition, we wanted to build a house bearing sustainability in mind for and even trap CO_2 with our house."

BRINGING AN ARCHITECT ON BOARD

They knew that they wanted the design of the house to be modern. Toward that design end and to ensure everything went smoothly on-site, Baufritz contracted an experienced architect, Alexander Kolbe, who had already been working for Baufritz for several years. He also submitted the draft plan to the authorities for approval. The Jacksons traveled to Bavaria to the factory only once prior to the construction of the house. They say they will never forget the day on which the first of a total of eleven container trucks packed with house components drove up to the site. All the neighbors had been forewarned, since the trucks made it impossible for any other vehicles to park or turn in the one-way street. It took only three days before the building was weather–proofed and the work on fixtures and fittings could begin. For the onlookers and others, the scene could have come straight from a motion picture.

GETTING CONSTRUCTION APPROVAL

The building supervisory authorities approved the new house because there had already been a house built in the 1960s on the 11,840-square-foot (1,100-sq-m) site. However, they didn't want the building to be much taller than the existing structure. The living space was increased to almost 3,122 square feet (290 sq m). This enlargement was permitted because the new home has a flat roof, which minimized the addition of height to the structure overall, even though the floors had already been raised to alleviate flood risk.

CONSTRUCTING ENVIRONMENTALLY

Organic mineral rendering (or stucco or plaster) covers the walls to achieve maximum thermal insulation standards. The house is built around the load-bearing framework of German kiln-dried structural solid wood. The insulation is organic HOIZ made of

There is more than 100 square feet (10 sq m) of windows in the roof, which light the entire stairwell and the corridors.

wood shavings either produced in making the house or obtained from FSC-certified wood growers who have also been awarded Cradle to Cradle® certification (see Glossary, page 288). Baufritz uses natural whey for fire prevention and soda-lye for fungicide to treat the insulation material. Laws in this area require deep foundations, to protect the building from flooding should the Thames overflow its banks.

The design of the Jacksons' two-story cube is a conscious antithesis to the many half-timbered houses in the area that are characterized by small windows and rooms. The entire expanse along the south-facing wall of their home is floor-to-ceiling triple-glazed windows, which help to keep the house warm in the colder months.

The Jacksons say, "The aim of the sophisticated energy concept of our home is to minimize the impact on the environment as much as possible."

Solar collectors on the roof heat the water, and photovoltaic panels generate electricity. A controlled ventilation unit with waste heat recovery makes use of the heat energy of the gas. The Jacksons have a rainwater harvester to collect water for flushing the toilets and for watering their garden.

In order to achieve a healthy and energy-efficient home, Kolbe and Baufritz used state-of-the art technology with energy-efficient heat sources and energy recovery ventilation. The result is a modern home that is a compelling example of twenty-first-century sustainable design.

The open-plan kitchen, dining, and living areas benefit from the
abundance of light from the floor-to-ceiling windows and skylights.
The appliances are all A-rated.

European Union (EU) Energy Label

A legislative act of the European Union established energy consumption labeling for many items, including appliances, lightbulbs, car tires, and so on. These labels, giving information on energy consumption, are required on certain items to be sold or rented. They indicate the energy efficiency of the item in classes from A, which is the most efficient, to G, which is the least. House Jackson contains A-rated appliances. Additional grades have been added with the improved efficiency of products now available, so there are also A+, A++, and A+++ grades used. Since 2010, there has been a new label available, which uses pictograms instead of words, in order to allow manufacturers to use a single label in a variety of countries. For additional information about this program, see http://ec.europa.eu/energy/efficiency/labelling/labelling_en.htm.

Facit House

Prefabricated Components

PHOTOGRAPHER:
Mark Cocksedge

DESIGNER:
Bruce Bell
Facit Homes

MANUFACTURER:
Facit Homes

BUILDER:
Alton Services MK Ltd.

LOCATION:
Hertfordshire, England

SIZE:
2,153 square feet (200 sq m)

CERTIFICATION:
Energy Rating A (92 percent efficient)

▶ GREEN ASPECTS:
Central vacuum
Dual-flush toilets
Low carbon footprint
Minimal waste in construction
Recycled materials

▶ ENERGY ASPECTS:
Cellulose insulation
Double- and triple-glazed, energy-efficient windows
Energy-efficient appliances
Heat recovery ventilator (HRV)
LED and CFL lighting
Low-energy gas boiler
Optimal solar orientation
Photovoltaic panels
Solar hot water panels
Wood burning stove

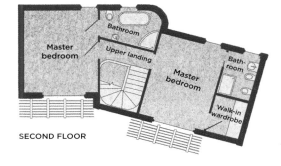

SECOND FLOOR

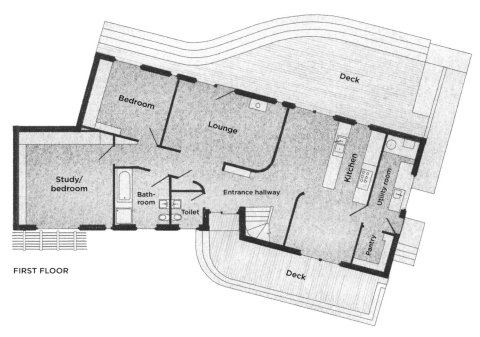

FIRST FLOOR

OPPOSITE The factory was set up on the property where the house was going to be built. The plywood components were digitally manufactured on site, connected in place, and then filled with cellulose insulation.

BELOW Large, south-facing windows help to keep the house warm in the winter, and solar shading keeps heat gain to a minimum in the summer.

When industrial designer Bruce Bell first spoke with Celia and Diana, they told him of their dream of building "a strikingly modern house" where they could enjoy their retirement. They looked at more than one hundred properties before falling in love with the lot, which is in an Area of Outstanding Natural Beauty (AONB)* in Hertfordshire, England. AONB status involves tighter than usual planning restrictions in order to preserve the character of these designated areas. The goal of this designation is to conserve and enhance the natural beauty of the landscape and to meet the need for quiet enjoyment of the countryside.

The plan for their new house took into account the optimal orientation for the structure, so that it would benefit from solar energy, fit in well with the site and neighboring houses, create minimal waste, and be as green as possible.

Because of planning and budgetary restrictions, the house was kept small. They compensated by designing the house with two dual-purpose rooms, which can be used as studies or guest bedrooms. Diana says, "The house is designed to work into old age for us, with the option to sleep and bathe on the ground floor if it becomes necessary, and easy disabled access via a ramp built into the rear decking."

---

* This is a countryside area of England, Wales, or Northern Ireland that is considered a significant landscape and is a designated area by Natural England on behalf of the government of the United Kingdom for natural conservation purposes (www.naturalengland.org.uk/ourwork/conservation/designations).

BUILDING WITH TIMBER

Diana's former job as head of research at Edinburgh Napier University involved close collaboration with researchers in the Timber Engineering Research Unit, and Celia has extensive experience helping friends in New England to renovate timber homes. Together they had also built a large timber frame extension on their previous house in Scotland. Although most houses in England are still being built out of masonry, Celia and Diana's experience with wood made it their material of choice for their new home.

BUILDING WITH PREFABRICATED BOX COMPONENTS

Facit Homes was looking for patrons to build the first prototype house, using the world's first on-site digital manufacturing process. Diana and Celia saw an article in a British self-building magazine inviting plot owners planning to build a house in the near future to have their home be a demonstration project. They decided to take a risk on this new method to build their home. The prefabrication method involves bringing the factory to the site rather than bringing the components from the nearby factory. Diana says, "We had confidence in the concept of using plywood components made on-site to construct the house, and we loved Facit's design."

Diana and Celia agreed to be pioneers with this new building system because the process was very quick and relatively easy, and they felt that manufacturing components on-site would allow any errors to be quickly rectified. It also met their criteria for a more environmentally friendly way to build, with no need for cranes or hoists, minimal waste, and less damage to the site than building with other methods.

Timber window shades keep the
house cool in the summer and
maximize solar energy in the winter.
They also cast a beautiful shadow on
the house.

BELOW The wood-burning stove is used to supplement the heating on the coldest days. There is an invisible sound system with speakers built into the wall.

BOTTOM The Wilder Creative Group designed custom cabinets and shelving, which were prebuilt in a London workspace and then installed on-site. The kitchen includes oak countertops, a spray-painted backsplash behind the stove, and energy-efficient stainless steel appliances (including an induction hob and a fan oven, which can provide separate heat zones if required).

BUILDING THE COMPONENTS

A shipping container with a computer-controlled cutting machine inside it was brought to the site, creating a mini-factory. Plywood was cut and components were quickly assembled, which could then be easily lifted and fit together like a LEGO set, making the house airtight. The size of each component was precisely cut according to Facit's trademarked computerized D-Process, which controls the cutting machine. Each component was numbered and connected with plywood staples. Cellulose insulation was later pumped into the components to make them very energy efficient. After the outer walls were completed, they were clad in part render (plaster) and part cedar. Instead of using standard cement-based render, lime render was used; it is more difficult to handle but is more eco-friendly and maintenance free. Recycled decking expands the opportunity for outdoor living in the warmer months.

OWNERS AS ACTIVE PARTICIPANTS

Diana and Celia contributed to the construction whenever possible. The builders gave them a variety of tasks, from laying pebbles under the foundation to painting foundation elements with bituminous paint. Diana says that after years of working in suits, "It was really nice getting dirty and being outside."

After the outer shell of the house was completed in eight weeks, Diana and Celia took over as project managers in controlling the budget and supervision of the various trades people: electricians, plumbers, and so on. The rest of the construction took five more months to complete.

The staircase was digitally manufactured off-site, delivered in parts, and then installed in the house.

ENERGY PERFORMANCE

The house was built to be airtight, with about 12 inches (305 mm) of insulation. Skylights in the ceiling adjust according to the weather and passively help to regulate the interior temperature. The solar panels provide energy for hot water. The electricity generated by the photovoltaic panels is used on-site or, if not needed, is fed into the national grid. Under a government incentive scheme, homeowners in England who are deemed to use half of the power generated are paid a sum in recognition of the other half returned to the grid. As part of this scheme, homeowners have to supply data on their energy consumption readings four times a year.

A low-energy boiler is used when needed and the wood-burning stove is fired up on the coldest days. The house has many large double- and triple-glazed windows and a high level of insulation so that a day of sunshine provides twenty-four hours of warmth, even on very cold days.

Diana says, "We had done major house renovations and extensions before but had not built a whole house. With the support of designer Bruce and Tadas Domarkas, the main builder, along with his brother Tomas (of Alton Services MK), and their teams, we were fairly confident of a happy outcome, built on time and on budget to a high standard. The whole team worked well together, with a spirit of problem solving rather than complaining, and it was exciting to be so closely involved in creating our own dream home."

The Edge

Steel Frame/SIPs/Modular

DESIGN/MANUFACTURER/BUILDER:
Boutique Modern

LOCATION:
Cornwall, England

SIZE:
880 square feet (82 sq m)

▶ GREEN ASPECTS:
400-gallon (1,514-liter) rainwater tank
FSC-certified hardwood cladding
FSC-certified oak cladding and flooring
Low-flow toilets
Permeable paving
Recycled materials

▶ ENERGY ASPECTS:
All-in-one system (see sidebar, page 37)
Automation system
LED and halogen lighting
Louvered panels for shade
Photovoltaic panels
Radiant heating
SIPs
Triple-glazed windows

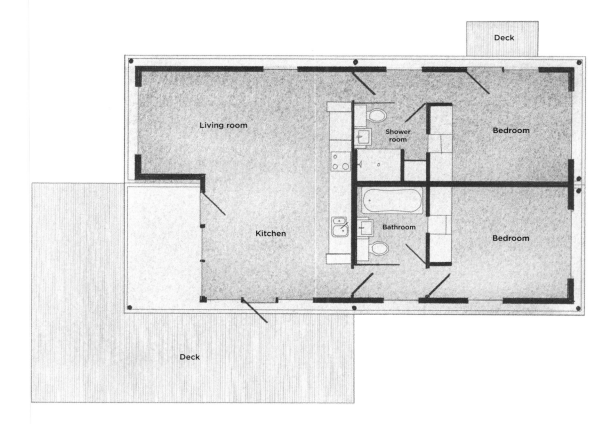

OPPOSITE The house was constructed in a factory in East Sussex.

BELOW The cladding is FSC-certified hardwood.

According to the manufacturer, "The design for this house was inspired by the iconic works of the mid-twentieth-century modernist designers." This house in Cornwall, about 300 miles (480 km) from the factory in East Sussex, was built as a vacation house. However, the company says they have built similar models for use as permanent residences.

BUILT TO LAST

Boutique Modern designs its homes for longevity using a very durable galvanized steel "super" structure. Technology and plumbing are in the center of the building, minimizing run distances and reducing exposure to damage.

HEATING AND COOLING

The envelope of this house provides for retention of heating and cooling with the use of SIPs, advanced framing techniques that limit air infiltration, and triple-glazed windows. The windows that stretch from floor to ceiling allow natural light to flood into the building's interior, limiting the electricity needed for lighting. The thermal performance of the envelope also means that the majority of heating is provided through solar gain.

Electric under-floor radiant heating is installed in the shower and bathrooms. An all-in-one mechanical system (see sidebar, page 37) provides ventilation with 90 percent efficient heat recovery and cooling throughout the house, as well as providing hot water. The photovoltaic panels on the roof run this combined ventilation, heating, cooling, and water-heating system.

Minimal damage was done to the site during the set, and the house was ready to live in after just a few days. The owners believe that they should live within the environment and not impose themselves on it, and consequently the Edge is designed to sit lightly on the land and to respect its surroundings.

OPPOSITE The bathroom off of one of the two bedrooms opens with a frosted glass pocket door.

ABOVE The clerestory window in the living room adds light while also allowing for cross-ventilation. The overhead lights are halogen, which give off an attractive bluish glow.

BELOW The dining room opens onto the patio, extending the living space. The flooring is engineered oak.

Evolutive Home

Panelized

PHOTOGRAPHER:
Courtesy of Concept Bio

ARCHITECT:
Mauro Veneziano
Concept Bio

BUILDER:
BA Bâtiment

LOCATION:
Mouans-Sartoux, France

SIZE:
3,552 square feet (330 sq m)

CERTIFICATIONS:
Passivhaus
BBC Effinergie
Bâtiments Durables Méditerranéen—
   Gold

BLOWER DOOR TEST:
0.58 ACH @ 50 Pascals

▶ GREEN ASPECTS:
Ecolabel certification for all paints, glazes, and
   varnishes
Permeable paving
Rainwater harvesting and storage
Wood fiber insulation

▶ ENERGY ASPECTS:
Cross-ventilation
Energy recovery ventilator (ERV)
Ground heat exchanger
High-efficiency windows
LED lighting
Optimal solar orientation
Solar hot water panels
Water wall for cooling

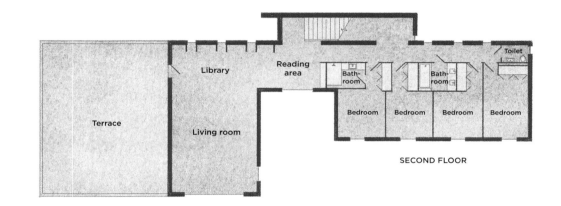

SECOND FLOOR

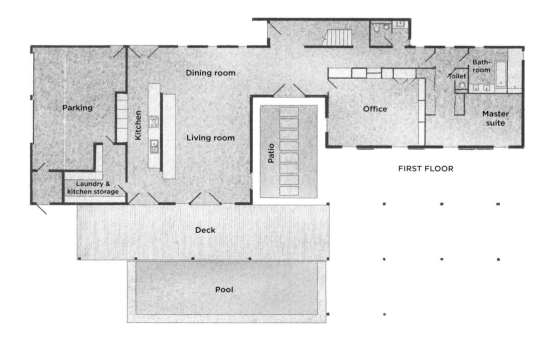

FIRST FLOOR

OPPOSITE Before the panels were erected, two concrete walls, which were intended to serve as thermal mass, were built to store energy that would aid in both heating and cooling the house. One of the concrete walls separates the living room and kitchen, and the other separates the staircase and the hallway.

BELOW Oak trees help to shade the house in the summer.

Frédéric Michel designed this Passivhaus for himself, his wife, Mares, and their three small children to show that "one can go very far in developing an ecological plan without abandoning comfort and aesthetics." He designed every aspect of the house to optimize its energy performance, to create a comfortable environment, and to require minimal maintenance. Michel also designed the house to serve as his office where he specializes in sustainable/energy construction. Two employees work in this space as well.

PASSIVE HEATING AND COOLING

A combination of construction strategies was used to minimize the need for heating and cooling. The house is oriented facing south. Some areas have a double orientation, such as the living and dining area and the first-floor working area. The hallways, which face north, have windows that offer a beautiful view of the mountains. The house was positioned to achieve maximum solar gain in the winter, and foliage helps to block some of the sun in the summer months.

Motorized blade shutters positioned outside the windows on the first floor react with sun sensors, which optimize the light inside and minimize the solar heat coming into the house, actively reducing the amount of sunlight that shines inside during hot summers. The "shade" cloth used for the awnings on the terraces also prevents hot summer sunlight from coming into the house through the windows.

Both wool fiber and wool insulation were used in the walls and ceiling to create an efficient building envelope. The outer facade of wood fiber functions as a heat shield, helping to prevent summer heat from warming up the inner wall insulation and also to prevent thermal bridging, which could be created by the wood frame walls. During the night, fresh air runs through the air blades, which are between the finished wall and the wood fiber, to cool down the wood fiber.

EXPERIMENTAL COOLING METHODS

Several of the methods used to cool the house are experimental. Michel designed a water wall for summer cooling and a groundwater system that couples with a heat exchanger to cool the house in summer and preheat the air in winter. The ground heat exchanger contains a brine solution (salt in water) that flows through six loops of tubing 1,640 feet (500 m) long. There are three pairs of loops positioned at different underground levels and in different substrates. In the summer, this system helps to cool fresh air and expel hot air. An air conditioner would consume a great deal of electricity, but utilizing the coolness of the earth keeps the house comfortable with minimal energy. In the summer, the ground temperature at a depth of 5 feet (2 m) to 9 feet 10 inches (3 m) below the surface is much cooler than the outdoor air. The ground therefore can cool air by absorbing the excess heat.

A ground-to-air heat exchanger transports the coolness of the ground into the fresh air very effectively with only a small brine-circulation pump. A small 40-watt pump can generate up to a 2-kilowatt cooling effect. By monitoring this system carefully, Michel plans to record useful data for improved cooling practices in the future.

Natural ventilation is achieved with the help of mirror pools. Warm air, which rises, is expelled out of the open swing windows on the first floor. The mirror pools cool the air through evaporation. Cooled air

BELOW The living room can be accessed from one side of the kitchen, while the dining room is accessed from the other.

BOTTOM The south facade of the living area looks out onto the garden and pool. The double-height glazing was designed to flood the large, open space of the double-height living room, dining room, and entranceway with daylight. There are also three vertical windows on the north side of the house, which offer additional light and views.

from the pools enters the house on the ground floor and rises through the staircase, up to the first floor to cool the upper part of the house.

During the winter, the ground-to-air heat exchanger preheats the incoming fresh air, and the solar energy kept in the hot water tank is used to heat the air blown into the house by the two-way flow ventilation system and energy recovery ventilator (ERV).

A COMFORTABLE HOME

According to Michel, there are several reasons why the house is so comfortable to live in: "The air quality is excellent and constant due to the fine ventilation system. Highly efficient insulation avoids the differences in temperature people feel in their feet and shoulders, which is the main cause of thermic discomfort. It also eliminates the uncomfortable feeling in many houses when being close to a cold wall or window; this does not exist in a Passivhaus. During the summer, we don't need to use air-conditioning to maintain a comfortable temperature level or suffer its bad effects, such as cold airflow and unpleasant odors. The energy consumption is kept to a minimum, and we don't have to worry about future increases in energy costs. Most important—we can save the planet for our children!"

The Evolutive Home is an exciting glimpse into what building for tomorrow could look like.

BBC Effinergie

This label identifies new buildings or parts of buildings with very low energy requirements that will contribute to the 2050 target to reduce emissions of greenhouse gases by four (meaning that by 2050 CO_2 emissions must be divided by four). The maximum energy consumption target for new residential constructions is kWh (ep) (ep stands for primary energy) set at 50/m²/year. Houses can be certified according to the permeability of the building envelope, providing reference values on a quality airtight construction. There are some financial benefits for meeting the criteria, such as tax credits, property tax reduction, and so on. For further information, see www.effinergie.org.

Bâtiments Durables Méditerranéen (or Mediterranean Sustainable Buildings)

This regional association created in 2008 helps to develop demand for sustainable buildings (residential, multi-housing, and commercial) in the Mediterranean region. The program recognizes a building's low-energy consumption with three levels—Bronze, Silver, and Gold—although it does not consider itself a certification program. The program provides guidance and assistance in facilitating sustainable structures with multiple online tools, advisors, and resource partners. For additional information, see www.polebdm .eu/batiments-durables-mediterranens.

Eco-certification

The Ecolabel (the official European Union mark for greener products) helps European consumers to distinguish greener, more environmentally friendly products (not including food and medicine) of high quality. For more information about this certification and to find products, see http://ec.europa.eu/ecat/.

The large patio on the south side of the house extends the living space in the warmer months.

BELOW At the entrance to the patio there is a mirror pool, which helps cool the house.

BOTTOM The hot summer sun on the south facade is controlled with awnings that have a patented fabric that absorbs and reflects 97 percent of the sun. Michel calls this a swimming "corridor" because it is small, at only 39 feet by 12 feet (12 m by 4 m). It is deep enough to swim in (4.6 feet/1.4 m), but shallow enough to minimize the water volume.

The Passivhaus in Bessancourt

Panelized

PHOTOGRAPHER:

Hervé Abbadie (unless otherwise noted)

ARCHITECT:

Karawitz Architecture

MANUFACTURER:

Finnforest

BUILDER:

Perspective Bois and RC Eco

CIVIL ENGINEERS:

DI Eisenhauer and Philippe Buchet

THERMAL ENGINEERING:

Solares Bauen

LOCATION:

Bessancourt, France

SIZE:

1,905 square feet (177 sq m)

RATINGS:

Passivhaus (first in the region of Île-de-
France and second in France)

BLOWER DOOR TEST:

0.48 ACH @ 50 Pascals

▶ GREEN ASPECTS:

Bamboo cladding

Gypsum fiberboard without glue

Low-flow faucets and showerheads

Low-VOC paints and stains

▶ ENERGY ASPECTS:

Cellulose and wood fiber insulation

CFL lighting

Cross-ventilation

Heat recovery ventilator (HRV)

High-efficiency appliances

Hot water panels

No heating system

Optimal solar orientation

Photovoltaic panels

Small heat pump

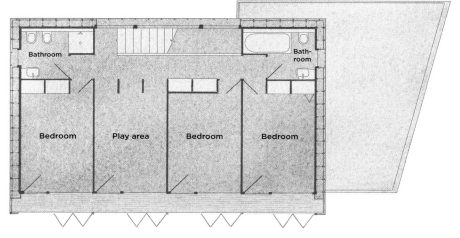

SECOND FLOOR

ABOVE The panels are being erected on-site.
(Photo courtesy Mischa Witzmann)

OPPOSITE Milena says, "The photovoltaic panels
on the roof make the house an energy-plus house,
according to the French standard."

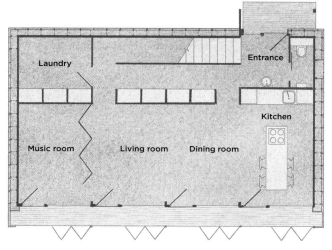

FIRST FLOOR

Architects Mischa Witzmann and his wife, Milena Karanesheva, decided to build a Passivhaus for themselves and their two children just 17 miles (28 km) northwest of Paris. In a town with structures that date back to the twelfth and thirteenth centuries, they wanted to build a house that would fit in with the old city but function with the latest technology. Mischa says, "Aesthetically, it is a sculptural and abstract replica of a traditional house, although it is designed to be more efficient."

NO HEATING SYSTEM

The house was designed to be comfortable without a heating system. The windows and prefabricated walls are so well insulated that the home's primary sources of heat can be the occupants and the sun. The heat recovery ventilator provides fresh air, exchanging the interior stale air, along with the warm or cool air already in the house, with fresh exterior air.

Keeping the house warm is accomplished by careful design. The house was sited for optimal solar orientation with the north side closed off, limiting heat loss, and the south opened to benefit from exposure to solar energy. A "spine" splits the front from the rear portions of the house, giving load-bearing support to the house and containing the mechanicals.

The southern portion of the house, which has a large amount of glazing, receives the most sun and was therefore designed larger. Most of the rooms in the house face south; only the bathrooms, staircase, and laundry face north. To prevent heat loss, there are few windows on that side of the house.

THE ENVELOPE

A second skin with open cladding in untreated bamboo envelopes the structure. This cladding, which will become gray over time, was chosen to mirror the look of the traditional barns in the Île-de-France region, where the house is located. Matching bamboo shutters are fitted on large bay windows to the south, which help control the amount of sunlight entering the house.

The foundations are the only concrete element; the entire structure is made of the assembly of very large solid wood panels, which were prefabricated in a workshop in Germany. The bamboo cladding and insulation were affixed to the panels in the factory to limit the construction time on-site.

Photovoltaic panels on the roof complete the energy-efficient design, producing 3,200 kWh/m^2 per year. The house consumes only 11 kWh/m^2 year for heating. Other typical houses in the area consume between 135 and 275 kWh/m^2 year.

OPPOSITE LEFT The bathroom faucets are low flow and the toilet is dual flush. There is an interesting contrast between the wood and the white elements.

OPPOSITE RIGHT The children's bedroom has lots of natural light. It is a very comfortable place to sit, play, and draw.

ABOVE The louvers open and close manually, but as they let in a lot of light, there is no need to manipulate them often. In spring and autumn some are opened or closed depending on the sun and the room temperature, but they generally stay open in the winter and shut in summer. Milena says, "The big windows are our radiators; the louvers are the regulator of the radiators." Along the southern facade of the house is a small catwalk of metal lattices, which serve as a balcony and a support for the folding shutters.

BELOW The living room is orientated to the south. The light green wall at the back is a folding wall, which separates the living room from the music room. Fluorescent light tubes are an efficient and attractive way to light up the room when there is no natural sunlight.

Fusion Bretagne

Log

PHOTOGRAPHER:
Gilles Plagnol

MANUFACTURER:
Honka Group

BUILDER:
2M Bois

LOCATION:
Brittany, France

SIZE:
1,432 square feet (133 sq m)

GREEN ASPECTS:
Dual-flush toilet
Low-flow faucets and showerheads
Massaranduba decking (see Glossary,
  page 289)
PEFC-certified wood
Rainwater harvesting used for toilets and
  landscaping
Red cedar cladding

ENERGY ASPECTS:
Cellulose insulation
Daylighting
Double-glazed windows
Natural ventilation
Wood stove

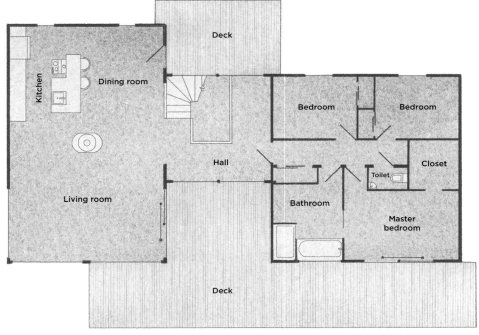

FIRST FLOOR

GROUND LEVEL

OPPOSITE The rear deck offers a beautiful view of the Atlantic Ocean. The house is situated on la Pointe du Raz, near Brest, about 390 miles (628 km) from Paris. There are picturesque bays, cliffs, and coastal villages to see in this region.

BELOW The cladding of the house is made from stone and red-tinted cedar, which is long lasting and requires minimal maintenance.

This house, with beautiful views of the Atlantic Ocean, was constructed with three cubes: one containing the living area, another containing the three bedrooms and single bathroom, and a middle cube that contains the staircase, entrance, and technical room. The beautiful cubic architecture combines wood, large glass surfaces, and stone in a maritime environment.

NON-SETTLING FUSION LOG HOMES

Unlike most log homes, in which the logs are apparent throughout most of the house, the system established by Honka allows the log surface to be left visible as just the inner or outer surface of the house. On Fusion Bretagne, it is visible on the inner walls.

Instead of using full logs, Honka engineered, cross-laminated, non-settling logs fused with a sealant that is free from harmful substances. Being laminated crosswise prevents the logs from sagging, and the sealant is virtually invisible and retains the wood's natural ability to breathe, which is important for maintaining the health of the load-bearing frame.

The outer sides of the log walls of this house are covered with ecological wood fiber insulation, 4¾ to 9½ inches (120 to 240 mm) thick.

The erection of these log frames is fast, because they are precisely factory manufactured and built with prefabricated logs. The air-tightness and strength of the walls, which are more than 11¾ inches (300 mm) thick, make the house energy efficient. The house's load-bearing walls are 5 inches (127 mm) thick. The external surface of the frame has 8 inches (203 mm) of wood fiber insulation. The facade walls of the Fusion Bretagne house are clad with red-tinted cedar wood and stone.

HEATING AND COOLING

Because the climate is mild in this area of western France and the home has such effective insulation, the only heating that is usually required is a wood stove. Only 11 square feet (1 sq m) of wood is required for warming the house during the winter.

An energy recovery ventilation system keeps the air fresh in the interior by exchanging the interior stale air for fresh exterior air, while also exchanging the heat (or cold in the summer). A thermodynamic water heater or geothermal system, which pumps thermal heat from the ocean, heats water for the house. Up to 75 percent of the hot water is heated with this geothermal heat restored from the ocean bottom, so only 25 percent is heated with purchased electricity.

A rainwater tank is used for filling the toilets and watering the garden.

AN INNOVATIVE SUSTAINABLE SOLUTION

According to Honka, "As a renewable natural resource, logs processed from Finnish pine forests also meet the criteria for ecologically sustainable construction. Because Finnish pine is slow-growing, it is hard and durable. Pine can withstand variations in humidity without splitting and is an excellent material for log houses."

In addition to being made from a renewable natural resource, the Fusion Bretagne's structural solution is completely without plastic foils, exploiting the natural properties of the wood that balance out humidity and improve the quality of the indoor air. For those who enjoy the rustic appearance of log homes, Honka has created a structure with multifaceted benefits, both environmental and aesthetic.

ABOVE The kitchen is open to the dining and living areas of the house. Appliances are stainless steel and the countertop is a black natural stone. The black details in the kitchen are consistent with other black furnishings and details throughout the house. Ceramic tile is a practical and beautiful flooring, covering the whole dining and kitchen area.

BELOW The warmth of the logs can be seen in the walls and roof of the house. The living "cube" of the house includes the living room, dining area, and kitchen.

Positive Energy ECOXIA House

SIPs/Modular

PHOTOGRAPHER:

Mandibule (unless otherwise noted)

ARCHITECTS:

Joseph Cincotta (USA) and
  Rémi Pellet (France)

BUILDER:

ECOXIA

LOCATION:

Yerres, France

SIZE:

1,030 square feet (96 sq m)

CERTIFICATIONS:

Passivhaus (under evaluation)

Bâtiment à Énergie Positive (BEPOS)

BBC-Effinergie+ (under evaluation)

BLOWER DOOR TEST:

0.39 ACH @ 50 Pascals

▶ GREEN ASPECTS:

Dedicated space for easy waste sorting
  and recycling

Dual-flush toilets

Linoleum flooring (all natural and biodegradable)

Low-flow faucets and showerheads

Low-impact foundation

Low-VOC paints and stains (Ecolabel
  A+ paint)

Rainwater harvesting

Recycled fiberboard

Renewable materials

▶ ENERGY ASPECTS:

All-in-one system (see sidebar, page 37)

Blown-in cellulose insulation

Energy monitoring

Energy recovery ventilator (ERV)

Heat pump

LED and CFL lighting

Motorized shutters

Photovoltaic panels

Radiant ceiling panels

SIPs

Triple-glazed doors and windows

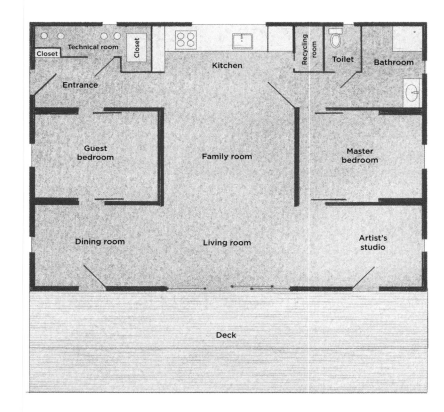

OPPOSITE The modules are side by side in the factory with most of the SIPs already in place. (Photo courtesy of Laurent Riscala)

BOTTOM ECOXIA's architecture is typical of bioclimatism (see Glossary, page 288), with a compact shape and a lot of windows facing south.

H enri Jacquin, a retired teacher, now an artist, loves Paris for its art scene and culture, so he wanted a pied-à-terre just outside the city center.

DECISION TO BUILD PREFAB

However, Jacquin says, "Just the idea of monitoring construction was impossible to manage due to the distance from my home in Brittany." When he heard about the house that the developers Laurent and Olivier Riscala of ECOXIA were building in a factory, to be assembled on-site in a very short time, he was immediately interested. It was reminiscent of the prefab house, provided by the United States at the end of World War II, where he lived with his parents in Lorient. He says, "When I understood what Laurent was achieving in energy efficiency and low impact on the environment, I realized I could leave my grandchildren not only a house, but also a scientific and artistic experiment."

DESIGNING FOR EFFICIENCY AND SUSTAINABILITY

Laurent says that to meet the requirements of the European Union to create zero-energy houses by 2020, "ECOXIA tried to imagine what housing of the twenty-first century could mean and developed a building system to meet those objectives at an affordable price."

He emphasizes the importance of not only an efficient design but also its implementation. He says, "You need to start with a building solution that brings excellent insulation and airtightness. If you add plumbing, electricity, home automation, ventilation, waterproofing solutions to the structural and insulating envelope, you get a complex system,

which requires a perfect installation of all the components to work well together."

A CONSTRUCTION SOLUTION

For the Riscala brothers, modular construction was the perfect solution to meet the standards they were hoping to achieve. Laurent says, "Modular offers a superior quality of construction, and all the benefits linked to an industrialization of the building process: better, faster, cleaner . . . and less expensive, especially in the long run, since modular companies have decreasing costs with additional volume."

Traditional wooden floors and ceiling, insulated with blown cellulose between the joists, are used for the modules. The overall height of the modules was not an issue, but the challenge was to design efficient thin walls, because it is difficult to have modules larger than 10 feet (3 m) wide in France and other areas of Europe and Japan because the roads are narrower than in North America. In France, the standard width for modules is below 8.25 feet (2.5 m) wide. Transportation is slightly more expensive for modules over 10 feet (3 m) wide, and if wider than that, special authorizations, special trucks, and escort vehicles are required. The cost of transportation will then more than double, which is why the modules for this house were kept at 9.7 feet (2.96 m) wide.

In order to be able to keep the walls narrow, the Riscalas opted to use structural insulated panels (SIPs) made with polyurethane (PUR) foam. They lined the inner walls with 80 percent recycled fiberboard and 20 percent cellulose, derived from recycled papers and mixed with recycled water. This board also has a high fire rating, excellent acoustic qualities, and a strong resistance to impact and

ABOVE The house was designed to be easy to maintain and to be environmentally healthy. The linoleum chosen for the flooring is made from all natural materials and is 100 percent biodegradable.

BELOW Matching handles, worktops, and hidden appliances create clean lines in the modern kitchen.

Radiant Ceiling Systems

Radiant ceiling systems are available as both electrical and hydro systems. One of the large advantages to a radiant ceiling system is it does not require a duct system, which can be costly and can leak energy. However, if central air-conditioning is required, one of the advantages to using this method is eliminated, as ducts would then still be required. Radiant ceiling systems are dust free, have a short warm-up time, and can cost less than some other heating systems, which require furnaces, ducts, filters, and flues. They eliminate drafts and are maintenance free because there are no moving parts. Each room can also be zoned individually, saving energy by heating only selected rooms where heat is required or maintaining varying temperatures in different rooms. These systems are also a cost effective and healthy way to retrofit an older house.

The heat that is emitted from either radiant floor or ceiling systems warms the mass in the room, rather than the air. It is often believed that since hot air rises, using radiant ceiling panels would not be effective. However, it is hot air that rises (convection); heat radiates traveling in all directions and transfers to the masses. It is also commonly believed that the objects in a room, such as a table or chair, shield the transfer of heat, but in reality the heat is bounced around and reradiated. In a closed environment like a well-insulated house, the walls, objects, and air eventually get to the same temperature in a very uniform and comfortable way. Therefore, having radiant ceiling systems can be as effective in heating a room as a floor system. The panels provided for the ECOXIA house were from Hora (www.hora.fr).

BELOW The two beams in the foreground of this image are the only visual clue that reveals the modular design of the house; the beams show the marriage of the two modules. The horizontal slots at the top end of the raised roof are the openings where the heat comes out from the radiant ceiling.

BOTTOM Sliding doors inside the house, such as here between the bedroom and the hallway that leads to the kitchen, conserve space, as there is no need to account for room for the doors to swing in and out.

The house is equipped with an automated system that controls the music, shutters, and other items in the house and can be accessed both on-site and remotely with a smartphone.

moisture. This combination of materials produced a wall that is only 9 inches (229 mm) thick but highly energy efficient. Windows are triple glazed to create a very tight envelope.

NOT JUST EFFICIENT BUT ATTRACTIVE

Laurent and Olivier Riscala wanted their first line of modular houses to have an attractive design, as well as a comfortable layout. They therefore worked with architects Joseph Cincotta in the United States and Rémi Pellet in France to create a design that was as functional and attractive as possible. Rémi also received help from young designers and engineers studying at the Université Evry Val d'Essonne and ENSTIB.

The house was monitored for a few months before Henri moved in. He now says that maintain-

ing a temperature of "20.5°C [69°F] without using heating on a sunny day in early March proves that Laurent's bioclimatic design works."

BUILDING INTO THE FUTURE

The house is fully monitored to function in conjunction with the weather conditions, and also to demonstrate the energy efficiency of the house.

The all-in-one system (see sidebar, page 37) includes a heat pump for heating and cooling the air and heating domestic water and an ERV to keep the air well ventilated in the house. Thirty percent of the ceiling includes a radiant heating system (see sidebar, opposite) that supplements the all-in-one system on the coldest days.

The heat pump supplies cool air, which is supplemented with natural ventilation from the tilt-and-turn windows. The energy monitoring system also determines the correct position of the motorized shutters, which block out the sun on very warm days.

The total cost for this house was $400,000, including the cost of research and development, which will benefit future owners of this design. The Riscalas have been granted two patents for the modular process for building this house: One of the patents is for the connection system, and the other is for the post-and-beam/SIP system.

Laurent says, "The overall result of this construction was beyond our expectations." Jacquin is very pleased with his studio, which easily maintains a comfortable temperature and has excellent acoustics. He says the house feels like a "healthy cocoon."

If the Riscala brothers' goal was to combine ecology, comfort, and economy, their vision for housing in the twenty-first century appears to be reached.

green[r]evolution Plus Energy House

Panelized

**MANUFACTURER/DESIGNER/
BUILDER:**

HUF HAUS

LOCATION:

Cologne, Germany

SIZE:

2,959 square feet (275 sq m)

CERTIFICATIONS:

Efficient House 55 (see sidebar,
   page 155)

Efficiency House Plus

▶ GREEN ASPECTS:

Dual-flush toilets

FSC- and PEFC-certified wood

Low-flow faucets

Low-VOC paints and stains

▶ ENERGY ASPECTS:

Cross-ventilation

Energy recovery ventilator (ERV)

ENERGY STAR–rated appliances

Geothermal energy

Heat pump

High thermal insulation

Large overhangs

LED lighting

Motor-driven venetian blinds

Optimal solar orientation

Photovoltaic panels

Prefabricated concrete ceiling panels

Programmable thermostats

Radiant floor heating

Solar panels

Triple-glazed, gas-filled windows

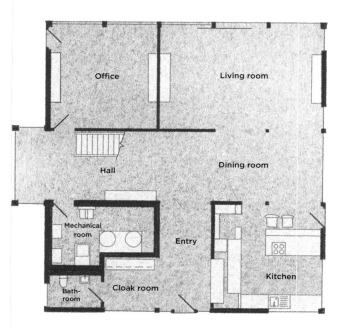

FIRST FLOOR

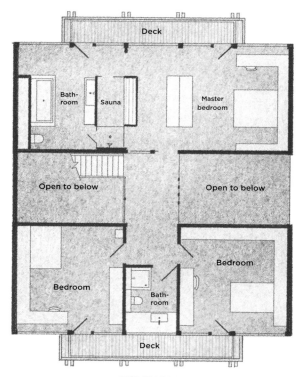

SECOND FLOOR

The south-facing facade is predominately glazed, which allows maximal winter daylighting and also creates a harmonious connection between interior and exterior living spaces. Large 5-foot (1.5-m) overhangs provide necessary summer sun shading.

This house in Cologne was built as a show house and was the first green[r]evolution Plus Energy House design built by HUF HAUS. This is the most energy-independent and energy-saving model that the company offers. Its powerful photovoltaic array, which produces clean solar energy, is a major contributor to this efficiency. Other important features are the elevated floor construction (meaning the distance between the top of the floor slab and the top of the finished floor is larger than average to allow for increased insulation thickness), providing R-34, and the extra layer of insulation in the roof, increasing it to R-63. In addition to the effective thermal insulation, this home also is extremely airtight. Thermal bridging has been reduced with a newly developed comprehensive air-sealing approach achieved through blower-door tests. It is also equipped with a state-of-the-art technology for controlled ventilation and heat recovery with mechanical heat recovery ventilation and under-floor heating.

These houses are built with glue-laminated timber frames that are independent of the inner, load-bearing panel structure. As a result, the exterior timber parts can be treated with wood preservative where necessary, without affecting the interior air quality.

HOUSE GLAZING

The HUF HAUS construction allows for frameless floor-to-ceiling glazing. The triple-glazed, argon-filled insulated glass units (which form the windows, turn-tilt doors, and sliding patio doors) are made of insulated glazing sourced from a local supplier that has an R-value of 9.52 and a U-value of 0.5W/m²K (see Glossary, page 290). The stainless steel spacers are filled with argon gas. The large-scale glaz-

ing is segmented by the post-and-beam structure, which also allows for transom lights and windows (these are horizontal windows that if fixed are called transom lights or if operable are called transom windows) above the main glazing and in the gables.

FLOOR AND CEILING CONSTRUCTION

The ceiling consists of large, solid, precisely prefabricated panels made of concrete, which is a common ceiling material in Germany. The advantages of using concrete are its ability to store thermal energy in the summer, creating a cool climate inside the house, and warmth in the winter; the avoidance of thermal bridging; and the acoustic benefit of creating excellent soundproofing. Construction above the concrete floor consists of 4-inch (102 mm) sound/thermal insulation topped with a 3.15-inch (80 mm) layer of concrete and floor covering for the floor above.

HUF HAUS installs a hydronic under-floor radiant heating system with pipes made of a multilayered metal composite, which operates at a low temperature. Area heating complements this system with air source heating pumps. Each room's temperature is controlled separately by a thermostat. Summer cooling without air-conditioning is possible by running chilled water through the radiant piping.

HEAT PUMP

Heat pump technology is an economical way of making a portion of the thermal energy surrounding the house available for heating or water heating purposes. HUF HAUS focuses on the sustainability of its heat pump systems in particular, which use very small amounts of energy to pull heat from the ground (in this case) or air, in order to heat or cool the home depending on the season.

BELOW The photovoltaic array has a capacity to produce 14.53 kWp of energy, complementing the energy-saving techniques used on this house. This house also has an innovative energy "storage" solution that can retain energy from the photovoltaic system. The energy can be saved until it is needed in the evening or morning hours with a superefficient, high-performance lithium ion battery, whose capacity is 8.8 kWh (approximately the size of an upright refrigerator). In the past, the energy gained from a photovoltaic array had to be used immediately or fed into the power grid.

BOTTOM This double-height space is a typical feature of HUF houses.

Energy Conservation Ordinance (Energieeinspar-verordnung/EnEV)

In 2002, the *Energieeinsparverordnung* (EnEV) or Energy Conservation Ordinance was adopted in Germany and established energy standards for new buildings. These standards apply to *all* new buildings. These energy-efficient homes require innovative heating technology based on renewable energies (such as solar, geothermal, biomass, wood, wind, and hydropower) and very good thermal insulation. This program is funded by KfW Bank in Germany and offers loans and grants to help achieve these standards in residential housing. The EnEV is part of the economic administrative law (*Wirtschafts-verwaltungsrecht*) in Germany. The EnEV rating is required as part of the building application process in order to get a building permit. The EnEV is calculated by the local structural engineer and then sent to the building authorities for approval. If the energy requirement is not fulfilled, the building of the house is not possible. For additional information about this program, see www.kfw.de.

SANITARY INSTALLATION WITHOUT HEAT LOSS

Hot water heated by the heat pump is stored in a tank located in the plant room. The hot water pipes are highly insulated to avoid any energy loss. A circulation pump, controlled by a timer clock, keeps the hot water moving through the water pipes, resulting in instant hot water when the faucet is opened. Only one heat pump is needed, even in cool winter months.

CROSS-VENTILATION AND DAYLIGHTING

Numerous transom lights and windows provide natural light and allow for draft-free ventilation. Glass panels are also located above solid wall panels, providing natural light in otherwise windowless walls.

PASSIVE SOLAR DESIGN

To control solar gains during the summer months, the house has large protective overhangs. The overhangs not only protect the house from solar gain but also protect the wood construction from the effects of weathering. All glazed panels have motor-driven exterior venetian blinds, except for those in the transom windows and the main entrance door. Their horizontal slats can be pivoted to control the amount of light passing through, providing flexible sun protection throughout the year. Such "low-tech" measures are valuable in maintaining an energy-efficient, comfortable indoor climate in the hot summer months.

The green[r]evolution Plus Energy House conforms not only to the standards of the Efficiency House 55 (see sidebar, page 155), but also to the standards of the new Efficiency House Plus, which was developed by the Federal Ministry of Transport, Building, and Urban Development. These standards stipulate that a house must generate more energy than it consumes per year. The Frauenhofer Institute in Cologne monitored this house to prove that the house did in fact generate more energy than it uses.

BELOW The three bedrooms on the second floor all open up to a balcony.

BOTTOM This spacious bathroom has cabinetry built by StilART from HUF HAUS. The faucets and showerheads are water saving, and the toilet is dual flush. The sauna, typically found on the ground floor or basement level, is located here for convenience.

Transom windows across the living and dining area provide an additional light source and offer draft-free ventilation.

House Bretschneider

TimberFrame/Panelized

PHOTOGRAPHER:

Michael-Christian Peters

ARCHITECT:

Georg Schauer

MANUFACTURER/BUILDER:

Baufritz

LOCATION:

Bavaria, Germany

SIZE:

1,556 square feet (145 sq m)

CERTIFICATION:

Effizienzhaus 70

   (see sidebar, page 155)

BLOWER DOOR TEST:

1.51 ACH @ 50 Pascals

▶ GREEN ASPECTS:

Dual-flush toilets

Low-flow faucets and showerheads

Low-VOC paints and stains

PEFC-certified lumber

Recyclable materials

▶ ENERGY ASPECTS:

A-rated appliances

Advanced framing (to minimize thermal
   bridging)

Air-to-water heat pump

Energy-efficient windows and doors

Heat recovery ventilator (HRV)

LED lighting

Louvered shades

Radiant heating

Rear awning

Wood shaving insulation (see sidebar,
   page 151)

Wood stove

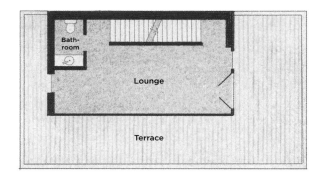

THIRD FLOOR PLAN

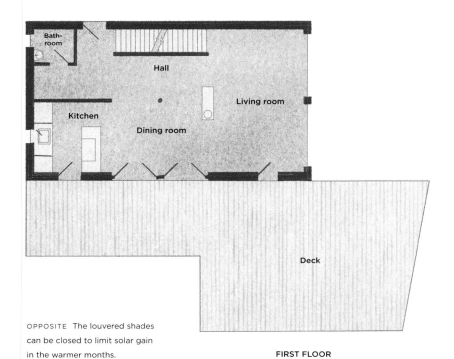

OPPOSITE The louvered shades
can be closed to limit solar gain
in the warmer months.

FIRST FLOOR

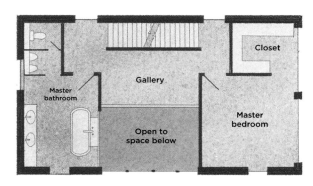

SECOND FLOOR

This modern cube design has clean lines and limited materials, features that are typical of Bauhaus architecture. The exterior of the house is made entirely from larch wood. Splashes of color can be seen only in the red doors and anthracite-colored windows. Larch shades cover the windows on the south side of the house, blending in with the exterior siding, making the house appear even more monochromatic.

The first floor serves as the family's gathering area with an open-concept cooking, dining, and living area, divided by a wood burning stove, which effectively heats the space. The staircase, not simply utilitarian, serves as a design feature with an all-glass handrail.

The second floor contains a bedroom, a dressing room, and a spacious bathroom with a freestanding bathtub. The top floor, the penthouse, serves as a refuge with a lounge and terrace.

The house took just four months to build after the foundation was put in, showing one of the great advantages of building prefab.

ENERGY EFFICIENCY

The house achieves a high level of energy efficiency with walls that are 14.6 inches (625 mm) thick, HOIZ insulation (see sidebar, page 151), triple-glazed windows, and an air-to-water heat pump. Because of these features, the homeowners' energy bills are modest even during the cold winters.

House Bretschneider, Germany

The rear of the house has multiple large windows to bring natural
light into the house and provide beautiful lake views.

BELOW The terrace, which is made from larch wood, looks out to Lake Ammersee.

BOTTOM The bathroom cabinets were custom built. The clerestory window above the bathtub provides light for the room but also maintains privacy.

HOIZ Natural Wood Shaving Bio Insulation

Organic HOIZ insulation is made either of wood shavings, which are by-products of the construction process, or from inspected FSC-certified wood forests. The insulation is treated with only natural products, such as whey and soda, to make it fire and fungus resistant. In addition, it is completely biodegradable and environmentally friendly. HOIZ has been certified by Cradle to Cradle® (see Glossary, page 288) and by Natureplus.

Natureplus

Natureplus is an international environmental organization whose goal is the "development of a culture of sustainability within the building sector."

The organization has developed a label that is awarded by a twelve-member executive committee. Products carrying this label, such as the insulation used in this home, have been recognized for their high level of quality in the areas of health, the environment, and functionality. For further information about Natureplus, see www.natureplus.org.

Cliff House

Timber Frame/Panelized

PHOTOGRAPHER:
Michael-Christian Peters (unless
    otherwise noted)

ARCHITECT:
Daniel Wagner

MANUFACTURER/BUILDER:
Baufritz

LOCATION:
Bavaria, Germany

SIZE:
2,411 square feet (224 sq m)

CERTIFICATION:
Effizienzhaus 55

BLOWER DOOR TEST:
1.51 ACH @ 50 Pascals

▶ **GREEN ASPECTS:**
Dual-flush toilets
Low-flow faucets and showerheads
Low-VOC paints and stains
PEFC-certified wood
Reclaimed wood flooring

▶ **ENERGY ASPECTS:**
Geothermal system
Heat pump
Heat recovery ventilator (HRV)
LED lighting
Photovoltaic panels
Radiant heating
Triple-glazed windows
Wood shaving insulation

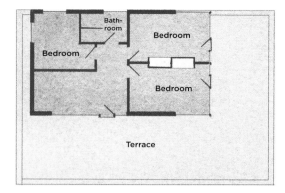

THIRD FLOOR

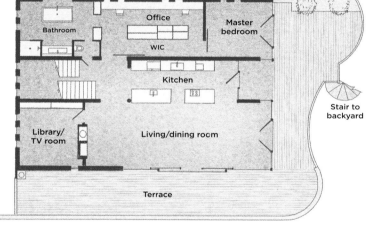

SECOND FLOOR

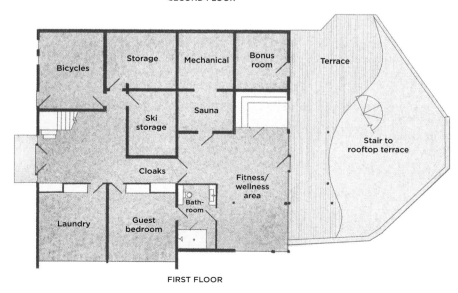

FIRST FLOOR

OPPOSITE The flatbed truck had to carefully navigate the narrow roads up to the site. (Photo courtesy of Baufritz)

BELOW Access to the house is through its north-facing side. To make the building fit in with the existing architecture, the owner chose terra-cotta because it is the same color as one of the walls of the fortress nearby. The natural larch cladding reflects the regional tradition of wooden cladding.

When the owner of the house had an opportunity to acquire this unusual 10,760-square foot (1,000-sq m) property, he knew it would be the perfect place for his family home.

THE DESIGN

He asked architect Daniel Wagner, whose work he was already familiar with, to design the house. A beautiful view of the Tyrolean mountain town of Kufstein can be seen from most of the rooms in the house. The three levels all have floor-to-ceiling windows to capture these beautiful views. The terraces on two levels expand the living space and allow for outdoor living.

THE CONSTRUCTION

Wagner selected Baufritz to build the house because he was impressed by the quality of their workmanship. The planning was finalized after just four meetings. Completing this house despite the challenges of this site was possible only because the developer, the architect, and Baufritz worked together to come up with the best available solutions.

One of the challenges in building this house was that building materials could only be delivered through the town gates, which were too small for Baufritz's double axle trucks. The prefabricated sections had to be reloaded onto smaller delivery transporter wagons to bring them up to the site. A special crane then lifted all the parts over the roofs of the existing buildings to the site.

HVAC

Radiant floor heating and wall heating provide comfortable indoor temperatures. Controlled ventilation

is also achieved with the use of a ventilation system with heat recovery. A solar heat pump uses thermal energy to heat and cool the rooms. The wood shaving insulation (see sidebar, page 151) makes a crucial contribution to creating a pleasant and comfortable environment. With outstanding heat insulation, triple-glazed windows, well-designed heating concepts (such as a heat pump and photovoltaic panels), and exceptional airtightness, the house, according to the family, generates more energy than it consumes. The owner defined his objective, "We want to reduce our consumption of fossil resources to a minimum."

When the LED lighting system lights up the house at night, it is clear that all of the work put into the thoughtful design has paid off; the house is an impressive sight.

OPPOSITE Two stainless steel "mono-blocks" form the sink section and cooking area in the kitchen. Cooking exhausts are extracted downward right at the gas hob and channeled to the outside via a ventilation duct.

BELOW AND BOTTOM The house is beautifully nestled into the hillside beneath the ancient castle.

The Effizienzhaus or Efficient House

This is a standard used by the German promotional bank KfW Bankengruppe to finance investments in energy-efficient residential buildings. The "Effizienzhaus" marks residential building with an especially low power demand. To receive this quality mark, the especially low power demand must be proved.

The numbers 40, 55, 70, 85, and 100 indicate how much energy a residential building requires compared to a standard new building constructed according to the statutory minimum requirements. Buildings that consume as much energy as a standard new building (i.e., 100 percent) are classified as Efficient House 100. Efficient Houses 70, 55, and 40 are significantly more energy efficient and may be certified with the Dena* Efficient House Quality Mark. The top energy-efficient house is Efficient House 40, which requires no more than 40 percent of the energy consumed by a standard new building. Hence,

---

* Dena is an acronym for "Deutsche Energie Agentur" (German Energy Agency): www.dena.de/en/about-dena/about-dena.html. Dena developed the standards for an "Effizienzhaus." These standards have to be observed in order to get the promotion by KfW.

the lower the number, the higher the level of energy efficiency.

The house-efficiency class affects the level of loans: The higher the level of energy efficiency, the higher the subsidy. For example, for a "Effizienzhaus 55," KfW grants a subsidy up to €13,125 (as of July 2013).

This standard was developed in accordance with the Energy Conservation Ordinance adopted by the Federal Cabinet in Germany in 2009 as part of an attempt to comply with the Kyoto Protocol of 1997 and meet the goal of achieving carbon neutral buildings by 2050. For further information see www.dena.de/fileadmin/user_upload/Presse/Pressemappen/effiziente_gebaeude/Broschuere_Effizienzhaus_Guetesiegel.pdf.

PEFC-Certified Wood

The Program for the Endorsement of Forest Certification (PEFC) is an international nonprofit, nongovernmental organization dedicated to promoting Sustainable Forest Management (SFM) through independent third-party certification. PEFC, unlike the Forest Stewardship Council (FSC), is an umbrella organization that recognizes and endorses other credible national forest certification systems. For further information about this certification program, see http://pefc.org.

LEFT The family wanted to have a modern, warm ambience and so chose three-hundred-year-old reclaimed timbers for the flooring.

RIGHT The double-panel front door leads to the first floor, which accommodates ski storage, a guest room with bathroom, a cloakroom, and a space for the heating system, among other things. The fitness and wellness area at the rear of the house leads straight onto the patio and into the garden.

BELOW The dining table is the meeting place for family and friends. "The tree trunk that forms the table top weighs 800 kilograms (1,764 pounds) and was lifted in by a crane while the house was still being built," explains architect Daniel Wagner.

OPPOSITE The master bedroom, dressing room, and bathroom are located along the length of the house facing the hill. A picture window looks out upon the cliff face so that, as the owner says, "It feels as if you could almost touch it when you are in the sunken bath."

Low-Energy House

Panelized

PHOTOGRAPHER:
Boris Storz

ARCHITECT:
Oberprillerarchitekten

MANUFACTURER:
Holzbau Haydn

BUILDER:
Gebrüder Schuhmann

LOCATION:
Frauenau, Germany

SIZE:
2,515.8 square feet (234 sq m)

CERTIFICATION:
KfW-Effizienzhaus-40-House
 (see sidebar, page 155)

BLOWER DOOR TEST:
0.52 ACH @ 50 Pascals

GREEN ASPECTS:
Dual-flush toilets
Low-flow faucets and showerheads
Permeable paving
Recycled materials

ENERGY ASPECTS:
A+++-rated energy-efficient appliances
Energy monitoring
Hot water panels
LED and CFL lighting
Log boiler
Optimal solar orientation
Radiant floor heating

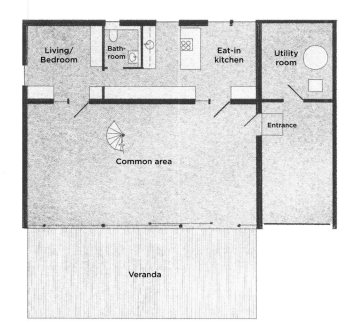

FIRST FLOOR

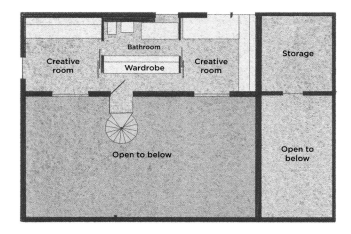

SECOND FLOOR

OPPOSITE To reduce heat loss, the northern side of the house has only a minimal number of windows.

BELOW The solar panels can be seen on the roof. The terrace, accessible through large sliding doors, seamlessly extends the living space into the garden.

Architect Jakob Oberpriller says, "Sun and light determine living and life in this low-energy house." The house takes the best advantage of natural light inside, while offering easy access to the outside.

A LOW-ENERGY DESIGN

The house was designed to only use renewable energy. The wide solar collector panels provide the domestic hot water as well as hydronic radiant floor heating when needed. The south-facing, floor-to-ceiling glass facade allows the home to passively absorb solar energy (predominantly in the autumn, winter, and the beginning of spring). These two aspects of the design provide most of the energy, which is supplemented with only 35 cubic feet (1 cu m) of wood, collected on the property for the fire stove. The solar collector shadows the south facade and the terrace in the summer minimizing direct sunlight.

If the weather is foggy or unpleasant outside, the residents can retreat from the large and open south-oriented room to the cozy northern side of the house; there are fewer windows on this side, which prevents heat loss in the winter.

The monitoring system shows that the passive system is functioning as designed and requires a minimal amount of additional energy.

A RURAL DESIGN

Inspiration for the structure comes from the historical designs of this rural and predominantly agricultural area with respect to proportion, scale, and materials. A translucent outer polyester skin, which looks like glass, is in sync with the long tradition of glass manufacturing in the Bavarian forest. The translu-

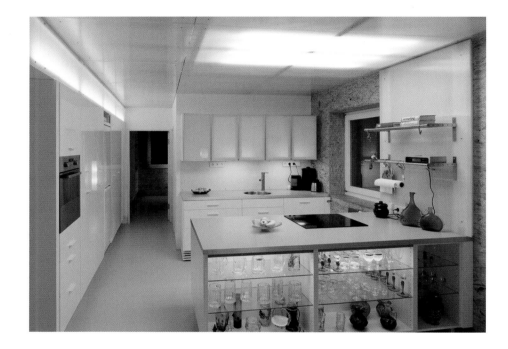

cent outer skin also gives the building an appealing clear, crystalline appearance.

Jakob's goal was to design a sophisticated, high-quality structure while maintaining a low budget, using prefabricated components and natural materials such as timber and wood wool panels, which fit in with the ecological concept of the house. Furniture was built into the walls to simplify the interior and minimize the need for purchasing additional furniture.

DESIGNED FOR ALL AGES

The house was designed with a fully accessible ground floor to meet the needs of a retiree who lives in the house and may not be able to access the steps in the future. The upper level was designed as a creative, light-filled workspace.

OPPOSITE The appliances are low-energy and rated A+++; the flooring is made from a concrete base plate with a coating of epoxide resin; the glass cabinets have an eggshell finish; and the luminous ceiling is polycarbonate.

BELOW AND BOTTOM The dining area is lit by LED spotlights and lanterns hanging above the table, which use CFL bulbs. The living and dining area has a spacious and open feel.

OVERCOMING A DESIGN CHALLENGE

Planning and construction of this house represented an exciting challenge. Meeting the Passivhaus standards and creating an energy-efficient, substantially self-sufficient, comfortable, contemporary home, while using solar energy, with minimal technology, minimal construction costs, and primary energy, was an exciting feat.

This house functions as the design intended, and its success has been publicly recognized. The house has won a number of awards, including the National Award for Residential Buildings 2013 by the Bavarian Department of the Interior, the Regional Architectural Award Lower Bavaria and Upper Palatinate 2009 by the Association of German Architects in Bavaria, the Association of German Architects Award for detached houses in 2010, the Timber Construction Award in 2011, and the People's Choice Award by the Association of German Architects in cooperation with Sueddeutsche.de in 2010.

Dream House

Panelized

PHOTOGRAPHER:
Peter Kiefer

ARCHITECT:
Bernd Neu

MANUFACTURER/BUILDER:
WeberHaus

LOCATION:
Near Cologne, Germany

SIZE:
3,337 square feet (310 sq m)

▶ **GREEN ASPECTS:**
Dual-flush toilets
Low-flow faucets and showerheads
Low-VOC paints and stains

▶ **ENERGY ASPECTS:**
Fiberboard insulation
Geothermal system
Glass wool insulation (see sidebar, page 85)
High-efficiency appliances
Large overhangs
LED and CFL lighting
Optimal solar orientation
Radiant heating
Triple-glazed windows

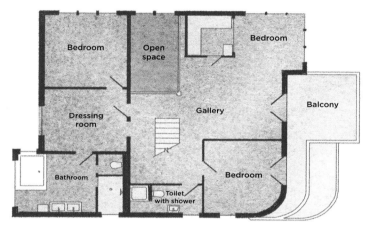

SECOND FLOOR

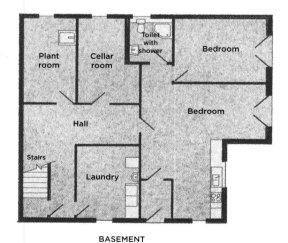

BASEMENT

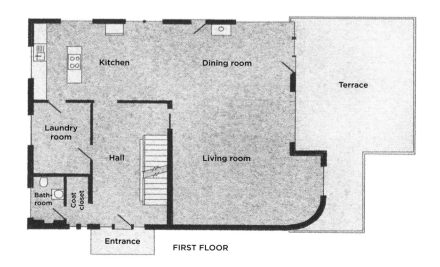

FIRST FLOOR

The northern side of the house on the ground floor has only a few small windows, in contrast to the southwestern side, which has many large windows to encourage solar gain.

The dream of this young couple was to build a home in a natural setting for themselves, their new baby, and their two cats. They also wanted to include a comfortable guest suite that could be used by their parents when they visit, and much later for their grown son, or as a rental apartment. Their goal was to have ample access to the outdoors and to seamlessly incorporate the house within its surroundings.

BUILDING THE DREAM

After about six months of searching, the couple found a property in a small town near Cologne, Germany, in a quiet residential area, at the edge of the forest, with nice views but steep slopes. To build on this structurally challenging slope, they needed to find the right company to construct their home.

After initial discussions with WeberHaus, the couple was convinced there were many advantages to building prefab. "WeberHaus allowed us a high degree of planning and a short construction period. Furthermore, it was clear to us that a prefabricated house can be designed very flexibly and individually according to our wishes."

The owners wanted to have many large floor-to-ceiling windows to enjoy the view of the valley, an open kitchen, and an energy-efficient and healthy home. They also wanted all three levels to open up to the exterior.

ENERGY EFFICIENCY

The family planned for the house to be energy efficient, exceeding the typical level of efficiency already offered by WeberHaus' eco-conscious designs. To accomplish this, they focused on creating both an efficient envelope and renewable energy with a geo-thermal system, which heats the radiant flooring and the domestic hot water.

The family took several months to plan their dream house with their architect and the WeberHaus engineers. After completing the planning phase, it took just six months until the family was able to move into their new home.

"We sit on the terrace in the summer and watch the sun go down right under our noses. In the autumn we sit in the reading corner in front of the crackling fireplace and have the feeling of sitting in a clearing," says the homeowner. "Hardly a week goes by that we do not notice how beautiful our home and surroundings are."

OPPOSITE The master bathroom faces east.

BELOW The kitchen and part of the dining room are on the southeast side of the house. The table faces south, looking out onto the patio.

BOTTOM The living room, which has a wood fireplace, faces southwest, offering a perfect view of the setting sun.

[Little] Smart House

Panelized

PHOTOGRAPHER:

Peter Kiefer (unless otherwise noted)

ARCHITECT:

Peter Rudloff

MANUFACTURER/BUILDER:

WeberHaus

LOCATION:

Baden-Württemberg
  (near Karlsruhe), Germany

SIZE:

1,421 square feet (132 sq m)

CERTIFICATION:

KfW-Effizienzhaus-40-House
  (see sidebar, page 155)

BLOWER DOOR TEST:

0.58 ACH @ 50 Pascals

▶ **GREEN ASPECTS:**

FSC-certified wood

Low-flow faucets and showerheads

Native plantings

No-VOC paints and stains

Permeable paving

▶ **ENERGY ASPECTS:**

All-in-one system (see sidebar, page 37)

Fiberboard insulation

Glass wool insulation (see sidebar, page 85)

High-efficiency appliances

High-efficiency doors

LED lighting

Optimal solar orientation

Photovoltaic panels

Triple-glazed windows

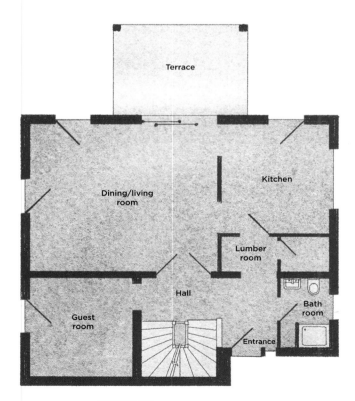

FIRST FLOOR

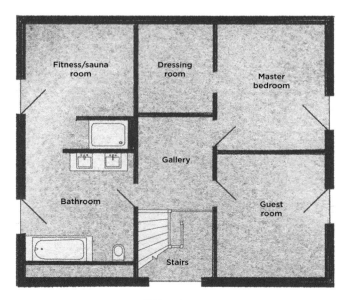

SECOND FLOOR

Nicole and Matthias renewed their vows after fifteen years of marriage and said yes to continuing their life together and to building their dream home. After visiting an exhibition at the World of Living in Rheinau-Linx, they decided that one of the houses built by WeberHaus was perfect for them because of their interest in environmentally friendly construction, coupled with high energy efficiency. They chose this fifth-generation house from WeberHaus that produces more energy than it consumes. Matthias was particularly concerned with energy efficiency, saying, "That's why we have opted for a plus-energy house that is consistently geared to produce energy even while reducing energy consumption."

BUILDING PREFAB

It took several months to complete the final plans for the house, but then it took just ten days for the factory to build it, approximately two days to erect the parts, and then about five months for the company to deliver the couple a turnkey home.

ADJUSTING THE HOME FOR COMFORT, SECURITY, AND ENERGY SAVINGS

Nicole and Matthias chose to include a building automation system. With this system they are able to automate the lighting, shutters, outlets, and so on. They can program the time and light intensity that determines when the shutters go up and down and when the lights go on and off. This serves their need for security, comfort, and energy savings. A tablet or a smartphone can be used to remotely operate the various system functions.

MINIMIZING THE USE OF ENERGY

The house is oriented to take optimal advantage of solar energy. The photovoltaic panels on the roof produce all the energy required for the house, and the surplus is fed back to the municipal grid, earning the owners some money back on their energy bill. Minimal heating and cooling is required because of the tight envelope created by the well-insulated walls that are approximately 12 inches (305 mm) thick. The heating, cooling, and ventilation system is one single machine (see sidebar, page 37). It recovers 95 percent of the energy of the outgoing air and warms up the water for domestic use. The air is exchanged every two hours without opening one single window, and thus no heat is lost in the winter.

With photovoltaic panels and battery/storage for the energy produced, the house is designed to be independent from the energy supplier. It is very comfortable; there are no cold or hot zones. An even temperature is maintained throughout.

OPPOSITE The doors are thicker and more insulated than traditional doors and are equipped with a nine-point security lock system (nine metal bolts lock the door).

ABOVE The living room and dining room are oriented to the south so they are light-flooded. Just outside this common space is the terrace, expanding the small living space into the outdoors.

BELOW The appliances in the kitchen are all energy efficient.

Borderline House

Prefabricated Insulated Reinforced
   Concrete Walls

PHOTOGRAPHER:

Assaf Pinchuk

ARCHITECT:

Guy Zucker

Z-A Studio

MANUFACTURER:

Rishon Cement Builders

LOCATION:

Shomera, Israel

SIZE:

1,200 square feet (111 sq m)

GREEN ASPECTS:

Dual-flush toilets

Low-flow faucets and showerheads

Recycled materials

ENERGY ASPECTS:

CFL lighting

Energy-efficient appliances

Energy-efficient windows

Solar hot water panels

Thermal mass of the concrete
   walls

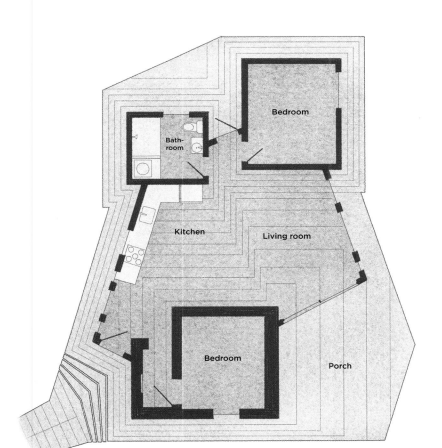

Bedroom

Bath-
room

Kitchen

Living room

Bedroom

Porch

OPPOSITE ABOVE This garage-type exterior door closes off large glass doors for thermal insulation and for security.

OPPOSITE BELOW The massive concrete walls, visible here in this side view of the house, function as thermal mass, absorbing solar energy in the day and releasing it when it is required on cool nights.

BELOW The entrance of the house is pale blue, which contrasts with the yellow sandstone color of the majority of the exterior.

When the owners of the Borderline House want to escape the hectic lifestyle of Tel Aviv, they go to their vacation home in Shomera, near the border between Israel and Lebanon. Located on a mountain overlooking a Mediterranean forest, they experience the serenity and meditative calm of being in the country. In the nearby area, they enjoy the excellent restaurants of northern Galilee and the Arab and Druze villages, which are all a five-minute drive away. They also enjoy swimming in the sea, which is just a thirty-minute drive from the house.

THE DESIGN

The architect Guy Zucker believes that homes today should be built small, built to meet the specific needs of the owners, and with zero air infiltration; the Borderline House follows these ideals.

Regional security regulations (for the zone in the north of Israel that is close to the border with Lebanon) dictated the use of concrete walls and ceilings for the rooms and that they be 20 inches (508 mm) thick, with limited openings. These regulations called for the strategic placement of the heavy concrete blocks, leaving openings for windows and doors. There are larger openings in the public spaces—the living room and kitchen—and fewer in the private areas, such as the bedrooms and bathroom. The large insulated concrete blocks were placed on the foundation and joined together with steel binding joints.

HEATING AND COOLING

The house needs limited heating and cooling equipment because the insulated concrete walls are very energy efficient. The orientation of the house, with a north and south exposure, provides adequate sunlight in the winter and less in the summer, as a result of the sun's angle. In addition, the winters are short and the summers are relatively cool on the mountain where the house is located. A ductless mini-split system (see sidebar, opposite) also helps cool the home.

A ZEN GARDEN STYLE

Based on typical Zen garden designs, the floor tiles in the public spaces, both inside and outside of the house, "ripple" around and between the blocks.

Zucker says, "When we were thinking of how the house would engage with the landscape, we were inspired by the Zen garden and how the small pebbles are combed around the big rocks, as if they are rippling around them, until they reach the edges of the garden. Since we conceptualized the concrete blocks as rocks or sandstones, we thought the floor tile pattern could ripple around them and create the pattern inside the house and out."

The soft blue of the flooring contrasts with both the color and feel of the massive concrete walls, creating a lighter mood for this vacation home. The floor pattern is a blue gradient formed using readily available ceramic tiles. The tiles are organized to ripple around the private areas of the house, extending to the exterior.

The area of the house that faces the forest and has a terrace is painted blue to evoke the feeling of sky and water, providing a lightness to contrast with the massive walls. The side of the house that faces the street is a yellow sandstone color.

With its carefully considered design aesthetic, this efficient and comfortable house is a peaceful weekend retreat for its owners.

BELOW The blue tile pattern emanates from the three private areas of the house—the two bedrooms and the bathroom. The air handler component of the mini-split system (see sidebar) can be seen high up on the wall.

BOTTOM The appliances in the kitchen are all low energy and the countertops are butcher block.

Ductless Heating and Cooling Systems or Mini-split Systems

Ductless heating and cooling systems, also known as mini-splits and ductless heat pumps, are growing in popularity around the world because they are a highly efficient heating and cooling option for homes. They do not require ducts, are small in size, cost less to install than traditional HVAC systems, and use a fraction of the energy, reducing utility bills by about 25 to 50 percent. The system is composed of three main parts—an indoor air-handling unit, an outdoor compressor/condenser unit, and a remote control that operates the system. Heat is transferred using refrigerant expansion and compression, in much the same way as a refrigerator works. During the colder months, heat pumps move heat from the cool outdoors into the warm house, and during the warmer months, heat pumps move heat from the cool house into the warm outdoors. They move heat rather than generate heat, so they can provide up to four times the amount of energy they consume. Because these systems don't have ducts, they avoid some of the energy losses associated with central forced air heating and cooling systems, particularly when the ducts are in unconditioned spaces. One outdoor condensing unit can be used for up to four indoor air handlers in different zones of the house, each controlled to meet the needs of certain rooms. The number of heat pumps required will depend on the size of the home and how well insulated it is. Each of the zones will have its own thermostat so only the occupied rooms can be conditioned, saving energy and money. For further information about ductless heat pumps, see http://energy.gov/energysaver/articles/ductless-mini-split-air-conditioners.

New Energy House

Panelized

PHOTOGRAPHER:
Federico Zattarin

ARCHITECTS:
Giulia Zordan and Domenico
    Gabaldo
Architetti Zordan Gabaldo

BUILDERS:
Rasom Wood Technology and
    Impresa Baraldo Luigi

MANUFACTURER:
Rasom Wood Technology

LOCATION:
Padua, Italy

SIZE:
2,368 square feet (220 sq m)

CERTIFICATIONS:
CasaClima A (see sidebar, page 178)
ITACA Protocol (see sidebar,
    page 178)

BLOWER DOOR TEST:
2.30 ACH @ 50 Pascals

GREEN ASPECTS:

Cross-laminated timbers (CLT) (see sidebar,
    page 197)
Dual-flush toilets
Ecological and long-lasting materials
Location close to public transport
Low-flow faucets and showerheads
No VOCs or formaldehydes in paints, adhesives,
    and finishes
Reclaimed materials
Recycled materials
Separate garage

ENERGY ASPECTS:

Advanced framing (to minimize thermal bridging)
Cross-ventilation
Energy recovery ventilator (ERV)
Geothermal preconditioning coil
Large overhangs
LED and CFL lighting
Optimal solar orientation
Photovoltaic panels
Solar heat exchanger
Solar hot water panels
Wood wool insulation

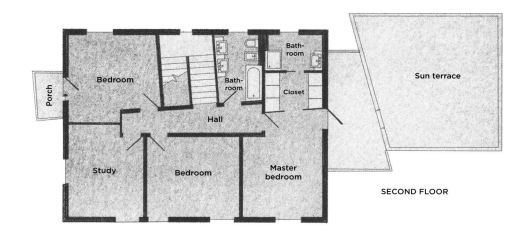

SECOND FLOOR

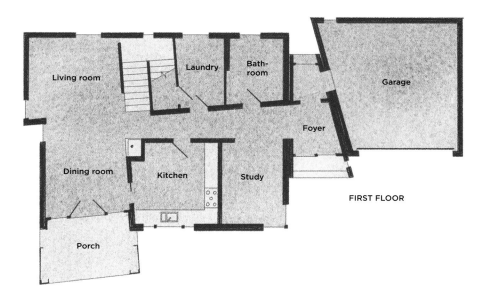

FIRST FLOOR

To create the exterior of the house, a plaster coating was put directly on the external surface of the insulated wood wool panels. The thick insulation is an important factor in why the house is so energy efficient.

The focus of architect Giulia Zordan's professional career has always been on sustainable construction and energy conservation. She became certified as a CasaClima expert in 2006 (see sidebar, page 178) and opened her own office with Domenico Gabaldo. In 2008 she also became certified as a Passivhaus Designer Architect.

GETTING THE HOUSE CERTIFIED

The house in Padua was Zordan's first house designed and built according to the standards of sustainability inspired by the ITACA Protocol (see sidebar, page 178) and CasaClima A certification. Although neither of these programs was compulsory, the owners and architects opted to become involved with them to test the quality of the design and construction.

Because of the high ITACA score of 2.67 that this house attained, the owners received a prize: money to help with the cost of construction, which amounted to about 3.5 percent of the total costs.

ENERGY EFFICIENCY

One of the most significant aspects affecting the energy efficiency of the house is the wood wool insulation, which at 5½ inches (140 mm) thick is a very thick insulation compared to most used in Italy. The U-value of the walls (the amount of energy that flows through them) is 0.178 W/(m²K), while the national requirement is 0.894 W/(m²K). The lower the U-value, the lower the amount of energy that escapes through the wall (see Glossary, page 289, for more information).

Heating and cooling needs were minimized in the design by positioning the house to get optimal solar advantage, taking into account preexisting and possible future construction, along with energy bal-

ancing of the windows and insulation. The location of the rooms was carefully planned in order to achieve optimal natural lighting and to minimize electricity consumption by taking into consideration the intended use of the rooms. For example, the kitchen faces southeast so breakfast can be prepared with the rising sun. The dining room has south and southeast exposure so the family can have dinner while experiencing the sunset. The porch faces east so it is in the shade in the afternoon and late afternoon, permitting the children to play or eat dinner outside. The children's rooms face southeast and southwest, so they get the most sunlight possible during the day. The master bedroom faces northeast, because it is used primarily for sleeping and daylighting is not important here.

HEALTHY AND SUSTAINABLE MATERIALS

The house was constructed primarily using natural materials from renewable resources, such as wood, and salvaged materials, such as wood wool fiber insulation, which is made from the waste material of wood elements. The environmental impact of the house over its lifetime was also taken into account by considering the recyclability of the parts at the end of the house's useful life.

The interior finishes were selected to minimize indoor pollution, so they contain no or limited quantities of volatile organic compounds (VOCs), which would directly affect the health of the occupants.

HEATING AND COOLING

Heating is provided in four stages, using the fresh airflow from an ERV. First, the fresh air is heated with geothermal energy as the intake vent passes it beneath the ground. Once inside the house, the heat

ABOVE The dining room gets a lot of natural light from the windows facing south and southeast.

BELOW The flooring is made from bay oak with a natural oil finish. The living room faces south and southwest and gets a good amount of natural light.

The interior of the house is modeled on a diagonal line that starts in the foyer and goes toward the south part of the house—the red wall is the physical manifestation of this design concept. Architect Giulia Zordan thought of the line as a guide from the darker, less sunlit inner part of the house to the illuminated, bright side of the house. The red wall passes near the warm hearth of the house, the fireplace, and reappears at the contact point with the south facade, splitting the south window into two parts.

ITACA Protocol

The ITACA Protocol is a system for the assessment of environmental quality for residential buildings. It is used by many regions in Italy. The evaluation is carried out by two groups: The first group evaluates the "resource consumption," measuring in the winter and summer, the production of domestic hot water, the quantity of natural lighting, the amount of electricity produced from renewable energy sources, the use of eco-compatible materials, drinking water consumption, and the capability of maintaining the performance of the building envelope. The second group checks for the incidence of "environmental burdens," analyzing factors such as greenhouse gas emissions, solid and liquid waste products, and the permeability of exterior areas.

Scores are given for the various criteria, ranging from -1 to +5. Zero is the standard for comparison with the current design practice, in accordance with the local laws and regulations. If a building's ITACA score is 0, it has the minimum performance required according to local code. If the score is -1, it means that something in the house is performing incorrectly. If the score is more than 0, it means that the house is better than what is required. The New Energy House scored 2.67.

This program is voluntary. For more information about this certification program, see www.itaca.org.

CasaClima

CasaClima is a public independent certification program, accredited in 2006 as a certifying agency of the Province of Bolzano. It is not involved in the construction process, but deals with the energy and environmental certification of building products. To date, the agency has certified nearly five thousand buildings, spread across the country. Third-party professionals evaluate not only the energy efficiency of the building but also the impact of the structure on the environment and health of the inhabitants. After inspection, the certifier releases a certificate and a CasaClima plate to be installed on the building. The agencies of other provinces, such as Florence and Friuli-Venezia Giulia, have decided to implement CasaClima Standards to improve the energy performance of their property assets. The model for CasaClima is growing, not only in Italy but also in Austria and Germany. This program is voluntary. For additional information, see www.agenziacasaclima.it/it/casaclima/1-0.html.

Terraces and patio decks are insulated in order not to create thermal bridges to the heated building envelope. Terrace railings are made of a metallic grid. The patio catches light in the morning, creating a pleasant place to have breakfast. The patio is shadowed in the evening, and allows for comfortable dining.

exchanger is used to extract the heat from the stale exhaust air and use it to warm the fresh intake air without mixing the two. Then a gas boiler heats hot water, which is distributed to radiators in each room through the ERV ventilation ducts. The fresh air from the ERV ducts passes over the radiator while mixing with indoor air from the room and finally provides both warmth and fresh outside air during the winter.

The solar thermal panels integrated with the natural gas boiler heat the water for the radiant system and domestic hot water. An airtight fireplace, with an ambient air heating circuit (separate from the path of the fumes), can be operated to meet peak demand. Air that is to be heated is taken from outside; it flows through pipes under the pavement, and comes into the fireplace. The burned air flows out through a chimney. Room air flows through a grid and reaches a cavity behind the thick metallic surfaces in the rear of the fireplace, becoming warmer, then flows back into the room again. Photovoltaic panels on the roof of the house partially meet the electricity demands of the house.

The house was not originally designed to have

an ERV. However, during construction the homeowners decided to include one, which vastly improved the energy efficiency of the house, raised their Casa-Clima certification from B to CasaClima A, while also improving the air quality in the house.

MONITORING THE HOUSE

The primary energy consumption of the house was monitored and calculated using electric energy and natural gas bills for the first year and a half. The result was lower energy consumption than was estimated when the house was designed. The house used 68.05 kWh/m² total energy consumption rather than 100.51 kWh/m², as estimated in the planning. Typical houses in the area use approximately 250 to 300 kWh/m².

AN AWARD-WINNING HOUSE

The house was awarded the New Energy honorable mention by the Chamber of Commerce, Industry, and Agriculture of Padua in collaboration with the Department of Electrical Engineering at the University of Padua.

EDDI's House

Light Steel Frame/Panels

PHOTOGRAPHER:
Daishinsha Inc.

ARCHITECT:
Edward Suzuki Associates and
  Daiwa House

MANUFACTURER/BUILDER:
Daiwa House Industry

LOCATION:
Nara, Nara Prefecture, Japan

SIZE:
1,554 square feet (144 sq m)

GREEN ASPECTS:
Bamboo flooring
Dual-flush toilets
Low-flow faucets and showerheads
Low-VOC paints
Recycled materials
Self-cleaning coating on exterior

ENERGY ASPECTS:
Air circulation paths in between exterior and interior
  finishes
Ceiling fans
Cross-ventilation with operable windows
Double-floor living space to act as a solar collector
Double-glazed windows
Exterior glass wool insulation
Fluorescent and LED lighting
Individual heat pump AC with exterior units
Silver roofing that reflects rather than absorbs heat
Solar panels

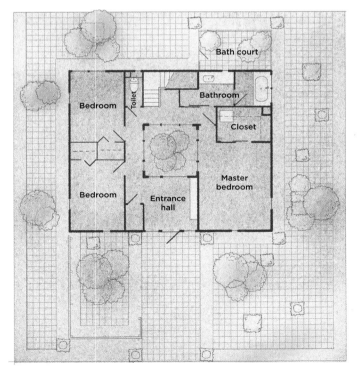

FIRST FLOOR

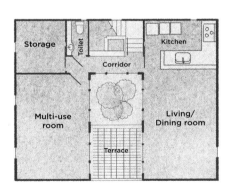

SECOND FLOOR

The exterior of the house is created from cement panels, a
low-maintenance material on which a self-cleaning coating is applied.

According to architect Edward Suzuki, EDDI's House is the first industrialized house in Japan designed by an architect (himself) and built by a major housing manufacturer, Daiwa House, in a "collaborative effort." The house is named for the architect's nickname, and it also stands for Edward Daiwa-House Design Innovation. The house pictured is a model home, but the company has already built more than three hundred similar homes in Japan.

HOUSE AS PRODUCT

This house, and many others like it, has been prefabricated and sold as a ready-made "product" in Japan. Because the home location is not known at the time of design, the architect has designed the house under the assumption that the site on which the house would be placed will not be surrounded by an environment with appealing views. Edward says this has proven to be true more often than not through his experience over the years; the house should therefore not look outward but inward.

Edward calls this design concept "go into go out," meaning that the house has an outdoor patio at the center of the house that each room looks onto. In addition, a balcony overlooks the central patio. This combination of open spaces creates an "interface" between the outside and the interior of the house that acts as a buffer between the two zones. Because of the way the house is designed, the surrounding environment will have little influence on the interior atmosphere. No matter how unfavorable the surroundings may be, the house can function comfortably within the mini-cosmos of its own boundaries. Should the outside conditions be favorable, however,

all that a future buyer would need to do is request additional openings to the outside.

PASSIVE HEATING AND COOLING

The house, with its central patio, is designed to allow sunlight in and cross-ventilation to provide maximum energy efficiency.

Occupants say they hardly turn on the heaters because enough light penetrates and heats the house by day. Likewise, in the warmer seasons cross-ventilation allows pleasant breezes to pass through the house; mechanical cooling is not necessary unless conditions are extreme.

EDDI's House now has five basic plans with at least fifty variations to accommodate the varying site conditions and characteristics required by different owners.

OPPOSITE   The kitchen and dining area are connected. Because of this open floor plan, the small space appears larger and better communication is possible between the rooms. Appliances are high efficiency and the countertops are Corian.

BELOW   The interior atrium is a two-story space that acts as a solar heat collector. It also provides natural light for much of the house, as most rooms face this central area.

B-House

Timber Frame/Kit Components

PHOTOGRAPHER:

Yoshikazu Shiraki and
  Hideo Nishiyama

DESIGN ARCHITECT:

Anderson Anderson Architecture

LOCAL ARCHITECT:

Nishiyama Architects

MANUFACTURER/BUILDER:

Tomisaki Construction

LOCATION:

Kyushu Island, Japan

SIZE:

1,100 square feet (102 sq m)

▶ GREEN ASPECTS:

Dual-flush toilets

Fiber cement siding

Low-flow water faucets

No-VOC paints

Rainwater harvesting

Small footprint

▶ ENERGY ASPECTS:

Concrete flooring

Daylighting

Energy-efficient appliances

Halogen and fluorescent lighting

Large overhangs

Natural ventilation

Photovoltaic panels

Solar hot water panels

Tankless water heater

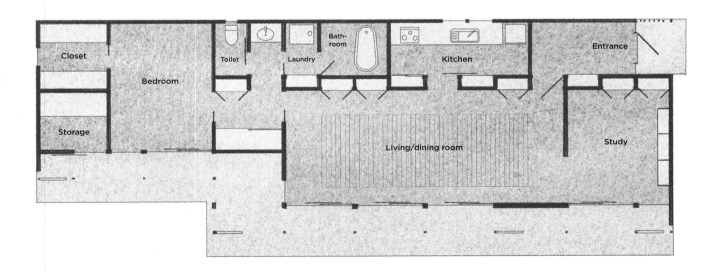

OPPOSITE The floor-to-ceiling operable glass window wall in the living room showcases the south view and lets in plenty of natural light. The room also includes custom built-in cabinets and a sliding door to the bedroom area.

BELOW Situated on a terraced, south-facing slope in a dense neighborhood, the house overlooks orange groves and has a beautiful view of Kumamoto Castle and the surrounding hills. The large exterior overhangs protect the house from overheating in the summer and allow the sun in when it is needed in the winter.

The B-House is a wonderful example of a very energy-efficient, eco-friendly house that was built on a modest budget. This two-bedroom, one-bath home was built for two public school teachers who wanted a very energy self-sufficient house on a construction budget of $154,000, an extremely modest budget by local Kumamoto standards. This required the close collaboration of the architects and the builder to achieve an off-site fabricated, timber-frame construction that was also high quality and met high sustainability standards.

The house was designed for indoor-outdoor living with large terraces and natural landscaping. Because of the simple materials used, such as timber, plaster, and concrete, minimal maintenance is required.

INCREASINGLY ENVIRONMENTALLY FRIENDLY

Rather than build the house fully energy independent from the start, the plan was to integrate additional energy-saving systems over the following five years, as the couple's budget would allow. These additions will include solar panels and a geothermal loop system.

The house has a water catchment roof system, which will collect water to be used for the landscaping. This catchment system will eventually be integrated with a future green roof.

TIMBER FRAME CONSTRUCTION

The timber frame and all major wood and steel parts were prefabricated in a factory in Kumamoto and were then brought to the site and assembled. In this way, the homeowners, architect, and contractor were able to control the budget, schedule, and quality of the timber and components with the utmost efficiency.

SOLAR OPTIMIZATION

All essential components of the sustainable design strategy were fully implemented in the original construction. The house was built to optimize solar energy. The high percentage of operable glass walls on the south side allows the owners to enjoy indoor and outdoor living, the beautiful views, and the prevailing summer winds, which cool the house. Heat loss in the winter is prevented with minimal glazing on the north side. The operable clerestory windows on the northern facade provide optimal daylighting in summer, without heat gain, and create a chimney effect. There is a natural ventilation draft that draws air through the home. These windows help exhaust the kitchen, bath, and sleeping spaces with cooling updrafts. Wide overhangs are beneficial throughout the seasons: They protect the house from the summer sun and allow the sun to warm the house in the winter.

Hydronic floor heating was installed in preparation for a geothermal system and solar thermal panels, which will eventually be integrated into this heating system.

The north face of the home has a steeply pitched roof section oriented for future photovoltaic panels facing south. The concrete flooring throughout much of the house provides thermal mass, which helps to heat the house in the colder months and cool it during the hotter times of the year.

The concrete portion of the living room's flooring around the periphery absorbs heat as thermal mass. The rest of the floor is oak wood. The sliding glass doors, which face south, provide natural daylight and ventilation.

EAST MEETS WEST

Anderson Anderson Architecture, whose office is located in California, worked in collaboration with Nishiyama Architects in Japan to design the house. The owners acted as translators for the collaborative process and were active partners with both firms in the design.

Peter Anderson of Anderson Anderson Architecture says, "Building design and construction is becoming increasingly complex because so many new problems and opportunities must be addressed at both global and local scales. Sustainable construction processes in the future will require collaborations such as the B-House, in which architects with various areas of expertise collaborate to use international construction technologies as well as local knowledge, local materials, and local fabrication and craft expertise."

Anderson says that collaborating on this house went smoothly, aided by the proactive clients: "We had an excellent experience collaborating with the local architect, engineers, manufacturers, and contractors on this project, with everyone cooperating very well in a team approach. All this was facilitated by very hands-on, bilingual clients, who were very engaged with all facets of the project. We have done a lot of international work for more than twenty years, so we've gotten quite used to anticipating what information is needed by all the parties, and in working with metric and other measuring systems that are used in each local area. We enjoy spending time in each of the places where we work, getting to know the local customs and building traditions, so we can make use of them where we can, and so we can know when it makes sense to introduce off-site fabrication as part of the complete project delivery system."

B-House is an exciting example of potential collaborations between organizations that take advantage of different companies' varied types of expertise. This is particularly useful today, when green and energy-efficient technologies are developing at such a rapid pace.

As seen from the study, this view
showcases the full length of the
house and the openness created by
the sliding glass doors.

LEFT This traditional Japanese-style wet room includes tiled walls, a freestanding soaking tub, and a shower. The clerestory windows provide privacy, as well as natural lighting.

RIGHT The bedroom's high clerestory windows on the north side of the house open to let warm air escape and bring in natural daylight. The floor is polished concrete, and the room is lit with halogen and fluorescent bulbs.

U-3 House

Kit Components

PHOTOGRAPHER:

Toshihisa Ishii of Blitz STUDIO (unless
   otherwise noted)

ARCHITECT:

Masahiko Sato, Architect-Show

MANUFACTURER/BUILDER:

Haraguchi Construction Corporation

LOCATION:

Fukuoka, Fukuoka Prefecture, Japan

SIZE:

1,934 square feet (181 sq m)

BLOWER DOOR TEST:

1.0 ACH @ 50 Pascals

▶ **GREEN ASPECTS:**

Dual-flush toilets

Low-flow faucets and showerheads

Low-VOC paints and stains

Metal roof

Permeable paving

Small footprint

▶ **ENERGY ASPECTS:**

Energy recovery ventilator (ERV)

Exterior insulation board

LED and CFL lighting

Low-energy appliances

Radiant heating and cooling

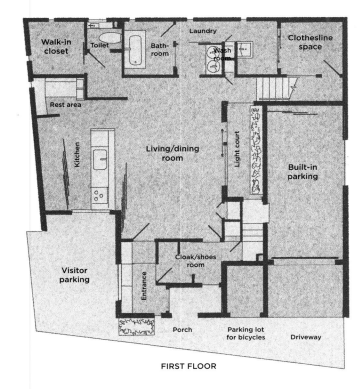

FIRST FLOOR

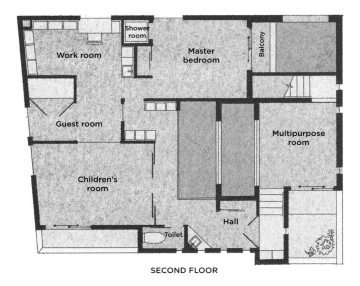

SECOND FLOOR

This house was built for a couple and their two daughters in the dense city center of Fukuoka. It took only three weeks for the house to be built in the factory, and then it was erected on-site in a day and a half.

PRIVACY AND LIGHT

Because the house is in a dense city area, the owners wanted the house to afford them a good amount of privacy from the outside world but still have a lot of natural light. To accomplish this, the house was built with a light court that brings ample natural light into the center of the house. Skylights and a series of narrow and clerestory windows that face the public areas also achieve that goal of daylighting throughout the home. The owners also did not want the electrical lighting equipment to be very visible, so the lights are recessed into the ceiling.

Although the house has a small footprint, it was designed to have a spacious appearance, with clean lines, natural light, and light interior colors. The wood floors and wall behind the dining table give the house a warm feeling, although the lines and colors are stark.

VENTILATION, HEATING, AND COOLING

The house is built with exterior insulation, which helps to close off any thermal bridging. Heating and cooling are both accomplished with a hydronic radiant system (see sidebar, page 138).

The house was designed with consideration to the styles of other homes in the neighborhood. In order to complement the look of the surrounding homes, which are in general sleek and modern, the architect selected an exterior made of dark wood paneling and stark white walls. This created a look

with clean lines but also with warmth and definition. The U-3 House is a worthy addition to the neighborhood—both beautiful and environmentally friendly.

OPPOSITE   When this newly planted garden grows, it will help protect the house from the hot summer rays.

LEFT   The light court allows natural light to flood into the living and dining area.

RIGHT   The dining room and kitchen flooring is natural solid cherry wood with an oil finish. For flexibility, the lights are mounted on a rail and can be moved freely.

BOTTOM LEFT   The stone flooring in the entrance leads into the living room, with display shelves and benches lining the wall. In this area of the house, the clerestory window allows for both privacy and natural light.

BOTTOM RIGHT   On the second floor, a communal sink was added for the whole family to share. The atrium railing contributes to the openness of the home. It is made of tempered glass, allowing for natural light to pass through it.

Energy Neutral Residence

Panelized

PHOTOGRAPHER:

Hans Peter Föllmi

ARCHITECT:

Pieter Weijnen of UPFRNT/FARO

MANUFACTURER:

MetsäWood

BUILDER:

J. J. A. Kerkhofs Montagebouw

LOCATION:

Amsterdam, Netherlands

SIZE:

2,583 square feet (240 sq m)

CERTIFICATION:

Passivhaus

▶ GREEN ASPECTS:

Compostable materials

Dual-flush toilets

Gray water system for washing machines and toilets

Herbal roof garden

Low-flow faucets and showerheads

No painting or preservatives

Rainwater harvesting

Recyclable materials

Wood fiber insulation

▶ ENERGY ASPECTS:

Adjustable sun screens

Cellulose insulation in the roof

Day/night ventilation

Deep-lying windows to optimize access by sun in winter and prevent access in summer

Energy recovery ventilator (ERV)

Groundwater heat exchanger

Insulated window framing

LED lighting

Manual exterior shades

Organic insulation (wood fiber, cellulose, and aerogel)

Pellet stove biomass heater

Phase-changing materials (PCM) in the adobe

Radiant heating

Solar hot water panels

Thermal mass (with clay plaster on walls and PCM by BASF)

Triple-glazed windows

Urban windmill

Ventilation heat exchange

Wind turbines

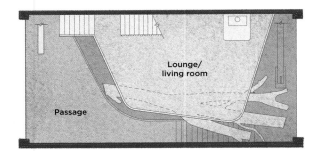

SECOND FLOOR

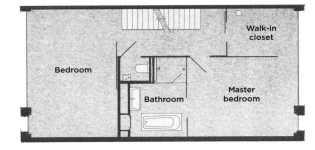

FOURTH FLOOR

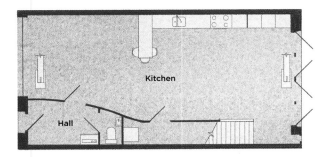

GROUND FLOOR

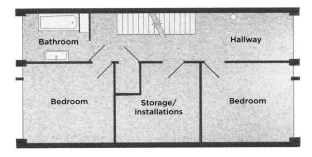

THIRD FLOOR

OPPOSITE The shou-sugi-ban larch wood is layered with bright orange planks. Solar collectors, which consist of double-glass tubes that minimize heat loss, form a cornice on the front facade of the house. A wind turbine is on the roof.

After the success of a mainstream sustainable residence in Steigereiland, a neighborhood of Amsterdam, architect Pieter Weijnen from UPFRNT pushed to build another house that would be able to reach an even higher level of efficiency. This new home that he built for himself, the Energy Neutral Residence, is exactly that, meaning it creates as much energy as it uses. The house is also built following Cradle to Cradle® principles (see Glossary, page 288), reducing CO_2 reduction to 100 percent. Most materials used in the house construction can be recycled if it is someday dismantled. Materials were also selected based on the following factors: proximity to the site, being locally produced, being developed by manufacturers carrying out environmentally friendly practices, and adherence to the parameters of the Passivhaus standards. Weijnen opted to use techniques that were very new, such as PCM, a phase-changing material for accumulating heat, and aerogel insulation (see sidebar, opposite). He also decided to push the local codes by incorporating a wind turbine into the design.

Using prefabricated construction, the house was completed in seven months, between March and September 2009. Components included CLT panels (see sidebar, opposite) and a more traditional panelized system that provides excellent insulation.

HIGH TECH HEATING AND COOLING

The Passivhaus standards were met in part by installing insulation with the value of R-10, triple glazing, 100 percent airtight connections (even the cat door is highly insulated), and heat exchangers. Integrated photovoltaic cells will be installed in the future on the roofline, and the wind turbine will generate enough electricity to supply both the nominal electricity demand and the heating of domestic water. Storing heat is difficult because the house has little mass, but the large boiler allows a sizeable amount of energy to be accumulated in its approximately 530 gallons (2,006 liters) of water. The heat exchanger, in combination with the high level of insulation and triple glazing, creates a comfortable internal air temperature. The fresh air supply comes from the outside and is preheated by a ground source heat exchanger, which is 2.7 feet (1 m) under the house. Warm water collectors supply energy for space heating and warm water. These are integrated in the cornice of the facade. If needed, the temperature in the house can be increased with the use of a pellet stove (see sidebar, page 41).

A HEALTHY HOME

In an attempt to keep all interiors healthy, the insulation is organic and the wood fiber is able to accumulate moisture and evaporate it slowly. "We call this a breathing house, in contrast to a house with glass or ceramic fiber insulation, which does not function in this way," Weijnen says. "And because of the accumulation of moisture, the house is very comfortable. The wood also creates a very good acoustic block to outside noise."

The exteriors were kept healthy, with no paints or stains used. The exterior of the house is seared wood (shou-sugi-ban) that requires no additional finishes. The interior of the house is treated only with an alkaline solution to keep it white, which also does not require harsh chemicals or finishes.

Cross-Laminated Timber (CLT)

Cross-laminated timber (CLT) is engineered wood constructed of wood planks laminated in layers at right angles to each other and glued together under great pressure to create panels that are used for prefabricated structural applications. Prefabricated panels are used in the construction of floors, walls, and roofs, and provide load distribution and dimensional stability in all directions. Panels often arrive at the construction site pre-cut for windows and doors. These panels provide positive environmental characteristics, such as carbon storage, low greenhouse emissions during the manufacturing process, and the ability to be recycled. CLT panels reduce construction time compared to some other building methods, weigh less than other building materials, allowing them to be installed with light construction equipment, and require a limited time to learn how to erect. Panels can be exposed and used as interior and exterior surfaces. For further information about the CLT used in this house, visit www.metsawood.nl.

Shou-Sugi-Ban (the Burning of Japanese Cypress)

Shou-sugi-ban is a traditional Japanese technique of burning cypress wood to make it more sustainable. Larch, which was used in this home, and other wood can also be treated in this way. The process involves burning the wood as a tube (three pieces of wood are bound to create a triangular tube and then the fire burns from the inside) or in the oven, just deep enough to get the black-silver finish. The wood is sometimes left in that natural state or finished with oil to bring out the gray, silver, or other tones. This process preserves the wood and makes it resistant to fire, rot, and pests. The burnt top layer not only preserves the wood but also eliminates the need for paint or impregnation. For further information, visit http://shousugiban .com or http://shou-sugi-ban.com.

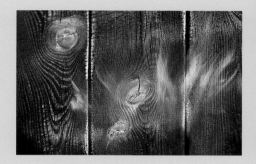

Larch wood is seared using the traditional Japanese burning technique of shou-sugi-ban.

Aerogel Insulation (or Frozen Smoke)

Aerogel is a silica-based substance that is manufactured by removing the liquid from the silica and replacing it with air, which makes up about 99.8 percent of the final product. Although it is one of the lowest density materials on earth, it is a highly effective insulator. It is about four times more efficient than fiberglass or foam. NASA first developed the practical application of aerogel for the use in spacecraft. There are currently two companies that manufacture aerogel for the construction industry. When aerogel strips 1.5 inches (3.8 cm) thick and 4.5 feet (11.4 cm) long, produced by Thermoblok, are adhered to the exterior side of framing studs in construction, the R-value of the insulated stud cavity is increased by 20 to 40 percent. They can be used around window frames and attached to studs to break thermal bridging (see Glossary, page 290). Aspen Aerogel produces rolls of material 0.2 to 0.4 inches (0.51 to 1 cm) thick and 57 inches (145 cm) wide. This product is used in wall cavities, roofing, and flooring, but because of the cost, it is more often used for commercial applications. Aerogel technology is still very expensive to produce, but can save the homeowner on energy bills over time. For further information, visit www.thermablok.com or www .aerogel.com.

LEFT The dining and kitchen area are located on the first floor. The ceramic tile floor is from a local source, which is Cradle to Cradle® certified (see Glossary, page 288).

BELOW The tree trunk is lifted into place on the second floor.

A TREE GROWS IN THE WEIJNEN HOME

A unique feature is the horizontal trunk that spans the length of the house. The tree was salvaged from one of the canals in Amsterdam, where it had to be removed for restoration of the quay. The living room balcony rests on the tree and is secured with steel cables.

Weijnen hopes his home will inspire others to build houses that are both sustainable and visually appealing. He says, "We hope this project will be an example for many other people and investors. Our Minister of Environment has visited the house to get an update on sustainable building practices." The Energy Neutral Residence was the first Passivhaus certified in Amsterdam. Since this house was built, others have been certified.

ABOVE The living room is located on the split-level second floor balcony.

BELOW To save space, a bathroom is incorporated into this bedroom on the third floor.

OPPOSITE ABOVE The pellet stove serves multiple purposes, providing heat for the shower and heating rooms on very cold days.

OPPOSITE BELOW Cantilevered steps lead up from the ground floor to the second floor. The steps are secured with steel to the wall.

First Light

Modular

PHOTOGRAPHER:

Jim Tetro (unless otherwise noted)

ARCHITECT/BUILDER:

Students at Victoria University of
Wellington

MANUFACTURER:

Mainzeal and the students

LOCATION:

Solar Decathlon 2011, Washington, DC

Waimarama, Hawke's Bay, New
Zealand

SIZE:

800 square feet (74 sq m)

▶ GREEN ASPECTS:

Compact size

Dual-flush toilets

Locally sourced materials

Low-flow faucets and showerhead

Recycled materials

▶ ENERGY ASPECTS:

Drying cupboard for drying clothes

Energy monitoring

Energy recovery ventilator (ERV)

Heat pump

Large overhangs

LED lighting

Optimal solar orientation

Photovoltaic panels

Solar hot water panels

Thermal mass

Triple-glazed windows and skylight

Wool insulation

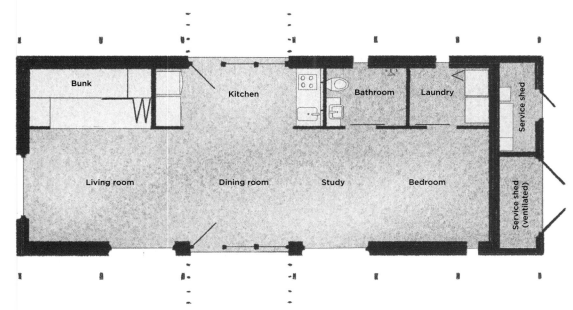

OPPOSITE The decking of the house is made from sustainably sourced Monterey pine, *Pinus radiata*. It both surrounds the exterior of the house and runs through the central interior space, which creates a link between the interior and exterior areas.

BELOW The timber canopy houses the photovoltaic panels and solar water heaters. It embodies part of the active and passive strategy behind the home's overall design, shading the glazing in summer months while the butterfly, slanted design aids the passive cooling of the photovoltaic panels. An innovative system was designed by the team that uses detachable cladding made of western red cedar. This removable cedar cladding clips to the outside of the house quickly and easily, which enabled builders to ship the house in modules covered in plywood to prevent damage to the cladding. The cladding was then installed on-site on top of the plywood.

New Zealand is one of the first places in the world to see the sun rise each day, thus providing the inspiration for the name of the house: First Light. The design of the house comes from the classic Kiwi bach (pronounced *batch*), a New Zealand vacation house, which has a strong connection to the landscape and is condusive to outdoor socializing.

The home was built by students at Victoria University of Wellington and was awarded third place out of nineteen teams at the US Department of Energy Solar Decathlon in September 2011. The team placed first in energy balance, second in architecture, and third in market appeal. The house was estimated to cost the team $300,000 to build; costs were covered by over a hundred sponsors.

BRIDGING THE INTERIOR TO THE EXTERIOR

The central section of the house functions as a bridge between the exterior natural environment and the interior of the house. This central area is used for socializing and entertaining, which reflects the Kiwi lifestyle. The large doors open up on both sides to allow passive cooling of the house during the summer. In the winter, the skylight allows sunlight to penetrate the space. The central portion of the house also bridges the sleeping and study areas with the living area.

WELL-INSULATED AND ADAPTABLE TO CLIMATIC CHANGES

The house was designed to be a net-zero dwelling, which means it produces as much energy as it uses. Wool insulation and triple-glazed windows create an efficient house envelope. The house was also designed to be adaptable to climatic conditions. Windows, doors, and shading screens can be manually operated to give the homeowner the freedom to control the indoor climate. Interior spaces are thermally zoned, reducing the loads on the HVAC system and making it efficient even when only some areas of the house are being used. The interactive monitoring system allows the homeowner to observe and optimize the energy usage. The system shows where energy is being used and displays peak energy use, peak energy production, water use, and weather data. Energy required to heat and cool the house is reduced by manually manipulating the space and systems.

PASSIVE BY DESIGN

The passive solar design principles have been maximized to optimize the house's performance and minimize the effect of New Zealand's changing climate. Large north-facing glass windows allow light to flood the interior space in winter and heat the thermal mass floor. In summer, the cedar solar canopy that also acts to support the solar array shades these windows. When the house was set in Waimarama, New Zealand, solar orientation was optimized. By designing the house to take advantage of passive measures, reliance on mechanical heating and cooling were vastly reduced.

PASSIVE AND ACTIVE VENTILATION

Natural cross-ventilation is achieved in the house by opening the doors on either side of the house. When it is too hot or cold to open the doors, a highly efficient ERV can be used to keep the air fresh in the house.

The living area offers an abundance of space. The sleeping bunks expand the capacity for overnight guests, with sliding doors that can also hide these beds. Ample storage is built into this custom unit. The walls of the kitchen and cabinets were lined with recycled rimu, a popular native timber from New Zealand.

Wool Insulation

In New Zealand, where there are more sheep than people, wool is used as a natural insulating material. In addition to being plentiful, wool has several other excellent qualities, including high thermal performance, reduction of sound transfer, and resistance to "slumping" or sagging (an important factor in a thick envelope construction). Because it is a naturally produced fiber, wool insulation requires less energy to produce than man-made insulations, such as fiberglass. Wool does not support combustion and does not irritate the eyes during construction and afterward, as fiberglass insulation may. Wool insulation is available as natural wool or as recycled wool produced by manufacturing processes, which is about 40 percent less expensive. First Light was built using recycled sheep wool insulation at a minimum of 10 inches (250 mm) thick for the floors, walls, and ceilings. For more information about the wool insulation used in First Light House, visit www.ecoinsulation.co.nz/insulation-solutions/ecowool.

Solar Decathlon

Since the Solar Decathlon began in 2002, thousands of students from colleges around the world have designed and created houses that are efficient at both collecting and converting sunlight into usable energy to compete in this event. The Solar Decathlon is an educational program of the US Department of Energy (DOE) and is organized by the National Renewable Energy Laboratory (NREL). The event occurs on alternate years in the United States. It took place in Madrid in 2012 and in China in 2013.

It is difficult not to be inspired by the innovative, beautiful, energy-efficient houses at the event, and by the bright students who give tours of their houses. They have impressive knowledge of the mechanics of their houses and explain all the systems and considerations behind the design decisions to visitors. The Solar Decathlon is a great educational opportunity for the public to experience the variety of prefabricated building methods, systems, materials, and techniques that can be used to build more sustainable, healthy, and efficient homes. There are ten contests within the competition: architecture, market appeal, engineering, communications, comfort, hot water, appliances, home entertainment, and energy balance. In 2013, affordability was added. With recent global economic struggles, it is understandable that affordability is a highly valued area in home construction today.

According to Richard King, the director of the Solar Decathlon, the program is wide-reaching. "Our outreach is in the millions. The three thousand students participating in this event will go out into the world, get jobs, and I believe will change the world. . . . Solar and energy-efficient houses will become the norm in our near future, not the distant future." For further information, visit www.solardecathlon.gov.

BELOW The house is currently set in a beautiful beach resort in Hawke's Bay overlooking Waimarama Beach. (Photo courtesy of Benjamin Jagersma)

BOTTOM The self-contained study unit creates a partial divider between the bedroom and living areas, granting privacy to the bedroom but maintaining an open feel to the house. The unit includes storage on either side of the pull-down workspace and can also be closed to create more floor space. All areas of the house, other than the central portion, have concrete floors that function as thermal mass to absorb the heat during the day and release it at night in the cooler weather. (Photo courtesy of Victoria University of Wellington)

HYDRONIC DRYING CUPBOARD

The team developed an innovative drying cupboard for this house, which requires very little power to dry laundry. According to the team, the drying cupboard uses energy stored in hot water to dry clothes as quickly as a traditional dryer. Hot water is pumped through a heat exchanger, which then heats the air inside the cupboard. Rails filled with hot air and hot water work to dry the clothes while a fan extracts humid air from the cupboard. This product was developed by LEAP, a "smart home" resource, but is not being produced currently for commercial use.

A LONG JOURNEY TO WAIMARAMA

The six prefabricated modules were assembled in less than seven days in Wellington. The house left by ship from the Port of Tauranga for its monthlong journey to the United States. On the same day it departed, the realtor Harcourts in Wellington sold the house at auction. The house garnered attention at the Solar Decathlon in Washington, DC, with more than twenty thousand people having toured it.

After the event, it was shipped back to Hawke's Bay in New Zealand, where it now sits on a hill overlooking Waimarama Beach. The house, with optimal solar orientation in a very sunny area of New Zealand, produces up to 40 kWh (kilowatt hours) per day. However, because of the efficient insulation and design of the house, it uses only about 6 or 7 kilowatts per day. This is drastically different from the on-average 26 kWh of power used per day by New Zealand families. Because of the home's energy efficiency, the homeowners receive a check for about $50 NZD ($41.49 USD) from the power company each week. The house currently serves as a rental property in this beautiful resort city.

NOW A SALEABLE OPTION

After graduating from Victoria University, four of the students who worked on this house teamed up with Guy Marriage, a registered architect and director of Building Science at Victoria University, and formed First Light Studio. They are currently selling several expanded versions of First Light.

i-PAD

Kitset

PHOTOGRAPHER:

Trevor Read (unless otherwise
    noted)

ARCHITECT:

André Hodgskin

MANUFACTURER:

iPAD

BUILDER:

Kuriger Builders

LOCATION:

South of New Plymouth, coast
    of Taranaki, New Zealand

SIZE:

538 square feet (50 sq m)

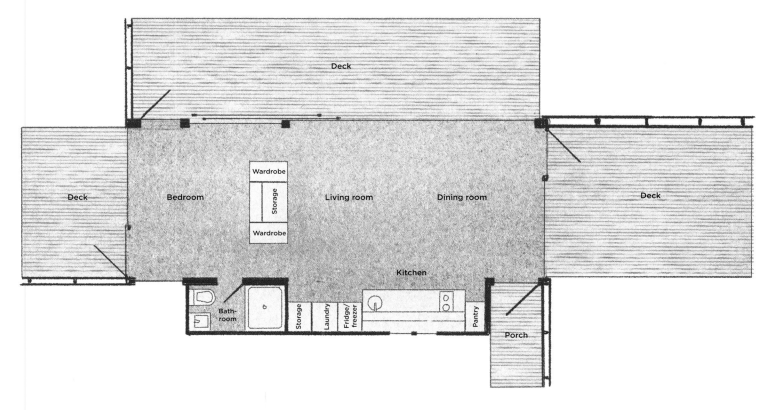

Architect André Hodgskin developed the concept of this light kitset (see sidebar, page 211) that can either be assembled in the factory or shipped as a kit with the components erected on-site by a licensed contractor. Hodgskin wanted to build a structure that would emphasize quality over quantity and appear simple but stylish. With the iPAD, Hodgskin achieved these goals.

The iPAD design framework grants owners the option for it to stand alone or be combined with additional components to meet the need for more space. André says these houses are "versatile yet affordable."

HOUSE BY THE SEA

This seafront iPAD is the holiday home of two Californian surfers who ride the Taranaki waves several times a year when they escape from Sausalito. The natural timbers are stained to evoke a subtle, weathered, seaside appearance, and it nestles sensitively in this sometimes-harsh coastal environment.

HEATING, COOLING, AND VENTILATION

Cooling occurs naturally in the house with the help of many operable glass doors. A small bioethanol burner is used for heating. A 4 feet (1.2 m) deep overhang prevents overheating in the warmer months, but allows direct sunlight to penetrate deeply in the colder months when the sun is lower in the sky. Unlike homes in the northern hemisphere, which get the best sun on the south side of their structure, this house, located in the southern hemisphere, gets the optimal sun in the northern portion. Because of this, additional glazing is added to the northern side and a minimal amount is applied to the southern side to

avoid heat loss. The house was also oriented for optimal solar energy.

PRICE TAG AND REWARD

This iPAD cost $149,000 NZD ($123,506 USD), excluding the cost of the land, shipping, construction on-site, and the required hookups for electricity and plumbing. In 2011, this iPAD at Porikapa Beach on the Taranaki coast won the New Zealand Architecture Award for Small Project Architecture.

OPPOSITE The bathroom features a duel-flush toilet and a low-flow showerhead and faucet. A heating bar keeps towels warm.

ABOVE The house can be opened up to take advantage of the ocean breezes and natural ventilation. The deck is made of a composite material (wood sawdust and recycled plastic), and the interior flooring is a laminate with a wood appearance.

BELOW Porches off the living area and bedroom allow for outside relaxation. Here, the owners are able to enjoy the natural landscape.

Califont LPG Hot Water Heaters

Instant liquefied petroleum gas (LPG), also referred to as propane or butane gas, water heaters require only a cold water hose and a bottle containing the gas. LPG water heaters do not require a water tank or an electricity supply. The califont (an instant gas water heater mounted externally) is connected to the LPG tank. When the tap is turned on, the torch-battery-powered ignition fires up automatically, supplying instant hot water. These heaters are fitted with a constant temperature-control device, so that a steady supply of hot water is available. If the heat rises above 167°F (75°C), a safety overheat device on the califont is triggered. A digital temperature meter displays the temperature and allows the water temperature to be set. Califonts are energy efficient and are economical to operate, and most often used in remote locations or on boats. The califont used in the iPAD comes from Rinnai (www.rinnai.co.nz).

Kitset (or Kit Components, Kit House)

A variety of terms are used to describe this prefabricated method of shipping most or all the premanufactured and prefinished elements required to assemble a complete house. Early examples of the kit house in the United States are the catalog homes sold by such companies as Aladdin and Sears Roebuck in the early 1900s. Kits have become more sophisticated over the years and the choice of materials has expanded, but the concept has remained the same. The advantage to this type of prefabrication is the ease in shipping the parts to far away or difficult locations, even to other countries. Other types of prefab components (such as modular), which are often larger and heavier, would be more difficult and expensive to ship. Components can be packed in one or two containers and shipped by boat, rail, or truck to locations where the materials required may not be readily available.

PRISPA

Modular/Panelized

PHOTOGRAPHER:

Santonja/Cubas

Cubas I+D+Art Studio (unless otherwise noted)

ARCHITECT/BUILDER/ MANUFACTURER:

PRISPA team: The Technical University of Civil Engineering of Bucharest (UTCB), "Ion Mincu" University of Architecture and Urbanism in Bucharest (UAUIM), University Politehnica of Bucharest (UPB)

LOCATION:

Solar Decathlon in Madrid, Spain, and Luncani, Romania

SIZE:

805 square feet (74.80 sq m)

▶ GREEN ASPECTS:

Clay plastering (inside)

Engineered wood

Gray water system

Low-flow faucets and showerhead

Off-the-shelf products

Small footprint

▶ ENERGY ASPECTS:

Air-to-air heat pump

Energy recovery ventilator (ERV)

Exterior shutters

Glass wool insulation (see sidebar, page 85)

Large overhangs

LED lighting

Photovoltaic panels

Smart home system

Solar hot water panels

Triple-glazed windows

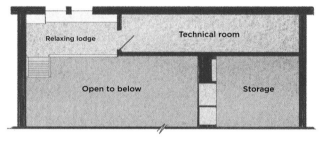

SECOND FLOOR

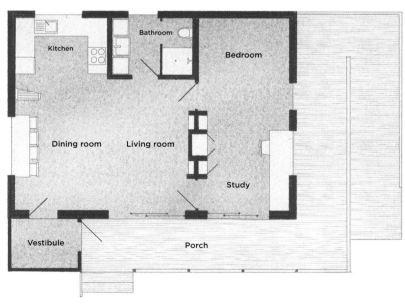

FIRST FLOOR

OPPOSITE The modular units used to build this home were transported to Madrid by truck for the Solar Decathlon. After the event, the house was rebuilt close to Bacău in Romania. (Photo courtesy of the PRISPA team).

BELOW The front southern porch protects the house from the summer sun, and when the sun is low in the winter, it comes through the frontal glazing to warm the house. The exterior walls are covered with a special new coating that is made from a silicate material. This material helps resist the elements while also minimizing maintenance. The roof is made with zinc.

PRISPA was the first house produced by a Romanian team for a Solar Decathlon event. It was built with traditional design but modern technology. The team wanted to build a house that used materials that are easily accessible, easy to maintain, and available at a modest price.

Prispa is the Romanian word for "porch," a traditional element of Romanian homes. The porch functions as a bridge between the interior and exterior of the house while also blocking the hot summer sun. In the winter, the low sun can enter the house and warm the interior black tiles, which work as thermal mass, releasing the heat later in the day when it is needed.

THE CONSTRUCTION

The house was constructed using structural prefabricated panels. The panels were made into I-joists and box studs, plated on both sides with oriented strand board (OSB), filled with mineral wool, and coated on the interior side with gypsum boards that meet the required fire protection. A vapor barrier membrane was then applied on the inner side of the panels for protection from moisture. For exterior cladding, a moisture-resistant baseboard, made of concrete and polystyrene, was added.

The majority of the elements that compose the house come from do-it-yourself (DIY) stores. The idea behind this was to make it easy to find all the components to build the home. In Romania, complicated materials have to be ordered from outside of the country. But for this house, the building materials, the tools, and most of the equipment can be found in any hardware store around the country.

The PRISPA team took one year to design and create the plans for the house, and it was prefabricated in three months. The total cost of constructing the home came to about $150,000 (€120,000). Since then, the process and design have been refined, and the house can be constructed in just thirty days and for a lower cost.

HEATING AND COOLING

The team used several approaches for heating and cooling the house. Natural ventilation is used in the evening with the windows opened to cool the house. The indoor humidity is absorbed by the clay walls, which also help to cool the interior. An air-to-air heat pump can be used when it is needed. The house also uses solar energy whenever possible. The sun heats up the stone flooring, which serves as thermal mass. In the evening, when the sun is down, some of that energy is released back into the room. The heat pump, as well as the radiant panels, can be used to warm the room when the temperatures are extremely low.

A FUTURE FOR PRISPA

Companies in France, Spain, and Africa expressed interest in selling this house design. Because of this, the team created a more industrialized version with an extra bedroom and bathroom, which would sell at a reduced cost of about $90,000 (€70,000). This version of the house has not as of yet been sold.

The prototype house used for the Solar Decathlon was sold before the competition in Madrid. Selling it enabled the team to raise the money they needed to complete their house and also solved the problem of where to assemble it after the event.

The owner who bought the house already owned land and was interested in prefabricated homes. The team was told that the owner received

LEFT The entertainment area's interior walls are coated with a natural clay finish that provides hygrothermic capabilities (it regulates humidity and acts as a thermal mass). Along the window areas for about 3½ feet (1 m), the floor is made of stone. Wood flooring dominates the room, but the stone was included to serve as thermal mass absorbing the sun's energy in the winter. An abundance of natural light reduces the need for electric lighting.

RIGHT Depending on the owner's preference, the kitchen can be either a closed or an open space. The balcony is an extra zone and offers numerous possibilities, such as a nook for reading or a sleeping loft for guests. The technical module is also accessed from this space.

approval to get credit for the electricity that is given back to the grid. This approval was a first, as net metering had never been allowed before in Romania. This was an important achievement that can be credited to the PRISPA team.

LEFT There is storage under the bed, in the wall cupboards, and in the open shelves in the upper wall. The students designed all the furniture in the house.

RIGHT This is a flexible area that can be used for reading, as a guest room, or just a private space. Here it is shown as a workspace.

The north shed roof functions as a windshield, protecting the home from the harsh Romanian winters, with strong winds and heavy snow. The east and west facades have triple-glazed windows, which allow in natural light but prevent heat loss. The sliding shades protect the interior from the hot summer sun.

Ecomo House

Modular PODS/Panelized

**ARCHITECT/BUILDER/
MANUFACTURER:**

Pietro Russo,
Ecomo

CARPENTER:

Tim Wolf,
Ecomo

LOCATION:

Franschhoek, South Africa

SIZE:

1,184 square feet (110 sq m)

▶ **GREEN ASPECTS:**

Australian blue gum flooring
(see Glossary, page 288)

Bamboo flooring

Built on stilts to protect the natural
environment

Dual-flush toilets

Gray water system

Low-flow faucets

No material waste during construction

Rainwater harvesting to flush toilets

Recycled polyester insulation

Water catchment tanks

▶ **ENERGY ASPECTS:**

Cross-ventilation

Gas cooking (with propane)

High-efficiency glazing

LED lighting

On-demand water heater

Photovoltaic panel ready

Solar hot water panels

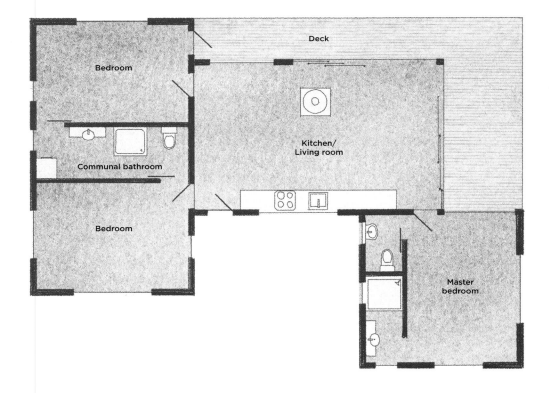

OPPOSITE The exterior cladding is North American cedar, which needs no maintenance, oil, or varnish. Over time, the cedar weathers to a silver-like color. The builders chose aluminum as the roofing material, which complements the cladding's color.

BELOW The house sits in a beautiful location among the mountains surrounding the town of Franschhoek. The French Huguenots previously inhabited Franschhoek, which in Afrikaans means "the corner of the French." After moving to the area, they discovered that the very rich soil was ideal for growing vines. They began to grow grapes, and today some of the best South African wine comes from this area.

The Ecomo House was built as a prototype for a client of architect Pietro Russo. It was originally planned as a temporary one-bedroom home that the client would stay in while a main house was built. However, during the design stage, the client fell in love with the modular and green concept and chose to increase the house to three bedrooms, deciding against building another main structure.

The house is located on a vineyard just outside the town of Franschhoek; the owners bought a piece of land from the wine estate Chamonix. The grapes on their land are still farmed by the wine estate. This farm is classified as a "lifestyle farm" in South Africa because the owners of the land do not farm it, but instead own the land for its beauty. It is a common practice for farmers to sell off parts of their property for financial reasons but retain the right to farm on it.

The client wanted to build the structure with as many natural materials as possible in order to minimize the impact the house would have on the land and to build it as quickly as possible. This could be accomplished by having all the components built off-site. They were built in Cape Town, which is about 31 miles (50 km) from Franschhoek. The factory completed all of the components in two weeks and assembled it on-site in two months.

A DIFFERENT KIND OF HOUSE FOR SOUTH AFRICA

The Ecomo House is a diversion from most other houses in South Africa, which are still built with brick and mortar. It is one of a few upscale prefab homes, and one of a few that has integrated green aspects in the country. Building this house prefabricated not only hassened construction time, but also minimized its impact on the property. The difficulty of finding capable artisans in these locations also contributed to Russo's decision to build the house with prefabricated components. He says that another advantage is that the client can add on pods at any time, increasing the size of the house.

Prefabricated homes are not new to South Africa. In the 1960s and 1970s, the government built a large number of low-income prefab homes. This gave the concept of prefab a bad reputation, which continues to persist. There are few companies that build prefab homes for an upscale market in the country, but this house might set a new example for future prefab architecture.

HVAC

Because of the generally mild weather, the heating and cooling requirements are minimal. The exceptions are when the summers get very hot—the temperature may go as high as 108°F (42°C) due to the location between the mountains—and on winter nights, when it may go as low as 32°F (0°C).

The house was oriented to take optimal advantage of the sun. With multiple strategically placed windows and doors, cross-ventilation is also maximized. Only a wood-burning fireplace is required in the winter. Solar hot water panels on the roof heat the water. Russo believes this house uses half the energy required by other houses in the area.

Electricity is required for only a few LED lights, an LED television, and the refrigerator.

JUST THE BEGINNING

Russo's company has since built eight additional prefabricated houses based on this original prototype.

As seen in the kitchen and dining area, the compact space is maximized with the open house plan and omission of any corridors or entrance halls. Australian blue gum is used for the flooring.

JP House

Modular

PHOTOGRAPHER:

FG+SG, Fernando Guerra and
   Sergio Guerra

ARCHITECT:

Carmina Casajuana, Beatriz G.
   Casares, and Marcos González
MYCC

MANUFACTURER/BUILDER:

Ageco Scotman

LOCATION:

Tragacete, Cuenca, Spain

SIZE:

1,550 square feet (144 sq m)

▶ **GREEN ASPECTS:**

Dual-flush toilet
Low-flow faucets and showerhead
Minimal waste in construction
Small footprint
Steel frame

▶ **ENERGY ASPECTS:**

Electric heat pump
High-efficiency fireplace
Mineral wool insulation
Optimal solar orientation
Sun screens

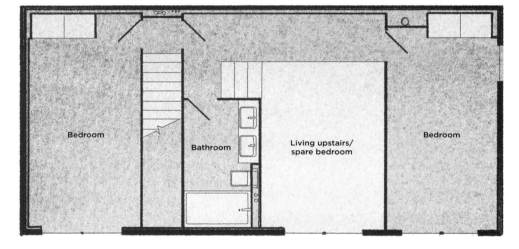

SECOND FLOOR

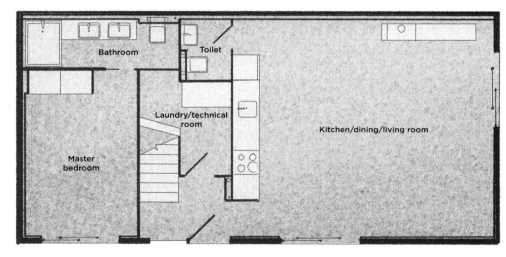

FIRST FLOOR

OPPOSITE ABOVE The steel frame was erected in the factory in Olmedo, 236 miles (380 km) from the site.

OPPOSITE BELOW One of the eight modules was carefully lifted into place among the existing structures of the village.

BELOW The house is surrounded by a stone wall that adds a historic character to this modern structure.

The JP House was designed for an urban family who wanted a second home in a remote village in central Spain for the weekends and holidays. The family was looking for a design that would be unique in comparison to the traditional houses in the area, but one that also fit in and complemented the aesthetics of the small town. For them, prefab construction offered appealing style options as well as a better chance that the construction could be of the highest quality.

MYCC architects say, "In most developed countries, it is very difficult to find craftsmen who still work in the traditional way. What is usually built are just cheap copies of rural houses that usually do not have an origin in that specific place." Rather than offering a poor version of traditional architecture, the JP House offers something new that doesn't look out of place with the structures in the rest of the village.

PLANNING THIS VACATION HOME

Built in an upper part of the village, the house was designed to be compact and fit in well with the surroundings. In addition to the 1,550 square feet (144 sq m) occupied by the house, there is also space for a terrace and outdoor areas.

Although the house was designed to have an open floor plan, areas throughout were designated for particular uses. The upper level has two bedrooms, a bathroom, and a separate living area for their teenage children to relax. The lower level includes the common areas and master bedroom.

The house is composed of eight modules of 194 square feet (18 sq m) and a small additional piece to extend the ceiling in the upper level living room areas.

The home's design takes full advantage of solar energy. All of the windows in the house face south and east. The material used for cladding the structure is a larch rain screen facade (see sidebar, page 69). This same larch material was used to construct two sliding doors. Adding to the feeling of spaciousness in the house, these doors can be opened to enjoy outdoor living but closed off when the house is not in use.

Although the house is in one of the coldest regions of Spain, it uses minimal energy because it is built so efficiently. A high-efficiency electric heat pump and wood fireplace are all that is required to keep the house warm on the coldest days.

OPPOSITE LEFT Extra ceiling height over the table gives the room delineation and an open feeling.

OPPOSITE RIGHT The cladding is a larch rain-screen facade. The decks are made of a wood polymer composite.

RIGHT The larch facade casts beautiful shadows inside the entranceway and on the stairs.

Villa EntreEncinas

Structural Cross-Laminated
  Timber Panels

PHOTOGRAPHER:

Tania Diego Crespo

ARCHITECTS:

Alicia Zamora and Iván G. Duque,
  Estudio de Arquitectura Duque y
  Zamora

MANUFACTURER:

KLH

BUILDER:

EntreEncinas Promociones
  Bioclimáticas S.L.

LOCATION:

Villanueva de Pría, Asturias, Spain

SIZE:

2,325 square feet (216 sq m)

BLOWER DOOR TEST:

0.39 ACH @ 50 Pascals

CERTIFICATION:

Casa Pasiva (Passivhaus)

▶ **GREEN ASPECTS:**

Bamboo flooring

Black water system

Green roof

Natural limestone flooring

No VOCs or formaldehydes in paints,
  adhesives, and finishes

No PVC in products

Plastered mortar facade of lime silicate

Rainwater harvesting

Recycled materials

▶ **ENERGY ASPECTS:**

Cellular glass insulation

Cork insulation

Energy monitoring

Heat recovery ventilator (HRV)

High-efficiency windows

Highly insulated

LED and CFL lighting

Solar hot water panels

Sun screens

Wood stove

FIRST FLOOR

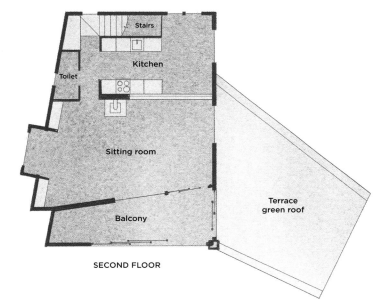

SECOND FLOOR

OPPOSITE   The green roof, which extends over part of the first floor, creates an almost seamless connection between the house and the surrounding landscape.

BELOW   The solar panels were placed on the southern exposure of the house to take full advantage of the available solar energy. The exterior facade is constructed with ventilated wood, limestone, and lime silicate plaster.

Villa EntreEncinas was built to Passivhaus standards and adheres to the criteria of bioclimatic architecture (see Glossary, page 288). The goal of the architects was to make the house as self-sufficient as possible. In order to achieve this efficiency, they created an integrated design that guaranteed almost zero energy consumption. They also selected materials and construction systems with a low environmental impact.

The house was built utilizing both active and passive renewable energy, as well as sustainable materials, free of toxic compounds. Even a black water sanitation system was installed because the house is in such a rural location. The challenge was achieving these goals with a budget similar to that of a conventionally built home.

DESIGNING FOR EFFICIENCY

Architects Alicia Zamora and Iván G. Duque first studied the climate and topography of the location before beginning construction. They designed a house that would respect the scale of the property and integrate well with the landscape. The plan also utilized solar energy and minimized energy consumption.

Zamora and Duque designed the house to be compact so as not to overwhelm the scale of the property and also to minimize the thermal requirements. They decided that part of the dwelling should be "hidden" to minimize its appearance. The balance of the house was designed with two floors that are open to the south and sit on the flat area of the lot. The height does not exceed that of the treetops on the property. The natural slope of the property and the many rocky outcrops serve dual purposes: acting as background for the rooms open to the south and maintaining privacy.

The upper floor, which is level with the top of the slope, contains the common living space: the living room, dining room, and kitchen. Conceived as the "day zone," these areas get the most daylight and an uninterrupted view of both the natural surroundings and the green roof. The ground level, which experiences less natural light, is the "night zone" where the bedrooms and bathrooms are located.

GREENHOUSE EFFECT

A gallery in the entire southern front of the first floor acts as a greenhouse, which serves many functions throughout the year. It performs well in varied environmental conditions. During the colder months, the limestone floors serve as thermal mass, absorbing the heat throughout the day and releasing it at night when heat is needed. In the warmer months, the glass doors can be opened to access the gallery area, creating natural ventilation and keeping the house cool.

BENEFITTING FROM BIOCLIMATIC AND PASSIVE DESIGN

Alicia says, "Architectural design should be the result of a complex process, which must synthesize climate analysis, the functional, the technical, and the aesthetic with user needs. Passive strategies related to reducing heating, cooling, lighting, and power should be combined with other priorities at an early stage of the project. The fact that the building can be designed under bioclimatic design parameters can reduce energy consumption by 40 to 50 percent free of charge." Energy savings for Villa EntreEnci-

BELOW The kitchen appliances are all high energy efficiency, and the countertops are made from 75 percent recycled material.

BOTTOM The glass separating the kitchen from the living room prevents smoke from entering the living room area and allows for natural light to flood into the kitchen.

nas exceed 80 percent compared with other Spanish houses located in similiar climates. The annual heating demand for this house is 12 kW/m²a and the annual cooling demand 0 kW/m²a. The typical house in this area requires 73 kW/m²a.

This house won the first prize in one of the most important competitions for national sustainable construction in Spain—Premios De Construcción Sostenible, España.

Villa EntreEncinas, Spain

Lugano House

Post and Beam/Panelized

PHOTOGRAPHER:
Lothar Rehermann
Grandpierre Design GmbH

DESIGNER/MANUFACTURER/ BUILDER:
HUF HAUS

LOCATION:
Carabbia-Lugano, Switzerland

SIZE:
3,423 square feet (318 sq m)

▶ **GREEN ASPECTS:**
Dual-flush toilets
FSC- and PEFC-certified wood
Low-flow faucets and showerheads
Low-VOC paints and stains
Quartz countertops

▶ **ENERGY ASPECTS:**
Air source heat pump
Cross-ventilation
High-efficiency appliances
High-efficiency thermal insulation
Large overhangs on the eaves
  and gables
LED lighting
Optimal solar orientation
Programmable thermostats
Radiant floor heating
Solar hot water and heating
Triple-glazed, gas-filled windows

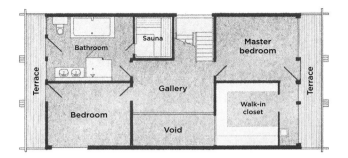

SECOND FLOOR

FIRST FLOOR

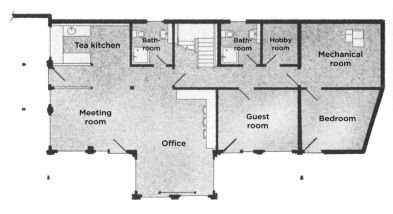

LOWER LEVEL

The house is located near Mount San Salvatore in Switzerland. The ceiling is made of fiber-reinforced drywall with a painted finish. The fully heat-insulated roof is constructed with beams made of high-quality laminated timber. The wide roof overhangs protect the house from the sun and the elements.

The major challenge in building the Lugano House was to achieve extremely low energy consumption despite the generous use of glass. This was achieved by using the appropriate advanced technology, including very energy-efficient glass, concrete ceilings, highly efficient insulated panels, and heat pumps.

PASSIVE SOLAR DESIGN

The house was situated on the mountain to take the best advantage of passive solar heat. The large overhangs protect the house from the sun in the summer, when the sun is high in the sky. In the winter, when the sun is lower, the sun's rays very effectively heat the house.

In addition to controlling passive solar heat, the insulated panels that form the walls of the house also protect the wood construction from the effects of weathering. For further protection from the sun, all glazed panels have motor-driven exterior venetian blinds (see sidebar, page 102), except for the transom windows above the doors and the main entrance door. The horizontal slats of the blinds can be pivoted to control the amount of light passing through, providing flexible sun protection throughout the year. Such "low-tech" measures are valuable in maintaining an energy-efficient, comfortable indoor climate in hot summer months.

As a result of these methods, energy costs are kept low, the indoor air quality is very healthy, and the house has a minimal impact on the environment.

PANELIZATION AND POST-AND-BEAM CONSTRUCTION

All exterior wall elements are fitted with a highly efficient thermal insulation layer, creating walls with an R-value of 34.5. Thermal bridging is reduced to an absolute minimum by advanced framing techniques. The wood panels, made of six layers of symmetrical cross-laminated and fully glued wooden planks from controlled forestry, guarantee high resilience and stability.

The exterior glue-laminated post-and-beam framework is independent from the inner load-bearing panelized structure. The advantage of this type of construction is that exterior timber parts can be treated with wood preservative where necessary without affecting the interior environment. As a result, this house already complies with the future energy efficiency requirements of the *Energieeinsparverordnung*/EnEV (See sidebar, page 143).

FIXED GLASS PANELS

The HUF construction allows for frameless floor-to-ceiling glazing. The triple-glazed, argon-filled insulated glass units are made of quality-controlled insulated glazing with a U-value of 0.5 W/m²K.

The glass and the air space are sealed by stainless steel spacers, which create a highly insulated cavity. The large-scale glazing is segmented by the post-and-beam structure, which also allows for fan-lights (also called transom lights, if fixed, or transom windows, if operable) above the main glazing and in the gables. Turn-tilt windows, the doors, and sliding patio doors all achieve an R-value of 9.52/U-value of 0.06 W/m²K.

FLOOR/CEILING CONSTRUCTION

The ceiling panels are made of prefabricated large-format concrete panels. This type of construction provides a few advantages: The ability to store thermal energy (as thermal mass) in the summer creates

The surrounding landscape is a beautiful backdrop for cooking in this fully equipped kitchen, filled with sand-gray lacquered cabinets. In addition to the basic appliances, there is a steamer and a warming drawer.

BELOW The living room looks out over a patio at the front of the house. The stainless steel heating stove is positioned in front of the windows, so that residents can enjoy looking at both the fire and the view.

BOTTOM The bathroom on the second level opens up to a terrace with a beautiful view of the hills. The faucets and showerhead are low flow. The shower and the bathroom furniture, a combination of blackberry-lacquered cabinets with white Corian surfaces, were tailor-made by StilART from HUF HAUS.

Heat Pumps

Heat pumps offer an alternative to furnaces and air conditioners. Using a small amount of energy, they can pull heat out of the air or ground (geothermal) to heat a house. The process can be reversed to cool a structure. They are more efficient than other types of HVAC systems because they transfer air instead of burning fuel. Heat pumps can vastly reduce utility bills. ENERGY STAR–rated heat pumps have a higher seasonal energy efficiency ratio (SEER), better energy efficiency ratio (EER) ratings, and a higher heating performance factor (HSPF) than standard models.

The functionality of a heat pump works as such: a compressor pumps air through an evaporator, which extracts thermal energy from it. The cool air is then released to the outside. The heat pump in the Lugano House has a particularly large evaporator, and the corresponding technology in combination with radiant floor heating makes this system work very efficiently with an impressive COP (coefficient of performance) value of 3.5.

Coefficient of Performance (COP)

Coefficient of Performance, or COP, is a term used to express the efficiency of a heat pump. The COP is a dimensionless number defined as the ratio of the energy output and the energy input. A typical heat pump's COP is 3. The one used in the Lugano House has a COP of 3.5. A conventional electrical resistance heater, in which all heat is produced from input electrical energy, has a COP of 1.

The lower level serves as an office for the owners. However, it was designed to be an independent two-and-half-room apartment, with its own bathroom, kitchen, and heating system. The apartment can be rented or may come in handy to house an au pair for the children, a separate space for the children when they are grown up, or for the grandparents. The apartment can be reached both by a separate entrance door from the outside or through the home's main entrance and down the stairs from the inside (but if necessary this can be closed off).

energy provides warm water for the radiant under-floor heating at the low operating temperature of 91°F (33°C).

HEATING

A hydronic under-floor heating system is used for warming the house. The heating pipes are made of a multilayered metal composite. Each room is separately controllable by a thermostat.

The heat pumps (see sidebar, opposite) use a portion of the thermal energy from the solar panels for space heating and water heating purposes, as well as cooling in the summer. Increasingly demanding legislation in Switzerland makes the use of renewable energy sources mandatory, and having heat pumps run by solar energy is an effective way to meet these stricter environmental standards.

A circulation pump keeps the hot water moving through the perfectly heated insulated warm water pipes, avoiding any energy loss. The result is instant hot water when the faucet is opened. A timer clock controls the circulation pump. To optimally utilize capacity and avoid unnecessary energy usage, two heat pumps are installed: a large one for winter and a small one for the warmer seasons.

CROSS-VENTILATION AND DAYLIGHTING

Transom lights and windows provide an additional natural light source and offer the opportunity for draft-free ventilation. These glass panels are also located above solid wall panels and provide natural light even in otherwise windowless walls.

The Lugano House is a beautiful example of interesting architecture with modern integrated technology and magnificent views.

a pleasant, cool climate inside the house, and there is no thermal bridging.

In addition to comfort, the concrete ceiling also provides excellent soundproofing. The ceilings are 11 inches (279 mm) thick. Construction above the concrete floor consists of sound/thermal insulation that is 4 inches (101 mm) thick topped with a concrete layer that is 3 inches (8 cm) thick and floor covering.

SOLAR PANELS

There are 150 square feet (14 sq m) of solar panels on the roof, which deliver hot water for personal use and heating support. The panels are connected to a 238-gallon (900-liter) warm water tank with a low storage temperature of 113° F (45°C). The solar

Casa Locarno

Timber Frame/Panelized

PHOTOGRAPHER:

Courtesy of designyougo

ARCHITECT:

Sebastian Gmelin and Mathis Malchow
designyougo – architects and designers

**BUILDER/ PREFAB TIMBER AND
FACADE MANUFACTURER:**

Veragouth S. A.

STRUCTURAL ENGINEERS:

De Giorgi & Partners Ingegneri
  Consulenti S.A.

LOCATION:

Solduno, Switzerland

SIZE:

1,916 square feet (178 sq m)

GREEN ASPECTS:

Dual-flush toilets

Grass roof

Heat exchanger

Native materials

Small footprint

ENERGY ASPECTS:

External shading with roof overhang and "skyframe"

Heat exchanger

High-efficiency windows and doors

Highly insulated

No conventional heating

Optimal solar orientation

Radiant floor heating

Solar hot water panels

Thermal mass of the concrete walls

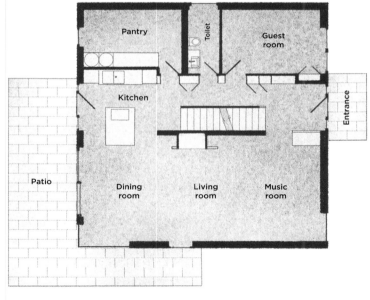

FIRST FLOOR

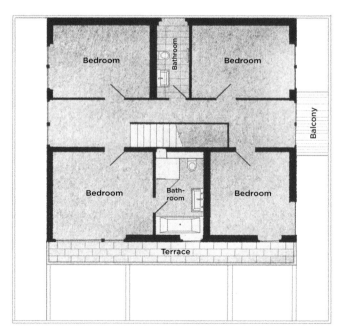

SECOND FLOOR

The skyframe and cantilevered roof allow the front of the house, which has beautiful views, to be more spacious with higher ceilings than the rear of the house.

The house is in Solduno, an old village with traditional stone-clad roofs, close to Locarno in southern Switzerland. Nestled into the steep mountains located at the rear of the house, it sits between Lake Maggiore and the town of Ascona.

PREFABRICATION

Due to limited accessibility of the site, walls and ceilings were prefabricated and flown in by helicopter. A light timber frame construction was chosen to allow large parts to be within the weight limits the helicopter could handle. Prefabrication also allowed for a high degree of computer-aided control over the design. The parts were built locally in Bedano, thirty minutes from the site, and transported by truck to a loading site nearby and then transfered to the helicopter for the short distance to the site.

DESIGN AND MATERIALS

The dominant feature of the exterior of the house is the larch wood "skyframe" (the extension over the first floor) and cantilevered roof, which gives the house a dramatic appearance. The architect describes it as "lifting the house off the ground, shaping the perception of the building, and furthering the integration into the dramatic setting." The larch has been left untreated and will weather naturally. The skyframe includes inclined surfaces at the top to ensure good water drainage. Another interesting feature of the exterior facade is the glass- or fiber-reinforced concrete panels, in three shades of blue. The architect describes them as "complementing the reflections of the windows and harmonizing nicely in dusk lighting."

SHADING

In addition to its dramatic appearance, the skyframe will create sufficient shading from the hot summer sun when it is filled in with plantings in the future.

CAPTURING THE VIEW

To take full advantage of the beautiful views, the windows are full height, and the roof rises toward the front of the house, creating high ceilings. Terraces across the front of the house connect the interior with the exterior, providing natural ventilation.

SUSTAINABILITY

The house was designed and insulated to low energy standards, and no conventional heating was installed. There are solar collectors on the roof, providing energy for the low-temperature under-floor hydronic heating and for domestic hot water. During the cold and cloudy winter days, additional energy is generated through a heat exchange incorporated within the fireplace. Energy from the solar collectors is preserved in a 106-gallon (401-liter) water tank in the basement.

The roof and walls have been insulated with up to 15½ inches (400 mm) of rockwool (see sidebar, opposite) and even the basement has been wrapped in a layer of insulation. The glass fiber–reinforced concrete panels of the facade are 0.31 inches (8 mm) thick and mounted with a space between them and the underlying timber frame walls to allow for good ventilation.

In recognition of its efficient and beautiful design, the house won the Green Good Design 2011 award from the Chicago Athenaeum.

BELOW With its full height glass wall and solid oak steps, the slender steel-frame staircase serves as a light divider between the kitchen and the entrance.

BOTTOM Solar panels on the roof warm water for both domestic use and the hydronic radiant heating system.

Rockwool Insulation

Rockwool insulation (also known as mineral wool, slag wool, or stone wool) is made from rocks and raw minerals that are heated to about 2,910°F (1,600°C) in a furnace through which air and steam are forced, creating streams of molten minerals that cool into fibers. The molten rock can also be rotated at high speeds in a spinning wheel, spinning off fibers much the way cotton candy is made. Air pockets in the intertwined fibers trap air and hold heat. Rockwool may contain food-grade starch as a binder and oil to decrease the formation of dust. It is a good heat insulator and sound absorber, is nonirritating, and has a high fire rating. Rockwool can be blown in or made into sheets. The R-value is approximately 2.5 to 3.7 per inch. For further information, see www.rockwoolinsulation.org.

BELOW The house has oak flooring. The downstairs has an open floor plan and unobstructed views of the beautiful scenery.

BOTTOM Some windows are frameless fixed glazing, including a glass corner in the dining area, creating a sense of proximity with the nicely landscaped garden.

The view from the balcony on the second floor is magnificent. The terrace doors have minimal thresholds, which allow the terraces to maintain the same floor level as the interior.

Laurel Hollow

Timber Frame/Panelized

PHOTOGRAPHER:

Courtesy of Yankee Barn Homes

DESIGNER/MANUFACTURER:

Yankee Barn Homes

BUILDER:

Gerard Mingino

INTERIOR DESIGN:

Jeffrey Rosen Interior Design

LOCATION:

East Hampton, New York,
   United States

SIZE:

3,500 square feet (325 sq m)

▶ GREEN ASPECTS:

Dual-flush toilets

Engineered quartz countertop

Locally sourced materials

Low-flow water fixtures

Pine siding

Sisal natural-fiber carpet

Sustainable Forestry Initiative (SFI)
   certified lumber

Zero-VOC paints

▶ ENERGY ASPECTS:

Advanced framing (to minimize thermal bridging)

Energy monitoring

ENERGY STAR–rated appliances

ENERGY STAR–rated windows and doors

Heat recovery ventilator (HRV)

High-efficiency HVAC

High-efficiency natural gas boiler

Insulated foundation with R-18 insulation

Insulated joists and sill plates

Natural cedar roof shingles

Polyisocyanurate insulation (see sidebar, page 246)

Programmable thermostat with moisture control

Tankless water heater

Underground space and hot water radiant in entire
   basement floor to lower whole house heat use

Use of natural stone over radiant to hold heat

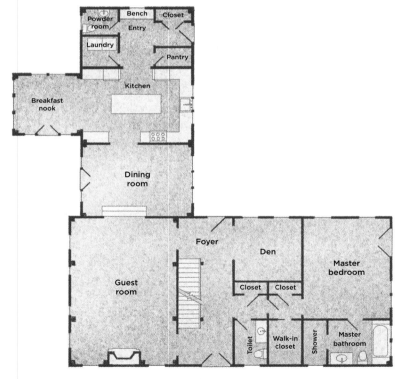

FIRST FLOOR

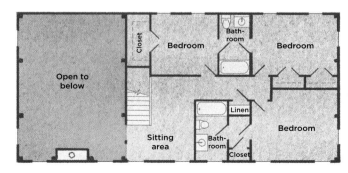

SECOND FLOOR

The house was designed to look like a barn and appear as though it has existed in its East Hampton, New York, location for years. The front entry is a courtyard, and the freestanding single-car garage creates one of the courtyard walls. The cupola over the kitchen and dining area is actually a skylight in the center of the kitchen. The landscaping is made from native favorites—boxwood, hydrangea, and privet—It has been simply placed to create privacy in this tight village lot and to soften the look of retaining walls. The gravel driveway is good for water infiltration.

Jeffrey Rosen built a house with Yankee Barn Homes four years earlier as a spec house and was really impressed with the quality and speed with which they could build houses. He was impressed not only with their beautiful designs and excellent construction but also with their environmental consciousness, using only certified wood, recycling materials (through Zero-Sort), and reviewing the corporate environmental policies and practices of potential suppliers.

The company later asked Jeff to become their creative director on other projects they were building. In 2010 he decided to build another spec house with them.

A PERFECT LOCATION

Jeff chose this particular lot in East Hampton because of its proximity to town and the ease of walking to its restaurants, stores, and other amenities. Jeff says, "I am a strong believer in village life, the ability to live somewhere without a car as transportation and walk to local shopping, activities, etc. I see the demand for this type of housing growing as the world becomes more stressful and technology becomes more invasive in our lives."

He chose a traditional design because of its location in the village, surrounded by shingle or board houses built between 1920 and 1940, with some dating earlier. Jeff says, "I wanted to build a house that reflected the character of the surrounding houses, something that did not look new, but embodied all the notions of a current lifestyle, modern in floor plan, economic in scale, efficient mechanically—essentially new, but old."

VERY EFFICIENT WALL PANELS

The house was built using the company's trade-marked wall and vented roof panels that have exterior wood sheathing over a rigid foam polyisocyanurate core (see sidebar, page 246) with foil facing to reflect radiant heat in the hot summers. Structural studs are added to the panels for strength and durability. The wall panels are built with the windows pre-installed, which saves time, reduces air infiltration, and creates a superior water barrier.

As both a spec builder on the east end of Long Island and the creative director of Yankee Barn Homes, Jeff is looking forward to starting another project using this same construction method. He says, "I know I can rely on quick production, the right mix of green elements (both lack of job site waste, but more importantly the strong passive savings gained from their own proprietary wall and roof panel systems), and excellent design elements and style."

OPPOSITE The windows create a strong vertical backdrop to the simple rectangular Gunite marble dusted pool heated by a natural gas heater. Bluestone pavers and stucco walls are used, creating flat areas for leisure on an otherwise hilly property.

BELOW The two-and-a-half-story post-and-beam living room has reclaimed yellow pine wide-plank floors stained a medium brown. Antique Swedish tin farming buckets are wired and hung upside down for lighting.

RIGHT The dining room is a step down from the living room, to accommodate the topography of the property as well as to add the architectural quirkiness and interest of an older structure. Barn doors, made to look antique, are built from Florida yellow pine. They hang from the same kind of track used for the exterior sliding doors, but here the track is painted black to accent the decorative black brackets seen throughout the house at timber structure joints. French doors lead to the pool area and terraces

BELOW The main part of the mudroom culminates with a window looking out onto the side yard with a window seat below. It's a comfortable perch and beautiful detail that can be seen from the kitchen. There is direct access to it from the driveway. The same stone floor as seen in the kitchen/breakfast area continues into this space.

Polyisocyanurate (or poly-iso or iso) Insulation

Polyiso is a closed-cell, thermo-set plastic, rigid foam-board insulation used primarily on the roofs and walls of residential and commercial structures. It offers high R-value per inch, third-party, thermal performance certification, compressive strength, nationwide availability, and high fire test performance. It has also shown to be an environmentally responsible material: It will not deplete the ozone layer or contribute to global warming. It is manufactured using recycled material (the amount is dependent on the manufacturer). Because it is stable at high temperatures, it can be used as a component in roof systems utilizing hot asphalt. It has low water absorption and low vapor transmission, making it an excellent insulating material. Yankee Barn Homes claims the R-values for True Wall Panels™ can be built to 37.2 and True Roof Panels™ to 66.5 using polyiso insulation. For further information about this insulation and to find suppliers, check the website of Polyisocyanurate Insulation Manufacturers Association (PIMA) at www.polyiso.org.

ABOVE This sunroom is an extension of the kitchen and is used as a breakfast area for all seasons, receiving natural light from all sides of the room. Reclaimed French limestone floors continue into the kitchen and mimic the look of exterior pavers.

BELOW The post-and-beam timber structure is visible in this cook's kitchen, contrasting with the modern kitchen appliances. The kitchen opens to the breakfast area, dining room, and mudroom area beyond. The countertops are quartz, and the ENERGY STAR–rated appliances are stainless steel. Industrial counter stools add to the vintage look of the room. Furnishings, such as the kitchen table and reclaimed timber beams, are antique pine.

Island Passive House

Panelized Walls/Modular Core

PHOTOGRAPHER:
Art Gray (unless otherwise noted)

DESIGNER/BUILDER:
Tessa Smith and Randy Foster
Artisans Group

INTERIOR DESIGNER:
Brenda Fritsch
Artisans Group

LOCATION:
San Juan Islands, Washington, United States

SIZE:
1,533 square feet (142.42 sq m)

BLOWER DOOR TEST:
0.55 ACH @ 50 Pascals

CERTIFICATIONS:
Passive House (PHIUS)
Energy Star

▶ **GREEN ASPECTS:**

Cabinetry with FSC-certified NAUF (no added urea formaldehyde) plywood
Dedicated recycling station
Drought-tolerant, native plantings
Dual-flush toilets
Fiber cement siding
Flexible interiors (to reduce need for future renovations)
Green Guard–certified quartz counters
Locally sourced materials
Low-flow faucets and showerheads
Metal roof
No carpeting (which can accumulate particulates)
Recycled content
Small footprint
Ventilation system
Wind-felled maple hardwood floors
Zero-VOC paints

▶ **ENERGY ASPECTS:**

Advanced framing (to minimize thermal bridging)
Daylighting
ENERGY STAR–rated appliances
Extra layer of OSB with liquid sealing
Heat recovery ventilator (HRV)
Induction cooktop
Integrated heat pump for space heating and domestic hot water
LED and CFL lighting
Natural cross-ventilation
No clothes dryer (indoor racks used)
Operable exterior shades at western exposure
Optimal solar orientation
Photovoltaic and solar hot water panel ready
Large overhangs
Super insulation
Triple-glazed windows

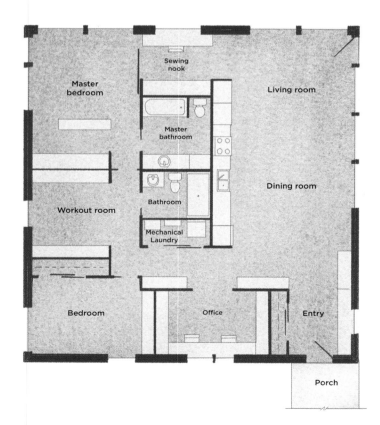

OPPOSITE The prefabricated parts are trucked from the factory to the site to be erected. (Photo courtesy of the Artisan Group)

BELOW This Passive House is solar oriented for maximum energy performance. The triple-glazed, over-insulated-frame, tilt-and-turn windows are mostly floor-to-ceiling, so even in the harshest weather the residents can have a connection with the outdoors.

Ned and Elaine planned to build a retirement house in the San Juan Islands, which they say remind them of their thirty-six years of living and teaching in remote villages on Kodiak Island in Alaska. Because of its location they knew it would have to be built resistant to high winds, hungry bugs, and the harsh marine climate. They wanted their house to be built using materials that are sustainable, insect resistant, and require minimal mechanical energy. Elaine says, "We knew we wanted to build a house that 'made sense,' but when we first started thinking about building, we had no idea where to start; the number of choices was overwhelming." Having traveled extensively, they knew they "liked the sunny patios and sense of the outdoors of houses in Mexico, the small, aesthetic spaces of houses in Japan, the prefab options of houses in Scandinavia, and solar panels and LED lights." When Elaine stumbled on the Passive House concept on the Internet, she felt a sense of excitement. "Here was the unified idea that brought all the disparate parts together to make sense! This would be a house based on hundreds of pieces of data that all related to each other. Rather than blindly choosing from a smorgasbord of unrelated options, we could design a building based on a verified energy model directly applied to our own unique property."

CHOOSING AN ARCHITECT/BUILDER

The Artisans Group, owned by Tessa Smith and Randy Foster, was selected to design and build the house because of their commitment to high-performance projects that are fiscally, socially, and ethically responsible. Tessa says, "The Passive House approach is the best way to achieve these goals." The Artisans Group oversaw all aspects of the proj-

ect, including the design, energy modeling, and construction.

DESIGNING AN ISLAND HOUSE

A low-pitched shed roof and solid-mass look seemed like the best option to complement the flat landscape. A limited number of windows were included on the front, north side of the house to avoid heat loss. Windows on the west side of the house are equipped with operable shades to limit excessive heat gain in the warmer months. Large windows on the south and east sides of the house provide a good source of solar energy and extensive views of the natural beauty of the area. Some of the windows are tilt-and-turn windows with a U-value of 0.13 (see Glossary, page 289) and are equipped with operable shades to limit sun exposure in the warmer months. Some of the windows are fixed to limit heat loss.

To limit the need for mechanical energy, the floor was built to R-60, the walls R-50, and the ceiling R-60 (see Glossary, page 289). All of these walls

OPPOSITE The house was strategically placed so that the client's favorite parts of the lot are visible from the home and were not destroyed during construction.

BELOW The windows are tilt and turn, making them easy to clean and allowing optimal natural ventilation.

were prefabricated in a factory in Satsop, Washington, and transported by truck and ferry to the site. Elaine and Ned were intrigued by this design, with its very circular traffic patterns, which didn't have dead-end destinations. The clever floor plan makes the house feel much larger than its square footage would suggest.

LIMITING THE NEED FOR HEATING, COOLING, AND VENTILATION

The tight envelope, well-placed and efficient glazing, large overhangs, and ENERGY STAR–rated appliances limit the need for mechanical energy in this house. It is equipped with a small heat pump and a ventilation system that is required to maintain a healthy interior environment, as well as meet the eligibility for Passive House certification.

The Washington State University Extension Energy Program provided some consultation and energy assessments for this house, although they will not continue to monitor it in the future.

PH COST FACTOR

Tessa says, "We saw a 0 percent cost increase to upgrade to Passive House on this project, compared to code-built custom homes on remote islands such as this one." In addition, the cost of heating and cooling the house is expected to be 90 percent less than other less efficient houses on the island.

Ned says, "Our home is like a symphony. Every element works together with every other element to create a feeling of harmony. The house has both aesthetics and common sense in one package. Each time we come home, the minute we walk through the front door, we know we are in the place we would most like to be in the world."

In this view of the living roon, the maple floorboards from naturally felled trees in the Seattle area are visible.

BELOW Because the owners don't like dark, walk-in closets, Tessa designed a closet and dressing area behind the bed's headboard that is filled with natural light coming in from the windows. The entrance to the room is a sliding glass door that keeps the room bright.

BOTTOM Elaine says the office has plenty of room to keep everything organized, and the soft northern light is perfect for computer screens.

Montana Farmhouse

SIPs

PHOTOGRAPHER:
Haily Donoven Seion Studio
(unless otherwise noted)

ARCHITECT:
Becki D. Miller
3 Point Architects

MANUFACTURER:
Premier Panels

LOCATION:
Gildford, Montana, United States

SIZE:
3,200 square feet (297 sq m)

▶ **GREEN ASPECTS:**
Passive orientation
Reclaimed materials (doors and windows, timbers and chalkboards)
Recycled materials (recycled metal roofing was used on the inside to create shed roofs over closets)

▶ **ENERGY ASPECTS:**
Concrete flooring (on main level)
ENERGY STAR–rated appliances
Geothermal heating
Insulated double-glazed windows
Radiant heating
SIPs

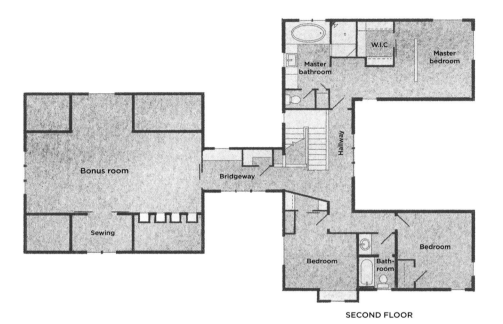

SECOND FLOOR

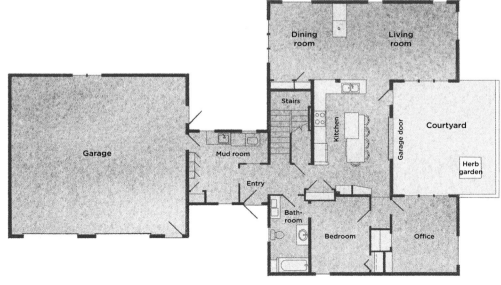

FIRST FLOOR

OPPOSITE ABOVE AND BELOW SIPs were erected to form the structure of the house. (Photo courtesy of the owner)

BELOW The exterior of the house reflects the typical farmhouse style of the area with a red facade and corrugated metal roof and siding. Red is the typical barn color, while the corrugated metal evokes the idea of a grain bin and elevators.

ecki Miller always had an interest in collecting antiques and reclaimed materials since her early childhood in rural eastern Montana. As a young child she spent many Saturdays attending auctions with her mother, where she honed her skill in finding items that she could later use or transform into something new and special. This interest continued through her architectural studies, and she opted to write her graduate thesis on abandoned homesteads in eastern Montana.

After completing college at Montana State University in Bozeman, she worked in Seattle, Washington, and Budapest, Hungary, before returning to Bozeman and opening her own architectural firm. When she married Justin, she moved from Bozeman to Gildford. One of her first projects after the move was to design and build a family home for herself and Justin (and eventually their two children, Rye and Piper). Her new home includes many of the items she had collected over the years and others she would buy along the way. Becki says, "Many of the items in our home I have had for years, knowing someday I would design a house to display them."

DECISION TO BUILD WITH SIPS

Becki used SIPs to design several residential and commercial projects before she built her own house, although her house was the first SIPs structure in this small town. Several curious local farmers came to watch the panels being erected. Later, she was asked to design other people's houses in town using SIPs. Becki says she opted to build with SIPs because, "I believe they are the future of home building; they are so fast to erect, green, and energy efficient." She clearly believes in this method and says building her own house with SIPs was a "given." "I believe in the

product, and it is more difficult to endorse it to your clients when you, yourself, haven't used it on your own home."

COST OF BUILDING

The cost for building the house was $120 a square foot, not including the cost of the land or landscaping. This low cost was possible in part because Becki and Justin did some of the work. Becki functioned as a general contractor, and Justin assisted the contractor. To expedite the process, Becki and Justin spent many weekends completing projects, such as insulating the roof and painting the interior.

The house orientation is southeast, which helps to utilize sun exposure in the winter and morning sun in the summertime. In colder months, the lower sun warms the concrete floors on the main floor and helps to radiate the heat. The tall two-story structure of the house on both sides of the courtyard provides shade in the summer months.

DESIGNED FOR CIRCULATION

Becki designed the house to circulate light and energy while still maintaining a close connection to the exterior. A small opening above the kitchen cabinets allows for natural light from the stairwell window to permeate into the kitchen. This opening is a favorite spot for the kids as they can stand on the landing and look out.

Becki says that when the gas fireplace is on, a large amount of heat flows up through the stairwell to help warm the upstairs. With over thirty windows, there are sweeping prairie views in every direction. There is a strong connection to the outside, regardless of which room people are in.

The homeowners fabricated their own concrete countertops for the kitchen and master bathroom. One of the counters, however, is a marble slab that was part of a table that Becki purchased at an estate sale. The metal around the kitchen sink is Galvalume, which is also magnetic. The green chalkboards around the island are a fun place for the children to doodle, and the one on the pantry is a convenient place to keep shopping lists and other notes.

The homeowners used built-ins wherever possible. Repurposed
window frames reclaimed from old Montana barns and homesteads
were used to create storage in the dining room for tableware used
for entertaining. The two cast iron columns on either side of the wine
rack were once part of a calf scale from Justin's family barn.

BELOW Many of the light fixtures are industrial in appearance, achieved with a galvanized look and simple form. The homeowners stained and sealed the concrete floors themselves, after researching the process and learning how to do it.

BOTTOM The house is located in north central Montana. The flat prairie landscape makes it ideal for dryland wheat farming. To the south are views of the Bear Paw Mountains, and to the northwest are the Sweet Grass Hills. The house and windows were orientated to take best advantage of these mountain views.

Montana Farmhouse, United States

Portland HOMB

Modular

PHOTOGRAPHER:

Michael Cogliantry

ARCHITECT:

Skylab Architecture

BUILDER/MANUFACTURER:

Method Homes

LOCATION:

Portland, Oregon, United States

SIZE:

3,930 square feet (365 sq m)

CERTIFICATION:

Energy Trust of Oregon's New
   Homes Program

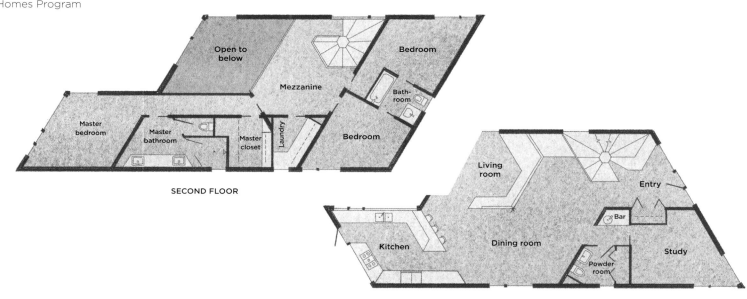

GREEN ASPECTS:

FSC-certified bamboo flooring

Low-flow fixtures

Low-flow toilets

Low-VOC products for air quality

Recycled carpets

Recycled plastic and bamboo decking

Sustainably harvested cedar siding

Zero formaldehyde in paints and adhesives

ENERGY ASPECTS:

Air-to-refrigerant fan coil–based
   AC system (mini split)

Air-to-water heat pump

ENERGY STAR–rated appliances

Highly efficient mechanical system

Heat recovery ventilator (HRV)

Hydronic radiant in-floor heating

LED lighting

Optimal solar orientation

Photovoltaic panels

Super-insulated building skin

SECOND FLOOR

FIRST FLOOR

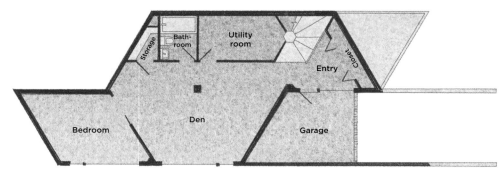

LOWER LEVEL

The front door is a splash of color on an otherwise monochromatic exterior. Materials, such as the vertical blackened cedar siding, were sourced locally.

In 2010, Seattle-based prefab builders Method Homes hired Portland's Skylab Architecture to design a new line of modular homes. Skylab's principal, Jeffrey Kovel, saw the potential in a prefab building model, designed as a flexible kit of parts, and decided to partner with Method to form HOMB in order to build not only residential housing but also commercial structures as well.

This first prototype was built at the Method factory in three months and completed in three months on-site in Portland.

A DIFFERENT TYPE OF MODULAR

The HOMB modules are composed of multiple triangular components that are laid on a triangular axis. The modules are designed as 100-square-foot (9.3-sq m) triangles and when joined together form parallelograms. In the Method factory, steel brackets and beams with bolted connections are used where the triangles come together to form a hexagon. Like other modular constructions, they are then transported by flatbed trucks to the building site and connected to each other.

This triangular configuration offers the manufacturer the ability to create large cantilevers and vaulted sections more easily than with traditional modules and to create a more unique appearance.

This first HOMB consists of two modular levels delivered in six units, composed of twenty-eight 100-square-foot (9-sq m) triangles.

The company says, "HOMBs of all sizes and applications apply the same design concept. The identical HOMB design could arguably be used for a 100-square-foot food cart or a 10,000-square-foot hotel."

ENERGY EFFICIENT AND ENVIRONMENTALLY FRIENDLY

Making this house energy efficient and environmentally friendly was an important aspect of the plan. To minimize heating and cooling costs, the house was built with a very tight envelope using advanced framing in the factory. Two-inch insulation and double-glazed windows with insulated frames were installed. The mini-split heating and cooling system (see sidebar, page 173) provides heating and cooling at a vastly reduced cost, and the photovoltaic panels on the roof provide most of the energy required to run the house. The air-to-water heat pump is used to heat both the domestic hot water and the water for the hydronic radiant heating system.

With protecting the environment in mind, the house was built with nontoxic stains and paints, certified wood, and materials that are plentiful and easily renewable, such as quartz and bamboo.

More than a thousand people toured this first HOMB during an open house in January 2013. The company's design and construction concept has generated a great deal of interest from architects, developers, neighbors, and prospective clients looking to build custom projects of their own.

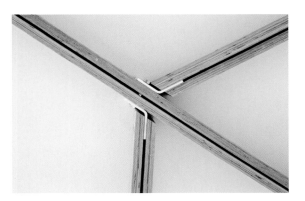

OPPOSITE The HOMB structural system design is based on equilateral triangular modules that form a hexagonal grid pattern when joined together. The exposed laminated veneer lumber (LVL) beams visually reinforce the HOMB structural system.

BELOW Appliances in the kitchen are ENERGY STAR–rated, and the countertops are quartz. The customized counters were triple mitered, adding complexity to their construction.

BOTTOM The second floor opens up to the living room below. The double-height vaulted space creates a dramatic effect.

Energy Trust of Oregon's New Homes Program

The New Homes Program works with builders to design, construct, test, certify, and market energy-efficient new homes. An approved verifier must be selected for technical support and confirmation of compliance with Environmental Performance Score (EPS)* requirements. Two inspections are made before drywall is installed and at the completion of the project. Performance testing after completion is also required to ensure that the systems and equipment function as they were designed to. For additional information about this program, see http://energytrust.org/trade-ally/programs/new-homes.

Laminated Veneer Lumber (LVL)

LVL is a high-strength engineered wood product that is produced by bonding together multiple wood veneers under heat and pressure. They are used for long unsupported spans in floors, ceilings, wide doorways, and the like. They are much stronger than solid-sawn wood beams and resist shrinking, warping, and splitting. They are assembled like plain lumber but there is no need to cut out defects in the wood, creating less waste. LVL beams come in lengths from 14 feet to 60 feet (4 m to 18 m), but can be created in any length, with the only restriction being transportation to the site.

---

* According to the Energy Trust of Oregon's website: "It is a measurement tool that helps define a home's energy consumption, utility costs, and carbon footprint based on energy use. It allows homebuyers to easily compare homes based on energy costs and efficiency."

Concord Riverwalk Cottage

Panelized

PHOTOGRAPHER:

Nat Rea

ARCHITECT:

Union Studio Architects

DEVELOPER:

Now Communities, LLC

MANUFACTURER:

Bespoke Corporation

BUILDER:

BOJ Construction

LOCATION:

Concord, Massachusetts, United
States

SIZE:

1,500 square feet (139.4 sq m)

**HERS RATING
(SEE GLOSSARY, PAGE 289):**

21

BLOWER DOOR TEST:

0.83 ACH @ 50 Pascals

CERTIFICATION:

Energy Star 5+

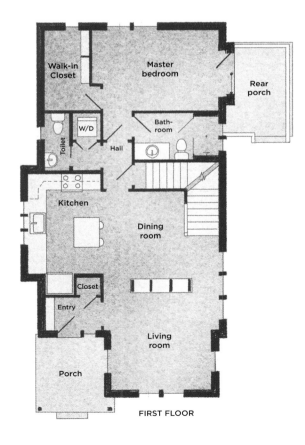

FIRST FLOOR

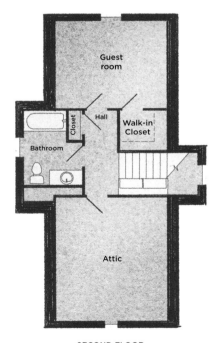

SECOND FLOOR

OPPOSITE The siding is fiber cement, mounted on strapping to create a rain screen (see sidebar, page 69) to ensure a long life. Permeable asphalt paving was used to allow storm water to infiltrate into the ground. A small portion of the grounds close to the house is for the exclusive use of the homeowners so they can personalize their outdoor living area.

▶ GREEN ASPECTS:

99 percent of construction debris was recycled

Drought-tolerant, native plantings

Dual-flush toilets

Locally sourced materials

Manufactured quartz countertops and recycled
tile

No- and low-VOC finishes

Recycled composite wood exterior trim and
decking

WaterSense-rated faucets, showerheads, and
appliances

▶ ENERGY ASPECTS:

Closed spray foam insulation

Energy-efficient lighting fixtures

Energy monitoring

ENERGY STAR–rated appliances

Heat recovery ventilator (HRV)

High-efficiency, air-sourced electric heat pumps

Insulated doors

LED and CFL lighting

Minimal glazing on north side

Optimal solar orientation

Photovoltaic panels

Polyisocyanurate board and rigid (XPS) foam insulation

Solar hot water panels

Triple-glazed insulated windows

Daniel Gainsboro, the developer of the Concord Riverwalk Cottage, says he has been fascinated by community creation for years. Growing up in an automobile dependent suburb of Boston, he says he was frustrated by the isolation and lack of community. When a colleague introduced him to the pocket neighborhoods (see sidebar, page 268) being created in Seattle by Ross Chapin, he decided to make a pilgrimage to check them out in person. "After experiencing the amazing sense of place they were able to create, I became determined to build an east coast version," says Daniel. In addition, he says, "Because of my own core value around waste, inefficiencies, and my frame of mind as a problem solver, I added the net zero possible energy and water conservation standards to the equation."

A BETTER PLACE TO LIVE

Daniel says he thinks pocket communities are superior to typical communities because, "They create community, provide a diversity of housing options, and attract a range of ages and family formations, which in turn creates a more sustainable and vibrant community with residents who value these qualities as well as being environmentally aware. Our community gardens are fully subscribed, and the outdoor fireplace is a constant draw for impromptu get-togethers."

Despite a challenging real estate market, the first eight homes were sold in three months. Daniel says, "The residents love their homes. They have formed strong bonds and several new friendships. One resident commented that he met more of his neighbors in the first ten days of living in Riverwalk than he had in the ten years he lived in his old community."

BUILDING PREFAB

When Daniel began planning the community, he initially wanted to build all ten houses with prefab construction. He had difficulty finding manufacturers willing to meet his requirements for air tightness, thermal efficiencies, and design at the price he planned. So he proceeded to build nine of the houses with on-site construction. But still determined to build prefab, he finally found a panelizer who was willing to meet his standards and budget and ordered the panels for the tenth house.

The same builder who built the site-built houses was employed to assemble the panels for this final construction. The panelized frames took two and a half days to erect and make weather tight, while the site-built houses each typically took three to four weeks to build. There was less impact on adjacent structures, and it was easier for the tradespeople to work effectively, because the erection time was reduced and there was less noise (less on-site cutting and nailing). The final house generated less waste, created less noise, and required less energy to construct the frame.

LESSONS LEARNED

Daniel says he learned a great deal from building this community: "The technical challenges pale in comparison to the social engineering aspects. Finding the right mix of residents who get and value it is critical. Providing residents with an energy-monitoring device makes them much more mindful of their energy consumption and introduces it into the daily conversation. People are willing to trade immediate access to their cars for living in a park-like, community-oriented setting."

Solar photovoltaic (for generating electricity) and solar thermal (for hot water) renewable systems are located on the south-facing roof to take the best advantage of solar energy. The locations of the windows were carefully planned to avoid clear views into the next-door neighbors' private rooms. All decks and porches were constructed using recycled composite wood.

BUILDING EFFICIENT HOMES

Daniel says, "Energy independence was a fundamental goal from the outset of the project." He decided to pursue a net-zero standard, which represents the optimum balance of cost, performance, reliability, durability, and user friendliness. He says it cost between 8 and 10 percent more to meet the net zero goal for these ten houses.

All the homes in the community are designed to accommodate a roof-mounted 5 kW solar photovoltaic array to meet the energy needs of the house. To accomplish this, the houses had to be designed to use 60 percent less energy to heat and cool than a similar-sized home. Not all the residents opted to include the solar panels on their homes. Residents without the roof-mounted system have average monthly electrical bills of about $135 a month. Residents with the complete renewable roof, including the Concord Riverwalk Cottage, have averaged about $0 to $24 a month. Daniel says, "Now that I know what I know about high-performance buildings, I would never build a home any other way."

RECEIVING A TAX CREDIT

The owners of the house received the $2,000 EPACT Energy Efficient Home Tax Credit, a Federal government tax credit for residences that are certified to have an annual level of heating and cooling energy consumption at least 50 percent below the annual level of a comparable house. One fifth of the 50 percent reduction must be attributed to the components of the building envelope, such as insulation and air sealing. A RESNET-certified third party rater must perform certification for this tax credit. (For more information, see www.resnet.us.)

Concord Riverwalk Cottage, United States

BELOW The pocket community consists of ten houses that share a common area. Parking is just outside the community. The Concord Riverwalk Cottage is the first one on the left.

BOTTOM In the kitchen, the countertops are quartz and the appliances are all ENERGY STAR–rated and WaterSense efficient.

Pocket Neighborhoods

Pocket neighborhoods are small clusters of houses in urban, suburban, or rural settings that arrange small footprint homes around a shared common area. These shared areas encourage interaction among neighbors. People who choose to live in these neighborhoods are generally seeking a stronger sense of community than they would have in a more conventional neighborhood. They want a more caring, supportive, safer, and connected community. Although the houses are generally close in proximity, they are designed to provide privacy with careful window placement and individual gates or gardens that designate private spaces. Parking for cars is usually located away from the individual houses, so residents must walk through the common areas to get to their homes. The Concord Riverwalk Cottage is one of ten houses in the Concord Riverwalk pocket community. For additional information, see www.pocket-neighborhoods.net.

The flooring is solid white oak that is prefinished with a water-based stain. The kitchen, living room, and dining room are arranged in an open plan and oriented toward the shared common exterior area. The large triple-glazed windows and high ceilings give the house a spacious feel.

Martis Camp Cabin

Modular

PHOTOGRAPHER:

Shaun Fenn (unless otherwise noted)

ARCHITECT:

sagemodern

MANUFACTURER:

Irontown Homes

BUILDER:

Gallagher Construction

DEVELOPER:

sagemodern

LOCATION:

Truckee, California, United States

SIZE:

3,250 square feet (302 sq m)

▶ GREEN ASPECTS:

100 percent of water runoff retained onsite

Best management practices to prevent erosion during construction

Electronic air cleaner to capture and remove 99.7 percent of pollutant air particles

Formaldehyde-free cabinets and casework

FSC-certified flooring

Low-flow faucets, showerheads, and toilets

Native plantings

Stone recovered during site excavation used for retaining walls

Zero-VOC paints (Green Seal certified)

▶ ENERGY ASPECTS:

Closed and open cell spray insulation

Double-glazed, low-E, thermally broken windows and doors

ENERGY STAR–qualified boiler for domestic hot water and radiant floor heating

ENERGY STAR–rated appliances

ENERGY STAR–rated HVAC System

Heat recovery ventilator (HRV)

LED lighting

Remote HVAC and lighting control

Ventilated roof assembly (to reduce summer heat gain and winter ice damming)

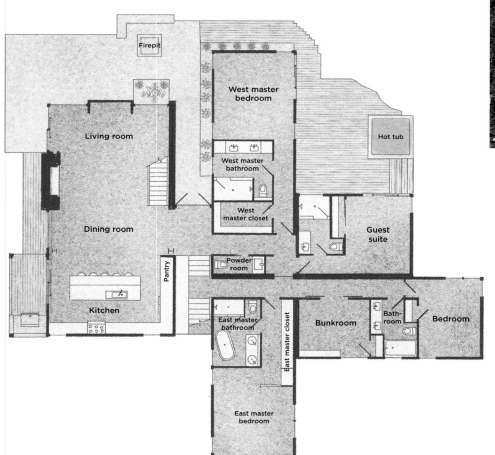

FIRST FLOOR

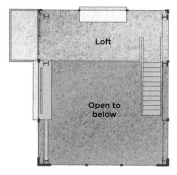

SECOND FLOOR

OPPOSITE The modules for this house were constructed in a factory in Utah. (Photo courtesy of sagemodern)

BELOW The home backs onto an eighteen-hole putting course. Two large pocket sliding doors hide behind the fireplace and media wall, opening the whole corner of the house to the exterior. The slate tile transitions seamlessly from the interior to the outdoors.

The family bought this vacation house because it had a great blend of mountain and modern architecture. Much thought was undertaken to help preserve the natural setting, and great care was taken in particular to preserve the trees, vegetation, and natural topography of the site. The house is composed of heavy timber and steel outside, cedar, slate, and stone inside to create a sense of place and permanence.

MODULAR CONSTRUCTION

The prefab approach greatly reduced the construction process's impact on the soils and environment.

The six modules and roof panels were built in the Irontown Homes factory in Utah. It took about twenty-two weeks to build the "boxes" in the factory, and they were then taken by flatbed truck approximately 600 miles (966 km) to the building site in Truckee, California. It took just one and a half days to erect the modules and just about eight weeks to complete the on-site construction.

Unique to this modular construction is the shed roof, which was produced as panels in order to get sufficient overhang to shed the snow in the winter and shade the house in the summer. The panels were placed on the roof in the factory to make sure they would easily connect, and then they were stacked for shipment to the site. Because of the restrictions in shipping heights imposed by the Department of Transportation, shipping the roof panels separately also allowed for more flexibility in ceiling heights and the architectural design overall.

The house was also designed to "climb up" the hill it was built on, so it was constructed with four different finish floor heights for the various modules. Factories generally build to one finish floor height, so Irontown had to carefully measure each module to ensure that it worked per the plan. The continuous heavy timber header along the length of the modules was designed to support the ventilated roof assembly.

OPPOSITE The clever roof design sheds the more than 250 inches (635 cm) of snow received each year. The butterfly entrance roof then collects the snow into a boulder retention basin to keep all runoff water contained on-site. The mountain modern aesthetic is carried through to the interior with a modern European design that is familiar to the family's French origins.

BELOW The large kitchen has a two-level kitchen island that can be used as a breakfast bar. The appliances are all ENERGY STAR-rated. Slate floors are used in the common areas to provide a durable yet elegant material that is used both in the interior and exterior.

The focal point of the home is the great room with its walls of glass that bring in the natural light and offer 270-degree views of the adjacent putting park, Lookout Mountain, and Carson Range. The steel wall opens up that entire side of the house to the outdoors. The second story loft offers a getaway to relax high up in the tree canopy. The outdoor deck off of the loft space is a great place to view the stars.

MAKING THE HOUSE ENERGY EFFICIENT

It was a challenge to make the house energy efficient with so much glazing. This was accomplished with highly energy-efficient windows and high R-value insulation. The efficient heating system includes an HRV that keeps the air fresh in the house without losing the interior heat already created. The radiant tile floor is a luxury during the cold winter storms.

COST CONSCIOUS AND ENVIRONMENTALLY FRIENDLY

Kam Valgardson of Irontown Housing Company says, "The house is a very good balance of luxurious finishes and excellent behind-the-wall construction. We were happy to partner with sagemodern on this project, a designer that creates high-quality houses with lower impact to the environment and the pocketbook."

Architect Paul Warner says, "The home was designed to blend in with the natural topography and pine forest. Great effort was taken during the design phase to reduce the impact on the natural environment. Constructing the home in a climate-controlled factory allowed the construction team to significantly reduce their time on the site to just a few months, in contrast to the traditional site-built construction project that would have a minimum of twelve months. This is a significant benefit in preventing soil erosion in the environmentally sensitive area of Lake Tahoe."

With careful planning by the architect and builders, this cabin represents a happy meeting of budgetary and environmental concerns.

Simblist House at Serenbe

Post and Beam/Panelized

PHOTOGRAPHER:

Chris Nelms

MANUFACTURER:

Empyrean International LLC

BUILDER:

Moon Brothers

INTERIOR DESIGNER:

Robert Gaul

LOCATION:

Chattahoochee Hills, Georgia, United States

SIZE:

3,750 square feet (348 sq m)

CERTIFICATION:

EarthCraft

▶ **GREEN ASPECTS:**

Bamboo floors

Drought-tolerant plantings

Ipe decking

Quartz countertops

Rainwater harvesting

Rubber roof

Walkable community

▶ **ENERGY ASPECTS:**

Advanced framing (to minimize thermal bridging)

Cellulose insulation

Concrete flooring

ENERGY STAR–rated appliances

Laminated tongue-and-groove roof structure with uninterrupted insulation panels

Large overhangs

LED lighting

Low-E, argon-filled insulated windows

Optimal solar orientation

Stack effect

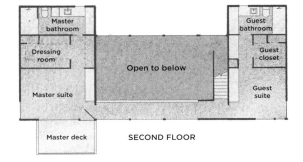

SECOND FLOOR

FIRST FLOOR

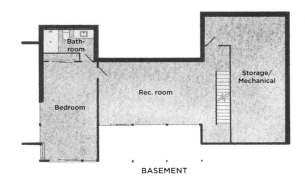

BASEMENT

OPPOSITE   The decking is Ipe, a very durable tropical wood, one of the hardest wood species and Class A fire rated.

BELOW   The siding on the exterior of the house is red cedar with mahogany trim. The rubber roofing provides great insulation. The outdoor railing is made of mahogany with stainless steel cables.

Sandy and Ron Simblist decided to build a house in Serenbe, initially as a vacation home and ultimately as their permanent home, after they were able to sell their house in downtown Atlanta. According to Ron, they were attracted to the burgeoning arts scene, sustainability of the area, and the organic farm. The environmental aspect of this community was an important factor along with the long-term plans of the Serenbe community, the people they met there, and its proximity to Atlanta.

Ron says, "Serenbe is a small, but growing, vibrant community. We feel very lucky to have found our way here. It's an amazing place to live!"

DESIGNING WITH NATURE

The Simblists presented a thorough plan with rendering and a video presentation to the management of Serenbe and were quickly able to begin construction of their house.

Ron says, "We were very conscious of integrating with our environment as opposed to imposing our house on a piece of land that may not have been appropriate." Even the bridge from the street creates an illusion of the house floating in the woods.

PANELIZED CONSTRUCTION

Ron and Sandy opted to build the house with panelized construction because it offered greater flexibility in design along with the precision of being built in a factory. Limiting disturbance to the land, quality control, and decreased construction time were all considerations.

All of the structural open-wall and roof panels, posts, beams for the timber frame, floors, ridged foam insulation for the roof, windows, and doors were engineered and fabricated in a factory in Mas-

sachusetts and assembled on-site. Cellulose insulation for the walls was provided by a local source. Also supplied by the manufacturer were interior and exterior trim and finish components, such as interior doors, hardware, preassembled railings, open and closed riser stairs, and so on. This ensured a high degree of control in terms of quality, pricing, and scheduling.

The local builder assembled the prefabricated building components and then finished the house using the manufacturer's finish package. Interior elements—such as drywall, paint, countertops, appliances, and so on—were supplied locally.

WATER HARVESTING

In order to harvest rainwater for on-site irrigation, an inclined butterfly roof drains water through a central scupper (or opening for draining water) along a 14-foot (4-m) cantilevered trough that spills into a retention pond below the home. During rainfall, the trough creates a plume of falling water.

LOCAL COVENANTS

As required by local regulations, the home is situated only 25 feet (7.6 m) from the street, and includes a large, welcoming porch, which encourages interaction with neighbors. The porch is reached by an elevated footbridge that draws in visitors while maintaining a form of separation for the home.

According to Ron, "Living at Serenbe is perfect for Sandy and me. The people and the surrounding environment are everything that we could ever want at this stage of our lives. Our beautiful home is the 'frosting on the cake' and would not have ever come to fruition without the great team of people who worked with us to achieve our goals."

BELOW The beautiful natural environment, visible throughout the home via large well-insulated windows, was an important factor that led the Simblists to choose the Serenbe community.

BOTTOM The kitchen cabinets were fabricated by the builder, the Moon Brothers. The countertops are made of quartz, and the appliances are ENERGY STAR–rated.

Serenbe Community

Serenbe is an example of New Urbanism, a design movement built on the principles of environmental sustainability and a healthy lifestyle. Serenbe's 1,000 acres (405 hectares) are in the heart of the Chattahoochee Hills, an area of 40,000 acres (16,190 hectares) protected with a master plan that calls for 70 percent green space. An organic farm on the property supplies much of the produce used in the community, and a biological wastewater treatment system operates in lieu of a sewer system to conserve water, create cleaner water, save energy, and reduce water bills. All of the homes are built to the standards of the EarthCraft House guidelines (see www.earthcraft.org), which include energy efficiency, low maintenance, enhanced air quality, water conservation, and resource-efficient materials and systems. The community includes traditional houses, live/work spaces, townhouses, restaurants, shops, an equestrian center, miles of walking trails, and a playhouse, and has recently expanded to include small farms. Central mail delivery stations eliminate unsightly mailboxes. Trash cans are located below ground, and garages are in the rear of houses to preserve the beauty of the area. Porches in the fronts of all houses encourage interaction among neighbors, and edible landscaping is prevalent throughout the community. For additional information about Serenbe, see www.serenbe.com.

The second floor walkway connects the bedrooms and bathrooms on either side of the house. The railings are mahogany with stainless steel cables.

The flooring in the living room and throughout the home is bamboo, a highly renewable resource. The windows were all produced in the factory and installed on-site.

Everett House

Panelized

PHOTOGRAPHER:
Anthony Rich

ARCHITECT:
Jonathan Davis with Davis Studio
  Architecture + Design

DEVELOPER:
Asani Development Corporation

MANUFACTURER:
Kingston Lumber (panels)

BUILDER:
PHC

LOCATION:
Grow Community, Bainbridge Island,
  Washington, United States

SIZE:
 1,840 square feet (171 sq m)

CERTIFICATION:
Built Green 5 Star

BLOWER DOOR TEST:
1.93 ACH @ 50 Pascals

▶ **GREEN ASPECTS:**

Bamboo flooring

Bike share program

Car share program

Community gardens with compost areas

Community play areas

Drought-tolerant, native, and edible plants

Eco-batt insulation

Locally sourced cedar siding

Low-flow toilets and fixtures

Low-maintenance exterior (cement and metal
  panels)

Low-VOC paints and finishes

Minimal PVC

No added urea formaldehyde cabinets and trim

No carpeting

No garage

One Planet–endorsed residential community

Recycled countertops (recycled paper and
  plant-based resins)

Recycled rubber and cork composite flooring

Renewable and recycled decking (bamboo
  composite)

Walking and biking trails connect to downtown

Walking community

WaterSense-rated plumbing fixtures

▶ **ENERGY ASPECTS:**

Cool roof (see Glossary, page 288)

Double wall system, with multiple thermal
  breaks

ENERGY STAR–rated appliances

Heat pump (for hot water and heat)

Heat recovery ventilator (HRV, ducted,
  whole-house air circulation and filtration,
  95 percent efficient)

High R-value insulation

Induction cooktop and convection oven

LED lighting

Liquid applied breathable waterproof air barrier

Optimal window orientation

Photovoltaic panels

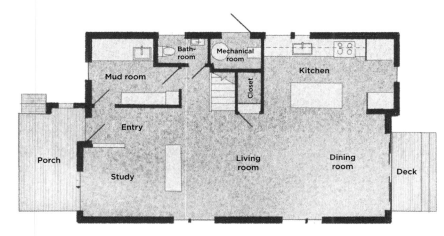

FIRST FLOOR

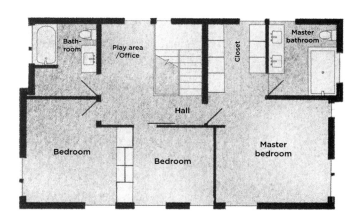

SECOND FLOOR

OPPOSITE The house is sheathed with fiber cement siding and
metal, which require minimal maintenance. Windows were positioned
for optimal solar gain and privacy in this close-knit community.
Plantings are all regional or edible, and paving is permeable.

The Grow Community on Bainbridge Island is the creation of architect Jonathan Davis, whose longtime goal has been to create an enclave of net-zero homes in an environmentally friendly community. Working with One Planet Living Community (see sidebar, page 286), Grow Community became the first One Planet–endorsed residential community to be built in North America. Jonathan designed the individual homes and multifamily townhouse apartments as well as the site and infrastructure layout.

The Everett is one of four model houses in the community. Future plans are for a total of fifty single-family homes and eighty-one rental townhouse apartments. Prices for the houses are in the $300,000 to $500,000 range, which is below market value for the island.

THE GROW COMMUNITY

In order to reduce the footprint of transportation (one of the One Planet goals) the eight-acre Grow Community is located walking distance from the ferry, making it easily accessible to downtown Seattle. Winslow, a thriving town with cafés, shops, a farmers' market, and other amenities, is adjacent to the community and easily accessed by foot or bicycle. This is a walking community with paths throughout, making it easy for residents to move about and connect with one another and the nearby town and neighborhoods. Community cars and bicycles are available for the residents to share, and cars are relegated to the perimeter of the site, separating them from the pedestrian paths and community spaces.

Homes are arranged in "micro-hoods," which are clusters of six to eight homes around a community space that includes a garden and informal gathering spaces. Community gardens are run as an urban farm with residents sharing responsibility for the upkeep as well as the crops that are grown.

BUILT EFFICIENTLY

The Everett is the largest of the four model houses. Like all the models, the house has an airtight, highly insulated envelope with R-35 walls, an R-60 attic, an R-48 flat roof, R-30 floors, and high-performance U-0.28 fiberglass and wood windows. Energy-saving appliances, LED lights, and a single mini-split ductless heat pump greatly reduce the energy needs of the house. An HRV is ducted to circulate warm or cool air throughout the house and provide five air changes per day.

The Everett achieves net-zero energy status with its grid-tied photovoltaic panels on the roof. The panels are optional when homeowners purchase the house, but Jonathan says all the buyers have opted to include them, making this essentially a net-zero community. Due to the net-zero design, the utility bills for the houses could be $0 per year, depending, of course, on the individual homeowners' practices for efficiency. All yet unsold houses will be wired for future installations, so that panels are easy to install at a later date, even if the homeowners opt not to include panels at the time of purchase.

BUILDING PREFAB

The Everett and the other two models were panelized and plans are to panelize future houses and rowhouse buildings as well. Building prefab is the

A zero-emission Nissan Leaf Electric car is powered by renewable energy using a 3.6 kW solar array, which is on top of the small community Welcome Center. This car and additional future cars will be available to be shared by residents.

best option on an island, such as Bainbridge Island, where materials are less readily available. Panelizing was also used for speed of construction.

Materials were chosen for their sustainability and low maintenance. Floorings, for example, are from fast-growing bamboo, recycled rubber, and cork. Fiber cement panels and corrugated steel siding were used, as both require minimal mainte-nance. Many of the materials were locally sourced, such as the cedar siding on the houses and the pho-tovoltaic panels. The result of using locally sourced,

Washington-manufactured panels is an extremely lucrative production rebate* of $0.54 per kilowatt produced.

Jonathan not only envisioned and designed the community but also is a resident with Mary Jo, his wife and business partner, their son, Everett, and their daughter, Dashwood.

---

* www.a-rsolar.com/net-metering-and-production-incentives

Appliances in the kitchen are the most efficient ENERGY STAR-rated available; there is an induction cooktop and convection oven; the countertops are made from recycled paper and plant resins.

One Planet

One Planet Communities is a nonprofit organization that has set out to create a network of the earth's greenest neighborhoods. These neighborhoods are designed to be as energy efficient as possible, but also have services, infrastructure, and design features that make it easy, attractive, and affordable for people to live in, in an environmentally friendly way. There are currently such communities in the United Kingdom and Portugal, and others are applying similar principles in South Africa, China, Australia, and Canada. The staff of this program help to create the projects, offering advice, support, planning, and eventually judging whether it meets the standards for the organizations endorsement. The program has ten guiding principles to structure the development, including zero carbon, zero waste, sustainable transport, sustainable materials, access to local and sustainable food, sustainable water and land use, and protection of wildlife. The goal of the organization is for these communities to be all net zero by 2020. This program was developed by UK nonprofit BioRegional Development Group and WWF International. For additional information about this program, see www.oneplanetcommunities.org.

The flooring is stranded bamboo, a highly renewable plant, and the lighting is created by LED bulbs, which are long lasting and use about 75 percent less energy than incandescent bulbs.

BIOCLIMATIC ARCHITECTURE

Bioclimatic architecture emphasizes the connection architecture has with nature. This construction style occurs when a building takes into account the climate and environmental conditions to achieve optimal thermal comfort in the house without depending on mechanical systems. Natural ventilation, optimal orientation of the structure for passive energy, natural daylighting, and deep overhangs that block the sun in the summer months and let the sun in on winter days when the sun is lower in the sky are all common features of bioclimatic architecture. Houses have been designed using these concepts throughout history. When heating and air-conditioning were very expensive (if even available), cross-ventilation was the best method for keeping a house cool in the warmer months. Similarly, in cooler months, early adobe houses, for instance, depended on thermal mass for heating, rather than on mechanical systems. Even with the wide range of mechanical systems and technology available today, these early methods of home design are often the preferred approach for creating environmentally friendly homes.

BLOWER DOOR TEST

The blower door test is a diagnostic tool used to measure the airtightness of a structure. A powerful fan is mounted in the frame of an exterior door. During a depressurization test, the fan pulls air out of the house, lowering the interior pressure and pulling air in from the outside through unsealed cracks and openings. A pressure gauge measures the amount of air pulled out of the house by the fan. Results of this test can determine if there are leaks in the air sealing, which can then be amended. Properly sealing a house will increase comfort, reduce energy costs, and improve indoor air quality. This test is required for certain certification programs, including ENERGY STAR and Passive House (Passivhaus). Passive House has the most stringent blower door test requirements, allowing a maximum infiltration of 0.6 air changes per hour (ACH) when measured at 50 Pascals pressure difference. Pascals are a measure of pressure. For reference, typical new houses will test between 4 to 6 ACH @ 50 Pascals, and typical existing houses will test between 8 to 10 ACH @ 50 Pascals. Results below 2.0 ACH @ 50 Pascals may be considered "tight," while 1.0 ACH @ 50 Pascals is a typical target for high-performance new construction.

BLUE OR SYDNEY GUM FLOORING (EUCALYPTUS SALIGNA)

Eucalyptus saligna grows in Australia in a variety of colors from soft to dark pinks and browns. It is naturally resistant to dust mites and other allergens. The trees can grow to a height of more than 213 feet (65 m). The wood is heavy, even textured, and easy to work with. If the trees are on the property, the Department of Water Affairs now requires that they be cut down because they "drink" too much water, and the surrounding indigenous vegetation has no chance to grow. By using the wood in homes, these unwanted trees are put to good use.

CEILING FANS

Ceiling fans create wind that carries heat away from the body, helping to evaporate moisture from the skin and driving down body temperature. Fans churning in an empty room, however, are just wasting electricity. In the warm weather fans run counterclockwise; in the cooler weather most fans can run in reverse, forcing warm air near the ceiling down to where the people are. If used correctly, fans can lower air-conditioning and heating costs.

COOL ROOFS

Cool roofs reflect the sun's radiation and emit absorbed heat back into the atmosphere. The roof remains cooler and reduces the amount of heat that is transferred to the house below it, decreasing cooling costs and increasing comfort for the occupants. TPO (thermoplastic polyolefin) is one of the popular cool roofing types used today. TPO is a trade name developed by Dow Chemical Co. for a combination of rubber and hot-air-welded seams made from ethylene propylene rubber. TPO is resistant to tears, impact, punctures, fire, and wind uplift, and is flexible enough to handle thermal expansion and contraction. Attached to the substrate material with adhesive, the roofing forms a strong chemical bond. TPO is considered an environmentally friendly material because it is recyclable, unlike some other types of roofing materials. For further information on cool roofs, see www.coolroofs.org.

CRADLE TO CRADLE® (OR C2C)

Cradle to Cradle (C2C) is a design concept based on natural principles—everything is a resource for something else; use renewable energy; and celebrate diversity. Cradle to Cradle certification is a program designed to support manufacturers in a process of continuous improvement. Such companies create materials and products that cycle continuously in one of two nutrient systems: biological (things that can safely return to the soil) or technical (things that can be upcycled in perpetuity). In their 2002 book, *Cradle to Cradle: Remaking the Way We Make Things*, American designer William McDonough, in partnership with German chemist Michael Braungart, developed this concept and popularized its importance. Their program identifies products and materials that are safe for humans and the environment. The program presently has four levels of certification—basic, silver, gold, and platinum—which are based on five categories, including material health, material reutilization, renewable energy use, water stewardship, and social responsibility. For further information about the Cradle to Cradle Certified program, check the website www.mbdc.com.

DIRECT VENT FIREPLACES

Direct vent fireplaces do not require a chimney and can be vented through a wall or through the roof. It is one of the most efficient types of fireplaces because it draws its combustion air from outside and does not consume warm house air, as most traditional fireplaces with chimneys do. Exhaust air is expelled through concentric pipes or through separate intake and exhaust vents. This type of fireplace eliminates drafts and heat loss and does not interfere with indoor air quality. There are also vent-free fireplaces available that do not require any venting.

HEAT RECOVERY VENTILATORS (HRV) AND ENERGY RECOVERY VENTILATORS (ERV)

When houses are built very airtight, there can be a shortage of fresh air in the house. One popular solution is a heat recovery ventilator, which can minimize energy loss and save on heating and cooling costs. The heated or cooled conditioned interior air is exchanged with the exterior fresh air, while transferring some of the heat and coolness generated in the home. Another alternative is the energy recovery ventilator, which functions in much the same way, but helps to control humidity. These are more often the ventilation choices in hot, humid climate areas. For additional information, see www.energysavers.gov.

HOME ENERGY RATING SYSTEM (HERS)

This is a national standard that was developed by the Residential Energy Services Network (RESNET), a not-for-profit association. It expresses the energy efficiency of a house compared to a reference house with the same dimensions, in the same climate, built according to the model energy code with a HERS rating of 100. A certified rating provider, working under the supervision of RESNET, determines the individual house rating. The rating is often used in determining eligibility for some programs, such as ENERGY STAR. Many older homes have a HERS rating over 100, but many new homes are being built more efficiently and are well under 100. The HERS

number indicates how much more efficient that house is than the reference house, so the lower the number, the more efficient the house is. For additional information about this rating, check the website www.resnet.us.

HYDRONIC AND ELECTRIC RADIANT HEATING

Radiant heat is becoming an increasingly popular heating alternative. It provides clean, even heat, warming objects in the room rather than heating the air, as forced-hot-air systems do. When installed correctly, radiant systems provide for greater comfort as heat is spread evenly throughout the heated area. The system can be zoned so only the areas being used are heated, increasing efficiency. Unlike forced-hot-air systems, with radiant heat no particulates and pollutants are being forced into the environment from the blown air. Additionally the system is noise-free. Radiant heating systems are imbedded in flooring, ceiling, or wall panels and can even be used to melt snow on driveways and sidewalks. Hydronic or hot water radiant systems can heat a pool, a spa, and domestic hot water.

There are two types of radiant heat—electric and hydronic. Though they basically work the same way, installations are vastly different, and operating costs are different as well. Hydronic systems are more complicated to install because they require a pump and special PEX tubing to circulate water heated by an electric, gas, or oil-fired boiler. They are easily adapted to hydronic solar panels, geothermal systems, and high-efficiency boilers because they do not require high temperatures to operate. Hydronic systems may be more expensive to install but are less expensive to operate. Electric systems are easier and less expensive to install but are more expensive to operate, making them impractical for heating an entire house but effective for small areas, such as bathrooms. One disadvantage of radiant systems is that they take longer to heat up an area than other types of systems. Whatever material the system is embedded in acts as a heat sink, absorbing the heat first, before the room does. Depending on how big the heat sink is (such as a cold foundation), this could take quite a bit of time. On the plus side, once the heat is turned off, the heat sink will take a similarly long time to dissipate the heat, keeping the area warm for longer. To learn more, visit www.radiantpanelassociation.org.

MASSARANDUBA (OR BRAZILIAN REDWOOD OR BULLETWOOD)

This is a tropical wood, generally from Central or South America, with a very fine grain, a reddish-brown heartwood, and a pale brown sapwood color.

It is very dense and hard, ranking among the most durable woods on the planet. It is a more economical alternative to Ipe and has comparable weather and insect resistance. It grows in a variety of conditions and soils, and is quite large, making it an abundant species that is readily available. The Massaranduba tree grows to heights of 100 to 150 feet (30 to 46 m) and has a wide trunk diameter of 24 to 48 inches (61 to 122 cm). The trunk is long and straight, which means straight-grain wood can be produced with minimal waste. Massaranduba also finishes well and polishes to a high shine. It should not be used in climates with sudden temperature and moisture shifts because the wood can check (split and crack) because of uneven shrinking; however, this can be controlled to some degree with finishes and oils.

PANELIZATION

The exterior and interior walls of a house and the roof and floor components are produced in a factory and are then shipped to the site to be assembled together like a jigsaw puzzle. Panels can include windows and doors but very often are shipped without those items already in place. Being built in a controlled environment, these component panels are not exposed to the elements and have less chance of later developing mold. Sophisticated machinery is often used in factories, which allows for more precise panels.

PASSIVE HOUSE

The Passive House (or Passivhaus in German) building energy standard, first established in Germany, is now being used in many countries around the world, including the United States. It focuses on reducing energy consumption for space heating and cooling by about 90 percent. The Passive House Planning Package (PHPP) is software that can be used to predict energy usage and losses for individual structures. The requirements are stringent and include maximum heat and cooling demand, total primary energy consumption, and a maximum leakage of air volume per hour at 50 Pascal pressure, which is measured with a blower door test. Passive Houses are designed with super-insulation, high-performance windows, an airtight building shell or "envelope," and the use of an energy recovery ventilator (ERV) to exchange the interior air with fresh outside air. Although some houses do include active solar systems, Passive Houses focus less on producing energy, but rather are designed to save approximately 75 percent of the entire energy used in a building compared to existing building stock. There are currently about thirty thousand structures built to this standard, and it is possible for this to become the energy standard in some countries by 2020. For further information, see www.passivehouse.us or Passivhaus Institut, http://passiv.de.

R-VALUE

R-value is the measure of thermal resistance to heat flow through a given insulating material. The higher the R-value of a material, the greater the insulating effectiveness. The R-value of a material depends on the type of material, its thickness, its density, and how it is installed. If thermal bridging is created around the insulation through the studs and joists, for example, the R-value of a material can be compromised. Proper installation is required to achieve the maximum insulation of a structure. The amount of insulation required depends on the climate and the exposure of a particular wall. For more information, see www.energysavers.gov.

THERMAL BRIDGING

This refers to thermally conductive or noninsulating materials (such as metal fasteners or floor slabs) that allow heat to penetrate or bypass the insulation so that the heat can transfer between the interior and the exterior. Materials that have better insulating qualities and can create a "thermal break" must be used to eliminate this bridge.

THERMAL MASS

Thermal mass is generally a solid substance (although it can also be a liquid) that can absorb and store warmth and coolness. Concrete, brick, and stone are examples of high-density materials that have the ability to store and release energy back into a space. In a home, flooring, fireplaces, and walls with a high thermal mass can help to heat and cool the interior space. In winter, the solar energy is stored during the day and released at night when the air temperature drops in the house as the material attempts to reach an equilibrium with the interior air. This heat released into the house reduces the energy required for heating the interior space. During the summer, heat is absorbed by the solid surfaces, keeping the space more comfortable during the day and reducing the need for air-conditioning.

U-FACTOR OR U-VALUE

The U-value rating represents the rate of heat transfer through building parts such as windows, doors, skylights, walls, floors, and roofs. It indicates how well these components conduct heat—a lower U-value indicates worse conduction and therefore better insulation and greater energy efficiency. A higher U-value indicates worse thermal performance. The commonly referenced "R-value" is simply the inverse of the U-value. U-value is measure in units of Btu/hr-ft2°F. In lay terms, this is the rate of heat flow per square foot, per degree of temperature difference between the two sides of the material or assembly. Typical targets for high performance new construction are:

> Windows: U-0.2 or less (R-5 or greater)
> Walls: U-0.03 or less (R-30 or greater)
> Roofs: U-0.02 or less (R-50 or greater)

OTHER IMPORTANT TERMS ARE DISCUSSED IN THE SIDEBARS ON THE PAGES LISTED BELOW:

RESOURCES

AUSTRALIA

Elsternwick

Photographer
Ben Johnson
+61 4 2570 6923
www.bjp.net.au

Architect/Manufacturer/Builder
Modscape
+61 3 9314 7769
www.modscape.com.au

Suppliers
Alucabond ACM
(aluminum composite panels)
www.alucobond.com

Dulux (low-VOC paints)
www.dulux.com

Embelton (floors)
www.embelton.com

Feltex Carpets
www.feltex.com

Gyprock (plasterboard)
www.gyprock.com.au

Rheem (solar hot water unit)
www.rheem.com

SHADowclad ECOply (structural
plywood siding)
www.chhwoodproducts.com.au

Dangar Island House

Photographer
Patrick Bingham-Hall
www.patrickbingham-hall.com

Architects
mihaus studio
www.mihaus.com.au

Sue Harper Architects
www.sueharperarchitects.com

Manufacturer
Mecando
www.mecando.com.au

Structural Engineer
Professor Max Irvine

Environmental Engineer
Andy Irvine
OTG Environmental Solutions
7700 Edgewater Drive, Suite 260
Oakland, CA 94621
United States
+1 510 465 8982
www.otgenv.com

Builder
Liam Flood
Project Manager, Maria Flood
To The Mil Pty Ltd.
www.tothemil.com.au

Steel Fabricator
Firdon Fabrications
+61 2 4964 8278

Suppliers
Aqua Clarus
(Simply Natural System for waste)
www.aquaciarus.com

BlueScope Zincalume Mini Orb
(steel sheeting)
www.bluescopesteel.com.au

James Hardie (ExoTec facade)
www.jameshardie.com.au/products/
exotec.html

Quantum Domestic (hot water unit)
www.quatum-energy.com.au

AUSTRIA

Plus Energy Passivhaus

Manufacturer/Builder
Elk Fertighaus AG
www.ebselk.co.uk

Suppliers
Fundermax (exterior siding)
www.fundermax.at

Nilan (ERV)
www.nilan.dk

Eliasch House

Photographer
Michael-Christian Peters
+49 8192 998470
www.peters-fotodesign.com

Architect
Georg Schauer
+49 8822 6821
www.architekt-schauer.de

Manufacturer/Builder
Bau-Fritz GmbH & Co. KG
+49 8336 9000
www.baufritz.com

Suppliers
Florim Ceramiche (floor tiles)
www.florim.it

Windhager (heating)
www.windhager.com

Solar Tube

Photographer
Bruno Klomfar
www.klomfar.com

Architect
driendl* architects
Mariahilferstraße 9
1060 Wien
Austria
+43 1 585 1868
www.driendl.at

CANADA

Nexterra LivingHome

Photographers
Finn O'Hara
www.finnohara.com

Joseph Hilliard
+1 574 294 5366
www.hilliardphoto.com

Developer
Gary Lands
Nexterra Green Homes Ltd
+1 416 482 4959
www.nexterra.com

Architect
Ray Kappe/Amy Sims
LivingHomes
+1 310 581 8500
www.livinghomes.net

Manufacturer
Hi-Tech Housing Inc.
+1 574 848 5593
www.hi-techhousing.com

**Green Consultant/Marketing
and Partnerships**
Laura Felstiner
www.laurafelstiner.com

Suppliers
AEG (induction range, oven,
dishwasher, washer/dryer)
www.aeg-appliances.ca

Aquabrass (bathroom fixtures)
www.aquabrass.com

Caesarstone (countertops)
www.caesarstone.ca

Ella + Elliot (children's furnishings)
www.ellaandelliot.com

Elte (rugs)
www.elte.com

Gus* Modern Design (living area
furniture)
www.gusmodern.com

Inline Fiberglass (windows)
www.inlinefiberglass.com

Liebherr (refrigerator and freezer)
www.liebherr-appliances.com

Jøtul (cast iron stove)
www.jotul.com/en-US/wwwjotulus

PARA (zero- and low-VOC paint)
www.para.com

Scavolini (kitchen cabinets)
www.scavolinigreenmind.it/index_
en.asp

Tembec (FSC-certified lumber)
tembec.com/en

WETSTYLE (bathtubs, sinks, and vanities)
www.wetstyle.ca

Beachaus

Design Architect
Chris Pardo Design: Elemental Architecture
http://elementalarchitecture.com

Manufacturer
Method Homes
www.methodhomes.net

Builder
InHaus Development
+1 604 377 4978
www.inhaus.ca

Suppliers
Bamboo Hardwoods (FSC-certified bamboo flooring)
http://bamboohardwoods.com

BlueLine (energy usage monitoring system)
www.bluelineinnovations.com

Bosch (appliances)
www.bosch-home.com

Caesarstone (kitchen countertops)
www.caesarstoneus.com

Control4 (SmartHome automation system)
www.control4.com

Daikin (air-to-water heat exchanger)
www.daikin.com

Kohler (guest bathtub)
www.Kohler.com

LifeBreath (HRV system)
www.lifebreath.com

Marvin Integrity Series (fiberglass windows)
www.marvin.com

Phillips (EcoVantage halogen and LED bulbs)
www.lighting.philips.com/ca_en

PowerPipe (48-inch drain water heat recovery system)
www.renewability.com

Speakman (ultra-low-flow showerheads)
www.speakmancompany.com

Toto (high-efficiency low-flush toilets)
www.totousa.com

Velux (operable skylight with rain sensor and SmartHome tie-in, which creates a solar chimney effect and passive stack ventilation)
www.veluxusa.com

Warmboard (radiant heating)
www.warmboard.com

Kitsilano

Photographer
Jacob McNeil
www.jacobmcneil.com/

Architect
Balance Associates
www.balanceassociates.com

Manufacturer/Builder
Karoleena Inc.
+1 877 366 8580
www.karoleena.com

Suppliers
Duravit (water fixtures)
www.duravit.us

Grohe (water fixtures)
www.groheamerica.com

Hi-Velocity Systems (air handler)
www.hi-velocity.com

Lakeview Geotech Ltd. (hydronic system)
www.lakeviewgeotech.com

LG (appliances)
www.lg.com

Marvin Windows and Doors
www.marvin.com

Two-pound Polarfoam Soya (spray foam insulation)
www.polyurethanefoamsystems.com

The Morris Island House

Photographer
Mathieu Girard
Studio Versa
+1 819 360 3686
www.studioversa.com

Architect
Jeff Armstrong
DAC International
38 Auriga Drive
Ottawa, ON K2E 8A5
Canada
+1 613 221 5946
www.dac.ca

Manufacturer
DAC International
+1 613 221 5946
www.dac.ca

Builder
Wade & Drerup
+1 613 432 6885

Suppliers
Atlas (Polyisocyanurate sheathing)
http://atlaseps.com

BIS (wood-burning fireplace insert)
www.lennoxhearthproducts.com/products/fireplaces/nova/

Durisol Building Systems (foundation)
http://durisolbuild.com

Hubbardton Forge (light fixtures)
www.hubbardtonforge.com

Icynene (insulation)
www.icynene.com

Jeld-Wen Windows & Doors
www.jeld-wen.com

Kenmore Elite (appliances)
www.kenmore.com

Laurysen (solid-birch cabinet doors)
www.laurysenkitchens.com

MP lighting (low-voltage halogen lighting)
www.mplighting.com

SICO (paint)
www.sico.ca

Silestone (quartz countertops)
www.silestone.com

Wicanders (cork flooring)
www.wicanders.com

CHILE

SIP Panel House

Photographer
Josefina Lopez Ovalle
Felipe Fontecilla
www.font.cl

Architects
Alejandro Soffia
+56 9 499 5445
www.alejandrosoffia.cl

Gabriel Rudolphy
www.gabrielrudolphy.cl

Panel Manufacturer
Tecnopanel
+56 2 2745 5940
www.tecnopanel.cl

Structural Engineer
Jose Manuel Morales

COSTA RICA

Casa Iseami

Photographer
Sergio Puccí
+506 8892 3351
www.photographyincostarica.com

Architect
Juan Robles
Robles Arquitectos
+506 2225 5418
www.roblesarq.com

Manufacturer
Centria
+1 800 759 7474
www.centria.com

Builder
CPS Construccion
Daniel Calvosa
www.cps-cr.com

Suppliers
Helvex (bathroom fixtures)
www.helvex.com.mx

Trex (louvers and deck)
www.trex.com

Versawall/Versapanel (insulated metal composite panels)
www.centriaperformance.com

DENMARK

Villa Langenkamp

Photographers
Thomas Søndergaard
+45 28 11 22 70
www.thomassoendergaard.dk

Martin Brandt

Architect
Olav Langenkamp
+45 40 73 96 20
www.langenkamp.dk

Builder
Olav Langenkamp
+45 40 73 96 20
www.uns4.dk

UNS4
Jens Peter Kjær Jensen
+45 22 91 57 70

Energy Calculations
Søren Pedersen
Passivhus.dk Ltd.
+42 25 31 92 11
www.passivhus.dk

Manufacturers
Ökologischer Holzbau Sellstedt
www.oehs.de

Foundation
Ole Vognstrup A/S
Martin Hansensvej 24
+42 20 23 84 53
www.ole-vognstrup.dk

Suppliers
Catalano (toilets and sinks)
http://catalano.co.uk/collection/verso

GAP SOLAR (honeycomb-like pattern cardboard)
www.gap-solution.at

Huber (faucets)
www.huber.it/de/armaturen.htm

Pazen Fenster + Technik GmbH (Enersign triple-pane windows)
www.enersign.com/en/Enersign_Fenster/

The worldFLEXhome

Photographer
Jens Markus Lindhe
Nyhavn 3
DK 1051 København
Denmark
+45 6015 0613
www.jenslindhe.dk

Architect
Arcgency
+45 6128 0012
www.arcgency.com

Manufacturers
Nordisk Staal
Industrivej 25
+45 2823 8096
www.nordisk-staal.dk

worldFLEXhome
+45 2834 8096
www.worldflexhome.com

Suppliers
Cembrit (exterior cladding)
www.cembrit.com

Danfoss (solar inverters)
www.danfoss.com

DEBA (prefabricated bathroom units)
www.deba.de

EcoVent (HRV)
www.ecovent.dk

Electronic Housekeeper (smart system)
http://ehweb.electronichousekeeper.com

Factotech (foundation)
www.factotech.dk

Falck Denmark A/S (alarm system)
www.falck.com

Holse & Wibroe A/S (bamboo facade)
www.holseogwibroe.dk

HTH/Nobia Denmark (kitchen)
www.nobia.com/Brands/HTH

Isover (glass mineral wool insulation)
www.isover-eea.com

JeldWen A/S (doors)
www.jeld-wen.biz

Junckers Industries (flooring)
www.junckers.com

Knauf Danogips (subfloors)
www.knaufdanogips.dk

Lacuna A/S (insulated folding door)
www.lacuna.dk

Nilan A/S (ventilation)
www.nilan.dk

Pro Tec (windows)
www.protecwindows.com

Skandek (roof elements)
www.roofingcentretas.com.au

Skandinavisk Byggeplast ApS (green roof)
www.genbrugsplast.dk

Solarglas A/S (solar cells)
www.energy-supply.dk
Thermia Atec (air/water heat pump)
www.thermia.com

Velux (skylight)
www.velux.com

ENGLAND

Archway Studios

Photographer
Candice Lake
www.candicelake.com

Architect/Builder
Undercurrent Architects
+44 786 644 0066
www.undercurrent-architects.com

Manufacturer
GZ Shipping

Suppliers
Pacific Green (furniture)
www.pacificgreen.net

Palmwood (exterior cladding and flooring)
www.palmwood.net

Camden Passivhaus

Photographer
Jim Crocker Architectural Photography
+44 798 575 1994
www.timcrocker.co.uk

Architect
bere:architects
+44 207 359 4503
www.bere.co.uk

Superstructure Engineering, Fabrication, and Erection
Kaufmann Zimmerei
und tischlerei gmbh
+43 5514 2209
www.kaufmannzimmerei.at

Contractor
Visco
Suffolk, England
+44 198 678 1355

Substructure Engineer
Rodrigues Associates
+44 207 837 1133
www.rodriguesassociates.com

Interior Decoration
Fiona Terry
+44 776 726 3411
www.fionaterrydesigns.com

Suppliers
Allgood (hardware)
www.allgood.co.uk

Double Good Windows (import agent for Bayer Windows and Doors)
www.doublegood-windows.com

Duravit (bathroom fixtures)
www.duravit.com

Green Building Store (HRV)
www.greenbuildingstore.co.uk

Hangrsgrohe (bathroom fixtures)
www.hansgrohe-int.com

HELLA KGaA Hueck & Co. (external venetian blinds)
www.hella.info

Intello Plus ProClima (airtightness membranes)
www.proclima.com/co/INT/en/intello_plus_pd.html

Kaufmann Holz (Profidecke timber panels)
www.archiexpo.com/prod/kaufmannholz/structural-glued-solidwooden-panels-60685-147522.html

Thef Joinerey (staircase)
+44 208 571 7440

Tuttoparquet (flooring)
www.tuttoparquet.co.uk

House Jackson

Photographer
Nicholas Yarsley
+44 124 224 2606
www.nicholasyarsley.co.uk

Architect
Alexander Kolbe
EvoDOMUS
Cleveland Heights, OH 44118
United States
+1 216 772 2603
www.evodomus.com

Manufacturer/Builder
Baufritz Limited
+44 122 323 5632
www.baufritz.de

Suppliers
Frank Neubrand (bespoke cabinetry)
www.neubrand-moebel.de

Facit House

Photographer
Mark Cocksedge
+44 786 667 1583
www.markcocksedge.co.uk

Designer/ Manufacturer
Bruce Bell
Facit Homes
+44 208 986 0241
www.facit-homes.com

Builder
Alton Services MK Ltd.
Milton Keynes
+44 772 496 9171
www.alton-services-mk.co.uk

Suppliers
Amina (built-in speakers)
www.amina.co.uk

Blanco (kitchen sink)
www.blancoamerica.com

Contura (wood-burning stove)
www.contura.eu

Hotpoint (oven, built-in microwave, warming drawer, and built-in refrigerator)
www.hotpoint.com

Ikea (utility room sink, cabinets)
www.ikea.com

Smeg (stove)
www.smeg.com/hobs

Sonos (wireless audio system)
www.sonos.com/system

Velfac (windows)
www.velfac.co.uk

Velux (skylights)
www.velux.com

Vent-Axia
www.vent-axia.com

Wilder Creative (kitchen)
www.wildercreative.co.uk

The Edge

Designer/Manufacturer/Builder
Boutique Modern
+44 127 391 1076
www.boutiquemodern.co.uk

Suppliers
Ecochoice (FSC-certified timber cladding)
www.ecochoice.co.uk

Internorm (windows and doors)
www.internorm.com/uk/internorm
.html

Mereway (kitchen and bath cabinetry)
www.merewaykitchens.co.uk

Nilan (All-in-one system)
www.nilan.dk

FRANCE

Evolutive Home

Architect
Mauro Veneziano
+33 4 42 26 83 45
www.mauroveneziano.com

Passivhaus Designer
Frederic Michel
Concept Bio
+ 33 4 37 26 23 31
www.concept-bio.com

Builder
BA Bâtiment
+33 6 30 90 77 41
www.ba-batiment.com
/realisations.htm

Suppliers
CREE (lighting)
www.cree.com

Internorm (windows and doors)
www.internorm.com

PAUL Heat Recovery (ERV)
www.paulheatrecovery.co.uk
/products/campus-500dc

netec (ground heat exchanger)
www.sole-ewt.de

Sarnafil (roofing membrane)
http://usa.sarnafil.sika.com

Serge Ferrari (awning fabric)
http://architecture.sergeferrari.com
/Shade-sails-buildings

The Passivhaus in Bessancourt

Photographer
Hervé Abbadie Photographe
+33 1 43 25 39 02
www.art11.com/artistes/asuivre/
artistes/A/abbadie

Architect
Karawitz Architecture
+33 1 43 58 62 08
www.karawitz.com

Manufacturer
Finnforest (now known as Metsä
Wood)
www.metsawood.com

Builders
Perspective Bois
+33 2 99 19 92 24
www.perspective-bois.com

RC Eco

Structural Engineer
DI Eisenhauer and Philippe Buchet

Thermal Engineer
Solares Bauen
+42 761 4 56 88 30
www.solares-bauen.de

Suppliers
Erco (lighting)
www.erco.fr

Genvex (HRV)
www.genvex.co.uk

ISOFLOC (cellulose insulation)
http://isofloc.com

Menuiserie André (windows)
www.andre-menuiserie.fr

Optiwin (windows)
www.optiwin.net

Osram (lighting)
www.osram.fr

Philipps (lighting)
www.philipps.fr

Ribag (lighting)
www.ribag.ch

SIKA Samafil (waterproof membrane)
usa.sarnafil.sika.com

Systaic (photovoltaic panels)
www.systaic.de

Fusion Bretagne

Photographer
Gilles Plagnol

Manufacturer
Honka Group
+35 8 20 5757 00
www.honka.com

Builder
2M Bois
France

Suppliers
Pro'fil Box (all-in-one system)
www.pro-fil.com/produits/profilbox

Purbond (adhesive)
www.purbond.com

Sparthem 9kW (woodstove)
www.spartherm.com/products
/stoves.html?L=1

Zehnder (HRV)
www.zehnder-systems.com

Positive Energy ECOXIA House

Photographer
Mandibule
+33 2 41 48 31 24
www.morganview.fr

Architect
Joseph Cincotta
LineSync Architecture & Planning
www.linesync.com

Rémi Pellet
France
+33 681 908 892

Builder
ECOXIA
www.ecoxia.fr

Engineering
CRITT Bois
+33 3 29 81 11 70
www.crittbois.com

ENSTIB
+33 3 29 29 61 00
www.enstib.uhp-nancy.fr

Universite d'Evry Val d'Essonne
www.univ-evry.fr

Thermal Designers
Society of Manufacturing Engineers
www.sme.org

SYS e.n.r.
+33 8 11 62 03 67
www.sysenr.com

Interior Designer
Sylvie Cardona
Paris
France
+33 6 16 39 64 62

Suppliers
Asanderus (wallpaper)
www.asanderus.com

Atouts Cuisines (kitchen cabinets)
www.atoutscuisines.com

Chêne vert (green bathrooms)
www.chenevert.fr

Fermacell (gypsum fiber board)
www.fermacell-drylining.co.uk

Hora (radiant ceiling and all-in-one
system)
www.hora.fr

Internorm (windows and doors)
www.internorm.com

LEGRAND (home automation system)
www.legrand.us

Onip (paint)
www.onip.com

SAITEC (polyurethane insulation for
floors and roof)
www.saitec.fr

SOLARDIS (manufacturer and installer
of solar panels)
www.soprasolar.com

Soprema (roofing, the EPDM
membrane)
www.soprema.us

Soprasolar (photovoltaic panels)
www.soprasolar.com

Vantem Panels (SIPs manufacturer)
www.vantempanels.com

Vitrafilm (home staging and
communication)
www.vitrafilm.fr

GERMANY

green[r]evolution Plus Energy House

Manufacturer
HUF HAUS GmbH u. Co. KG
+49 26 26 761 200
www.huf-haus.com

Suppliers
B&B Italia (furnishings)
www.bebitalia.it

Braas (Tegalit roof system)
www.braas.de

Duravit (bathtub)
www.duravit.com

Gaggenau (kitchen appliances)
www.gaggenau.com

Royal Mosa, Series Terra Tones (tile
flooring)
www.mosa.nl

Schüco International KG (photovoltaic
system)
www.schueco.com

StilART from HUF HAUS (kitchen
built-ins and furnishings)
www.stilart-moebel.com/en/stilart
/stilart-furniture-for-huf-haus.html

Voltwerk VS 5 Hybrid from the Bosch
Group (energy storage)
www.voltwerk.com

Zehnder (towel radiator)
http://zehnder-systems.com

House Bretschneider

Photographer
Michael-Christian Peters
+49 8192 998470
www.peters-fotodesign.com

Architect
Architect Georg Schauer
+49 8822 6821
www.architekt-schauer.de

Manufacturer
Bau-Fritz GmbH & Co. KG
+49 8336 9000
www.baufritz.com

Suppliers
Duravit (toilets)
www.duravit.com

Graniti Fiandre (floor tile)
www.granitifiandre.com

Hans Grohe (faucets)
www.hansgrohe.com

Herba (doors)
www.zimmertueren.de

Vaillant (heat pump)
www.vaillant.co.uk

Cliff House

Photographer
Michael-Christian Peters
D-86938 Schondorf a.Ammersee
Germany
+49 8192 998470
www.peters-fotodesign.com

Architect
Daniel Wagner
www.architektur-wagner.com

Manufacturer/Builder
Bau-Fritz GmbH & Co. KG
+49 8336 9000
www.baufritz.com

Supplier
Werkhaus (kitchen cabinets and
furniture)
www.das-werkhaus.de

Low-Energy House

Photographer
Boris Storz
+49 89 16783933
www.boris-storz.de

Architect
Oberprillerarchitekten
Jakob Oberpriller and Doris Heym
+49 87 0291480
www.oberprillerarchitekten.de

Builder
Gebrüder Schuhmann
+49 99 223998
http://www.schuhmann-bau.com/

Carpenters
Haydn Holzbau
+49 85 8291101
www.haydn-holzbau.de

Joiner
Karl-Heinz PLEDL
+49 9942 94310
www.schreinerei-pledl.de

Suppliers
Fliesen-Wenig (tiles)
+49 9920 903874

Martin Pankratz (locksmith)
+49 9926 1393
http://martin.pankratz@gmx.de

Peter Poczewski (windows)
www.pepo-glas.de

Reissner GmbH (heating, ventilation,
sanitary, and electrostatic systems)
www.reissner-gmbh.de

Dream House

Photographer
Peter Kiefer
+49 1713 210858
www.pkiefer-fotograf.de

Architect
Bernd Neu
+49 2761 97470

Manufacturer/Builder
WeberHaus GmbH&Co. KG
+49 7853 83627
www.weberhaus.de

Suppliers
KeraTür (doors)
www.keratuer.de/keratuer.php

Niveau (windows)
www.niveau.de

Ruegg (fireplace)
www.ruegg-cheminee.com
/ww/ff/pub/produkte/cheminees
/neu__pi.cfm

Tecalor (heat pump system)
www.tecalor.de

[Little] Smart House

Photographer
Peter Kiefer
Germany
+49 7814 1338
www.pkiefer-fotograf.de

Architect
Peter Rudloff
+49 7853 292

Manufacturer/Builder
WeberHaus GmbH&Co. KG
+49 7853 83627
www.weberhaus.de

Suppliers
EnOcean Alliance (home automation
system)
www.enocean-alliance.org/en/home

Hansa (bathroom fixtures)
www.hansa.com

KeraTür (doors)
www.keratuer.de/keratuer.php

Lithon Plus (permeable pavers)
www.lithonplus-steinmanufaktur.de

Miele (dishwasher)
www.miele.com

Neff (refrigerator)
www.neff-international.com

Niveau (windows)
www.niveau.de

Proxon (all-in-one system)
www.proxon.de

ISRAEL

Borderline House

Photographer
Assaf Pinchuk
www.apinchuk.com

Architect
Guy Zucker
www.guyzucker.com

Manufacturer
Rishon Cement Builders
Israel

Suppliers
Amcor (AC split system)
www.amcor-solar.co.il/len

Klil (windows and doors)
www.klil.co.il

Nirlat (paint)
www.nirlat.com

Tadiran Group (appliances)
www.tadiran-group.co.il

ITALY

New Energy House

Photographer
Federico Zattarin
+39 0422 968455
www.photo-zone.it

Architect
Architetti Zordan Gabaldo
Giulia Zordan and Domenico Gabaldo
+39 0444 785218
www.zordangabaldo.it

Builders

Impresa Baraldo Luigi (concrete
basement structure and insulation)
+39 0445 364845

Rasom Wood Technology (wooden
structures, insulation, and finishing)
+39 0462 764483
www.rasom.it

Suppliers
Fiemme 3000, Predazzo (flooring)
www.fiemme3000.it

Pluggit (ventilation and heating
system)
http://int.pluggit.com/en/befresh
/befresh.html

Pluggit Gmbh (ERV)
www.pluggit.com/it

Rasom Wood Technology (cross-
laminated panels)
www.rasom.it

Ruegg (fireplace)
www.ruegg-cheminee.com

Schüco Italia (photovoltaic panels)
www.schueco.com/web/it

JAPAN

EDDI's House

Photographer
Daishinsha Inc.
+81 03 3405 5135 (Tokyo Office)
+81 06 6976 7752 (Osaka Office)
www.daishinsha.co.jp

Architect
Edward Suzuki Associates & Daiwa
House
+81 03 5770 5395
www.edward.net

Manufacturer
Daiwa House Industry
+81 06 6342 1369
www.daiwahouse.com/english

Suppliers
Corian (countertops)
www2.dupont.com

LIXIL (components parts)
http://global.lixil.co.jp

B-House

Photographer
Hideo Nishiyama
+81 096 351 1215
www.hn-aa.com

Yoshikazu Shiraki
+81 096 285 3447
www.whitrees.com

Design Architect
Anderson Anderson Architecture
+1 415 243 9500
www.andersonanderson.com

Shop Architect
Nishiyama Architects
+81 096 351 1215
www.hn-aa.com

Manufacturer/Builder
Tomisaka Construction
+81 096 362 4345
www.tomisaka.co.jp

Suppliers
Miele (dishwasher)
www.miele.com

Modernica (furniture)
http://modernica.net

Ofuro (soaking tub)
www.japanesebath.com

YKK (windows)
www.ykkap.com

U-3 House

Photographer
Toshihisa Ishii
Blitz STUDIO
+81 092-526-2479
www.h3.dion.ne.jp/~stblitz

Architect
Masahiko Sato
+81 092-526-2479
www.architect-show.com

Manufacturer/Builder
Haraguchi Construction Corporation
Fukuoka City, Japan

Suppliers
Advan (stone for entrance)
www.advan.co.jp

Daiko (lighting)
www.lighting-daiko.co.jp

Mitsubishi (ventilator)
www.mitsubishielectric.com

Osmo (paint)
www.osmona.com

SK Kaken Co., Ltd (exterior coating)
www.sk-kaken.co.jp

Tostem (windows)
www.tostem.com.cn

Toto (appliances and bathroom
fixtures)
www.toto.co.jp

THE NETHERLANDS

Energy Neutral Residence

Photographer
Hans Peter Föllmi
Föllmi Photography
+31 65 26 46 701
www.ic4u.org

Architect
Pieter Weijnen
Coöperation For Up-Architecture
+31 20 26 00 145
www.upfrnt.com

Manufacturer
MetsäWood (Lenotec CLT wood for
construction)
+31 55 53 86 610
www.metsawood.nl

Builder
J. J. A. Kerkhofs Montagebouw
Hendrik-Ido-Ambacht

Construction Advisor
Pieters Bouwtechniek, Almere
+31 36 53 05 299
www.pietersbouwtechniek.nl

Sustainability Advisor
Trecodome
+31 20 30 50 940
www.trecodome.com

Installation
Aitec & Wiessenekker
+31 31 762 1784
www.aitec.nl

Suppliers
Denios (rainwater tank)
www.denios.nl

DonQi (urban windmill)
www.donqi.nl

Elco Heating Solutions, Kerkrade
(vacuum tube collector)
www.rendamax.elco.nl

Kreon / Artemide (lights)
http://artemide-flos-foscarini.blogspot
.com/2013/01/kreon-lights-artists
-creation.html

Haaksbergen (windowsills and panels)
www.tifaoverbeek.nl

Homatherm (insulation)
www.homatherm.com/uk

Insulair (insulation)
http://insulaireinc.com

Insulcon (insulation)
www.insulcon.com

MetsäWood (bearing walls and
facade)
www.metsawood.com

Microtherm (vacuum insulation panels)
www.microtherm.be

Mosa (tiles)
www.mosa.nl

Phase-change microcapsules (PCM)
by BASF (heat collection capsules in
clay plaster)
www2.basf.us/corporate/080204_
micronal.htm

Siematic (kitchen cabinets)
www.siematic.nl

SOLE by KNV (groundwater heat
exchange)
www.knv.at

Timmerfabriek Overbeek (windows,
doors, and builder of facade)
www.tifaoverbeek.nl

Warmteplan (insulation materials)
www.warmteplan.nl

Xavi Eco-o-Bouwbedrij (clay plaster
supplier)
www.xavieco.com/index.php

Zagerij de Vree (wood for facade)
www.houtzagerijdevree.nl

Zwarthout (shou-sugi-ban wood)
www.zwarthout.com

NEW ZEALAND

First Light

Photographer
Jim Tetro
+1 703 268 5514
www.jimtetro.com

Manufacturer
Mainzeal Building Certainty
(construction)
www.mainzeal.com

Designers

First Light Studio
+64 4 385 3789
www.firstlightstudio.co.nz

Students of Victoria University of
Wellington
School of Architecture
Victoria University of Wellington
New Zealand
+64 4 463 6250
www.firstlighthouse.ac.nz

Lighting Designer
Stephenson & Turner
+64 4 472 7899
www.stephensonturner.com

Suppliers
Eco Insulation/Ecowool (sheep's wool
insulation)
www.ecoinsulation.co.nz
/insulation-solutions/ecowool

Eco Windows (windows and doors)
www.ecowindows.co.nz

Fisher & Paykel (appliances)
www.fisherpaykel.com

Flexus (concrete floors)
www.flexus.co.nz

Herman Pacific (canopy and cladding)
www.hermpac.co.nz

Leap (plumbing supplies and solar hot
water panels)
www.leapltd.co.nz

Metro Glasstech (glazing)
www.metroglasstech.co.nz

Mitsubishi Electric (photovoltaic
panels)
www.bdt.co.nz/home

NZ Wood (lumber)
www.nzwood.co.nz

Rental property
www.firstlighthouse/accommodation.
co.nz

Schneider Electric (electrical supplies
and building automation)
www.schneider-electric.com/site
/home/index.cfm/nz/

Switch Lighting (LED lighting)
www.switch-lighting.co.nz

Tring Interactive Energy Monitoring
System
www.tring.co.nz

Verda Outdoor (decking)
www.verda.fr/outdoor

iPAD

Photographer
Trevor Read
+64 6 758 5899
www.trevorread.co.nz

Architect
André Hodgskin
Architex
+64 9 377 4691
www.architex.co.nz

Manufacturer
iPAD
+64 9 309 9135
www.ipad.net.nz

Builder
Kuriger Builders
www.kurigerbuilders.co.nz

Suppliers
Aluminum Taranaki (windows and
doors)
www.aluminiumtaranaki.co.nz

American Standard (bathroom basins
and toilet)

BIOLYTIX eco (sewerage system)
www.biolytix.com

Ecosmart (bioethanol burner)
www.ecosmartfire.com

Kingspan (ceiling panels)
www.kingspanpanels.com

Lightplan (lighting)
www.lightplan.co.nz

Newton Gordge Cabinetmakers
www.newtongordge.co.nz

Rinnai (califont)
www.rinnai.co.nz

SMEG (appliances)
www.smegusa.com

Tanaki (cabinetry)

Vantage Aluminum Joinery
www.apinz.co.nz

Wooden Floor Company (laminate flooring)
www.woodenfloors.co.nz

ROMANIA

PRISPA

Photographer
Santonja/Cubas
Cubas I+D+Art Studio
+34 619 859 765 (Ricardo Santonja)
+34 616 114 610 (Alberto Cubas)
www.santonjacubas.com

PRISPA team
"Ion Mincu" University of Architecture
and Urbanism in Bucharest (UAUIM)
Strada Academiei 18-20
Bucharest
Romania
+40 21 307 71 12
www.uauim.ro/en/university

The Technical University of Civil
Engineering of Bucharest (UTCB)
+40 21 242 12 08
www.utcb.ro/tuce-en.html

University Politehnica of Bucharest
(UPB)
+ 40 21 402 91 00
www.upb.ro/en

Suppliers
Bog art (cranes)
www.bogart.ro

Bosch (tools)
www.bosch.com

Electrolux (appliances)
www.electroluxappliances.com

Holzindustrie Schweighofer (wood
flooring and other wood elements)
www.schweighofer.at

Kronospan (wood panels)
www.kronospan-worldwide.com

PHILIPS (television)
www.philips.com

Rheinzink (roofing)
www.rheinzink.com

Rothoblaas (ironsmith and tools)
www.rothoblaas.com

Saint-Gobain (Rigips drywall and
concrete panels, SG glass, Weber
exterior coating, Isover glass wool
insulation and vapor barrier)
www.saint-gobain.com

Sir Safety (Health & Safety material
and equipment)
www.sirsafety.ro

Sunerg Solar Energy (photovoltaic
panels, inverter, solar panels, hot water
boiler)
www.sunergsolar.com

Valcon Roofs (roofing)
www.valconroofs.ro

Valrom (piping)
www.valrom.ro

SOUTH AFRICA

Ecomo Home

Architect/Builder/Manufacturer
Pietro Russo
Ecomo
+27 72 445 9373
www.ecomohome.com

Carpenter
Tim Wolf
Ecomo
+27 72 445 9373
www.ecomohome.com

Suppliers
Alubuild Pty Ltd. (Aluminum windows
and doors)
+27 021 9496527

Isotherm (recycled polyester
insulation)
www.isotherm.co.za

Ledzshine (LED lighting)
www.led-z.com
Solar Geyser (solar hot water panel)
www.solar-geyser.com

Stable Marketing (cedar cladding)
www.stablemarketing.co.za

SPAIN

JP House

Photographer
FG+SG
Fernando Guerra Sergio Guerra
http://ultimasreportagens.com

Architect
MYCC
www.mycc.es

Manufacturer/Builder
Ageco Scotman
www.algecoscotsman.com

Quantity Surveyor
Raul Olivares

Suppliers
IKEA (kitchen furniture)
www.ikea.com

JUNG (electric)
www.jung.de/en

Quick Step (flooring)
http://us.quick-step.com

ROCA (bathroom fittings)
www.in.roca.com

Simonin (larch rain screen)
www.simonin.com

Smeg (refrigerator)
www.smeguk.com

Villa EntreEncinas

Photographer
Tania Diego Crespo
www.taniacrespo.com

Architect
Alicia Zamora and Iván G. Duque
Estudio de Arquitectura Duque y
Zamora
www.estudioduqueyzamora.es

Manufacturer
KLH
Zulziri S.L + Biohaus Egorri S.L.
www.klh.at

Builder
EntreEncinas Promociones
Bioclimáticas S.L.
www.entreencinasbioclimatica.es

Blower Door Test
Micheel Wassouf
Energiehaus-scp
www.energiehaus.es

Suppliers
Bosch (refrigerator and washing
machine, rated A+++)
www.bosch-home.com

Caparol (silica siding)
www.caparol.es

Duron Paints & Coverings (interior
paint)
www.duron.com

Eco by Cosentino (countertops)
www.ecobycosentino.com

EPDM (roofing)
www.epdmroofs.org

IKEA (kitchen furniture)
www.ikea.com

Livos (wood stain)
www.livos.com

Moso (bamboo flooring)
www.moso-bambu.es/parquet/
bamboo-elite

Muebles Joya (furniture and lighting)
www.mueblesjoya.es

Rika (wood stove)
www.rika.at/en/esprit

Siemens (dishwasher, rated A+++)
www.siemens-home.com.au

Wolf (solar panels)
www.wolf-heiztechnik.de

Zinco (green roof)
www.zinco-greenroof.com

SWITZERLAND

Lugano House

Photographer
Grandpierre Design GmbH
Visuelle Kommunikation
www.grandpierre.de

Designer/Manufacturer/Builder
HUF HAUS GmbH u. Co. KG
www.huf-haus.com

Suppliers
Axel Meise (lamps)
www.architonic.com/pmpro
/axel-meise/8100467/2/2/1

B&B Italia (furnishings)
www.bebitalia.it

Boley (fireplace)
www.boley.nl

Caesarstone (ceramic tile)
www.caesarstoneus.com

Gaggenau (kitchen appliances)
www.gaggenau.com

Hans Grohe/AXOR (bathroom and
kitchen fittings)
www.hansgrohe.com

Ingo Maurer (lamps)
www.ingo-maurer.com

Jaso (American cherry parquet
flooring)
www.jaso.de

Siematic (main kitchen cabinets)
www.siematic.de/Startseite_DE.htm

Stiebel Eltron (heat pump system)
www.stiebel-eltron.de/en
/privatkunden/

StilART from HUF HAUS (built-ins in
the office kitchen)
www.stilart-moebel.com/en/stilart
/stilart-furniture-for-huf-haus.htm

Casa Locarno

Architect
designyougo - architects and
designers
+49 30 303 43385
www.designyougo.com

Structural Engineers
De Giorgi & Partners Ingegneri
Consulenti S.A.
+41 91 796 37 00
www.degiorgi.ch

**Prefab Timber and Facade
Manufacturer**
Veragouth S.A.
+41 91 935 79 79
www.veragouth.com

Suppliers
4B (windows)
www.4-b.ch

Eternit (fiber-reinforced cement
composite panels)
www.eternit.ch

Flos (lighting)
www.flos.com

Jenni Energietechnik AG (solar panels
and hot water storage)
www.jenni.ch

UNITED STATES

Laurel Hollow

Designer/Manufacturer
Yankee Barn Homes
+1 800 258 9786
www.yankeebarnhomes.com

Builder
Gerard Mingino General Contractor,
Inc.
+1 631 289 8643

Interior Designer/Architect
Jeffrey Rosen Interior Design
+1 212 717 1964

Suppliers
American Olean (bathroom tiles)
http://americanolean.com

Andersen (windows)
www.andersenwindows.com

Benjamin Moore Paints
www.benjaminmoore.com

Cabot (stains)
www.cabotstain.com

Crown Point Cabinetry
www.crown-point.com

GE Appliances (stove, wine
refrigerator, dishwasher)
www.geappliances.com

Hudson Valley (bathroom lighting)
www.hudsonvalleylighting.com

Philips Lightolier (lights)
www.lightolier.com

Sub-Zero (refrigerator)
www.subzero-wolf.com

Zero-Sort (recycling)
www.zero-sort.com

Island Passive House

Photographer
Art Gray Photography
+1 310 663 4756

Designer/Builder
Tessa Smith and Randy Foster
The Artisans Group
+1 360 570 0626
www.artisansgroup.com

Interior Designer
Brenda Fritsch
The Artisans Group
www.artisansgroup.com

Engineer
Carissa Farkas
Carissa Farkas Structural Engineering,
PLLC
+1 206 683 3197
www.cfarkasstructural.com

**Mechanical System Consultant and
Installation**
Brian Pruett
CSM Heating & Cooling (HRV)
+1 360 754 5220

Consultation
Tadashi Shiga
Evergreen Certified Principal
+1 206 491 7111
www.evergreencertified.com

Washington State University Extension
Energy Program
+1 360 956 2000
www.energy.wsu.edu

Suppliers
Architectural Hardwoods (epi for
exterior wood detail)
www.awi-wa.com

Artcraft Lighting
www.artcraftlighting.com

Beech Tree Woodworks (cabinetry
and custom tables)
+1 360 349 1558 or +1 206 724 1573
www.beechtreecustomcabinets.com

Benjamin Moore Paints
www.benjaminmoore.com

Best Range Hoods (hood)
www.bestrangehoods.com

Blanco (kitchen sink)
www.blancoamerica.com

Caesarstone (bath countertops)
www.caesarstoneus.com

Custom Bilt Metals (roof)
www.custombiltmetals.com

Daikin AC (heat pump)
www.daikinac.com

Design within Reach (furnishings)
www.dwr.com

Don Freas (sculptures)
+1 360 357 2850
www.donfreas.com

ET2 (bath ceiling fixtures)
www.et2online.com

Fisher & Paykel (single-draw
dishwasher)
www.fisherpaykel.com/us

Forecast Lighting (vanity light
fixtures)
www.forecastltg.com

Garden Artisan (paving and
landscape)
+1 360 317 7587
www.gardenartnz.com

GE Appliances (induction cooktop)
www.geappliances.com

Hinkley Lighting
www.hinkleylighting.com

James Hardie (siding)
www.jameshardie.com

Jeffrey Alexander (decorative
hardware)
www.hardwareresources.com

Kohler (bathroom sinks)
www.kohler.com

LBL Lighting (dining room light
fixture)
www.lbllighting.com

Liebherr (appliances)
www.liebherr-appliances.com

Lynden Door (interior doors)
www.lyndendoor.com

Meyer Wells (reclaimed maple floors)
www.meyerwells.com

Moen (tub and shower fixtures)
www.moen.com

Pental Granite & Marble (backsplash
and tub/shower tiles)
www.pentalonline.com

Radianz (kitchen counters)
www.staron.com/radianz/eng/index
.do

Sanijet (jetted tub)
www.sanijet.com

Schlage (interior door hardware)
www.schlage.com

Sliding Door Company
www.slidingdoorco.com

Small Planet Workshop (air sealing
tape)
www.smallplanetworkshop.com

Studio 23 (exterior front entry)
+1 360 705 0770
www.olymetal.com

Task Lighting (under-cabinet lighting
and angled outlet strips)
www.tasklighting.com

Tech Lighting (hall, office, bedroom,
and sewing nook light fixtures)
www.techlighting.com

Toshiba (LED lightbulbs not provided
with lighting)
www.toshiba.com/lighting

Toto (dual-flush toilets, vanity sinks,
and faucets)
www.totousa.com

Zehnder (HRV)
www.zehnderamerica.com

Zola Windows (windows and exterior
doors)
www.zolawindows.com

Montana Farmhouse

Photographer
Haily Donoven Seion Studio
+1 406 265 3300
http://hailydonoven.zenfolio.com

Architect
Becki D. Miller
United States
+1 406 376 3230

Manufacturer
Premier SIPS by Insulfoam
+1 800 275 7086
www.premiersips.com

Builder
Dale Pimley
+1 406 292 3390

Suppliers
Distinctive Lighting (lighting)
www.distinctivelighting.com

Kitchenaid (cooktop and oven)
www.kitchenaid.com

Kenmore (hood and refrigerator)
www.kenmore.com

Minot Builders (Marvin windows)
+1 406.761.7530

Portland HOMB

Photographer
Michael Cogliantry
+1 917 449 6933
http://michaelcogliantry.com

Architect
Skylab Architecture
+1 503 525 9315
http://skylabarchitecture.com

Builder/Manufacturer
HOMB Modular
http://welcomehomb.com

Method Homes, LLC
+1 206 789 5553
http://methodhomes.net

General Contractor
Rainier Pacific
+1 503 223 2465
http://rainierpacificdevelopment.com

Suppliers
Anderson Window
www.andersonwindows.com

Bamboo Hardwoods (hardwood
flooring and composite decking)
www.bamboohardwoods.com

Blue Frog Solar (micro solar inverters)
www.bluefrogsolar.com

Caesarstone (countertops)
www.caesarstoneus.com

Daikin (mini-split system)
www.daikin.com

Duravit (tubs and sinks)
www.duravit.us

Flor Carpet Design Squares (custom
tiled carpet)
www.flor.com

Hans Grohe/Axor (bathroom and
kitchen fixtures)
www.hansgrohe-usa.com

In House PDX (built-in furniture)
www.inhousepdx.com

Juno Lighting Group (LED lighting)
www.junolightinggroup.com

Meyer Wells (cedar siding)
www.meyerwells.com

Mr. Sun Solar (solar installation)
www.mrsunsolar.com

Pesznecker Brothers Inc. (stairs
fabrication)
www.peszbros.com

Portland Cement Company (bathroom
tiles)
+1 503 490 2226

Portland Energy Trust (energy
certification)
http://energytrust.org

Roseburg (framing lumber)
www.roseburg.com

Smith & Vallee (custom cabinetry)
www.smithandvallee.com

Sunmodo (solar racking)
www.sunmodo.com

Ultimate Air (HRV)
www.ultimateair.com

Washington Window and Door
(E-Series windows and doors)
www.washingtonwindowanddoor.com

Concord Riverwalk Cottage

Photographer
Nat Rea
+1 401 338 6827
www.natrea.com

Architect
Union Studio Architects
+1 401 272 4724
http://unionstudioarch.com

Developer
Now Communities, LLC.
+1 978 369 6200
www.nowcommunities.com

Manufacturer
Bespoke Corporation
30 Brighton St.
Belmont, MA 02478-4172
United States
+1 617 932 1754

Builder
BOJ Construction
+1 508 747 5447
www.bojconstruction.com

Mechanical Engineer
Jordan Goldman
+1 617 720 5002
www.zeroenergy.com

Building Technologist
Marc Rosenbaum
+1 508 693 4850
www.southmountain.com

Suppliers
Grohe (faucets and showerheads)
www.grohe.com

Hubbardton Forge (lighting)
www.hubbardtonforge.com

James Hardie (siding)
www.jameshardie.com

Mitsubishi Electric Corporation (air-
source heat pumps)
www.mitsubishielectric.com

Paradigm Windows
www.paradigmwindows.com

Renaissance Electronic Services (solar
thermal system)
www.res-llc.com

Sunbug Solar (photovoltaic panels)
http://sunbugsolar.com

Toto (toilets)
www.totousa.com

Trex (decking)
www.trex.com

Venmar Ventilation Inc. (HRV)
www.venmar.ca

Martis Camp Cabin

Photographer
Shaun Fenn
+1 510 282 0660
http://shaunfenn.com

Architect/Developer
sagemodern
http://sagemodern.net

Manufacturer
Irontown Homes
1947 North Chappel Drive
Spanish Fork, UT 84660
United States
+1 877 849 1215
www.irontownhomes.com

Builder
Gallagher Construction
+1 530 550 7500
http://gallagherconstructiontahoe.com

Suppliers
American Slate (slate flooring)
www.americanslate.com

Cooper Industries (Halo lighting)
www.cooperindustries.com

DuChâteau Floors (wood flooring)
http://duchateaufloors.com

Lochinvar (boiler)
www.lochinvar.com

Renewaire (HRV)
www.renewaire.com

Sierra Pacific Windows (windows and
doors)
www.sierrapacificwindows.com

Thermador (appliances)
www.thermador.com

Western Window Systems (sliding
glass doors)
www.westernwindowsystems.com

Simblist House at Serenbe

Photographer
Chris Nelms
+1 678 368 4444
www.theVSIgroup.com

Builder
Moon Bros. Inc.
+1 404 377 6006
www.moonbros.com

Interior Designer
Robert Gaul Architectural Design
+1 917 783 6990

Suppliers
Ann Sacks (tiles and bathroom
flooring)
www.annsacks.com

Benjamin Moore (paint)
http://benjaminmoore.net

Caesarstone (kitchen counters)
www.caesarstoneus.com

Flos (lighting)
www.flos.com

Hans Grohe (rainwater showers)
www.hansgrohe-usa.com

Miele (dishwasher, washing machine,
clothes dryer, ovens)
www.mieleusa.com

Moon Brothers (custom-built cabinets)
www.moonbros.com

Plyboo (bamboo flooring)
www.plyboo.com

Sub-Zero (refrigerator)
www.subzero-wolf.com

Toto (toilets)
www.totousa.com

Walker Zanger (glass tiles and slate)
www.walkerzanger.com

Wolf (stovetop)
www.subzero-wolf.com

Y Lighting
www.ylighting.com

Everett House

Photographer
Anthony Rich Photography
+1 310 729 7349
www.anthonyrich.com

Architect
Jonathan Davis
Davis Studio Architecture + Design
+1 310 572 6055
http://davisstudioad.com

Developer
Asani Development Corporation
+1 206 780 8898
www.asanillc.com

Manufacturer
Kingston Lumber (panels)
+1 888 557 9663
www.kingstonlumber.com

Builder
PHC Construction
+1 206 780 4060
http://phc-construction.com

Suppliers
Air Generate (AirTap Hybrid heat
pump for hot water)
www.airgenerate.com

Bamboo Hardwoods (flooring)
www.bamboohardwoods.com

Blue Frog Solar (micro inverters)
http://bluefrogsolar.com/aps-inverters

Expanko (rubber and cork composite
floor)
www.expanko.com

GE (induction cooktop)
www.geappliances.com

iTek Energy (photovoltaic panels)
www.itekenergy.com

James Hardie (fiber cement siding)
www.jameshardie.com

Marvin (windows and doors)
www.marvin.com

Meyer Wells (cedar siding)
www.meyerwells.com

Mitsubishi (mini-split ductless heat
pump)
www.mitsubishicomfort.com

Paperstone (countertops)
http://paperstoneproducts.com

Zehnder (HRV)
www.zehnderamerica.com

Editor: Laura Dozier
Designer: Darilyn Lowe Carnes
Production Manager: True Sims

Library of Congress Control Number: 2013945688

ISBN: 978-1-61769-083-9

Copyright © 2014 Sheri Koones
Foreword copyright © 2014 Robert Redford

Printed and bound in the United States
10 9 8 7 6 5 4 3 2 1

Abrams books are available at special discounts when purchased in quantity for premiums and promotions as well as fundraising or educational use. Special editions can also be created to specification. For details, contact specialsales@abramsbooks.com or the address below.

THE ART OF BOOKS SINCE 1949
115 West 18th Street
New York, NY 10011
www.abramsbooks.com